WITH vs AT

Two Prepositions That Changed My Life

KYLA MITSUNAGA

Edited by Luke Lavin

Book Cover Photo by Tara Booth

Book Cover Design by Bo Tsang

Interior Design and Formatting by Jovana Shirley, Unforeseen Editing, www.unforeseenediting.com

Dedicated to + Inspired by all of my students past, present + future.

For my mother, grandmothers, and the many generations of women before them.

WITH gratitude to my mom, dad, Miu, Bobo, LG, Edgar, and mi familia.

TABLE OF CONTENTS

The What

The Why

The How

Everything Begins WITH YOU

WITH People: Dealing WITH Your Community

WITH Respect for Women: The Most Important Part of Any Community

Being WITH Your Emotions

Traveling WITH a Culture/Country

FOREWORD BY MINJEONG

Whenever we have a chance to meet new people, Kyla almost always introduces me as "the first student who visited her during office hours." If you are that person who I'm meeting for the first time, you might think it is not a common way to describe someone. But if you give a second thought to it, soon you will see that it is what Kyla values the most-interaction with her students.

The reason I came to her office, stood in front of it, and even cared to knock on her door was neither because I was more courageous to talk to a foreign professor than other students, nor because I had enough confidence to think that I could talk to professors whenever I wanted to. I simply needed and was desperately looking for someone who could listen to me and give me advice on my future. That frustration of not being able to see what was ahead of my life and desire for help led me to create a unique relationship with Kyla. When I first met her, even though I was a senior in college I still had no idea what I should do or what I truly wanted to do. Maybe that is why I went to talk to Kyla, someone who has made decisions about her life on her own terms and enjoys all of the rewards of her own decisions. If that cool person happened to be a professor as well, I'm sure you would want to talk to her too.

So when I first visited her on that particular fall day of 2011, I was thinking that maybe she would give me clear answers-which path I should take, what job I should get, etc. But instead, she asked *me* a question: "Forget about what people do, what people tell you you should do. What is it that you truly enjoy doing and feel like you could do for the rest of your life?"

Since then, Kyla has been my good friend and an awesome teacher whom I can even discuss private matters like family issues and my deepest concerns that I could never tell anyone. I am so glad that I can congratulate her on yet another accomplishment --this book--*with* her students and show my gratitude to her.

She is someone who has been a great mentor throughout my 20s, when I was struggling to understand who I really was and find my own answers for my own life. I am well aware that a number of us in our 20s and even 30s have no luxury to reflect on what we truly want with our lives, because far too many times we are too stressed to find jobs and survive in this competitive Korean society or elsewhere around the world.

If looking for jobs at big corporations and getting into better schools are what you really want, I believe it will be all worth investing your life in them even though you may go through a grueling process. But if you're not happy with that life you thought you have always wanted, how about creating a little bit of time and reflecting on your own life?

I truly hope that this book finds you well and delivers my friend, Kyla and her students' sincere desire to help you. Or maybe you can just drop by her office for a chat? Either way, I can guarantee you'll start liking her "HAPPY VIRUS" if you haven't already caught it by the end of this book!

Minjeong and I enjoying hot chocolate | Cambridge, MA. | Winter 2013

LETTER TO STUDENTS

Dear Students (I use this term loosely to incorporate my past students, present students, future students and any one I have ever learned/taught WITH, and every one in between who has taken the time to teach me something),

This book is my gift to you. I hope by the time you have finished reading this book, you will have learned WITH me, and been as inspired by this book, as I have been WITH you—your inspiration was the catalyst to write this book. It was not an easy journey, but sometimes the most challenging journeys are the ones most worthwhile.

I want to express here to be WITH yourself and those around you as much as possible. I wish for you a life of not only "successes" but also "failures" as you define them WITH yourself. I wish for you a life where you get your heart broken, pick yourself up again, and fall in love WITH yourself, and WITH others. I wish for you a life of helping others see the importance of learning and teaching WITH.

But most importantly, if you take away nothing from this book, but how incredible it feels to be truly WITH yourself, to be true to yourself, and listen to your heart, then I think I have done something great – WITH you. And the stronger your foundation WITH yourself is, the more you'll be open to working WITH people across genders, races, ethnicities no matter how different they may be on the outside.

Thank you in advance for reading this and being WITH me.

I love you.

Wishing you Happiness,

Kyla

AUTHOR'S NOTE

Why A Book?

(December 2011)

"You should write a book, Kyla." Jae-kyung and Ji Hye encouraged.

It was our very first book club meeting and we had spent the majority of the night over dinner and then over tea in *Hapjeong* chatting away about everything but the book we were supposed to have read prior to our meeting. Jae-kyung and Ji Hye were former students of mine from the Foreign Language Institute (FLI) at Yonsei—my first job in Seoul. Jae-kyung was a mother of two boys. Her husband did all of the cooking, which he mostly learned from watching NHK cooking shows in Japan. She was warm and kind and her laugh rivaled my own. Ji Hye was a senior at Yonsei (at the time), but seemed to be mature beyond her age. She even read *real* paper books. She was committed to helping others, and this was exemplified in her volunteer experiences in Uganda and her wanting to become a nurse at the time.

Jae-kyung and Ji Hye had an affinity for books—real books—not ebooks or books on Kindle. They always had books to recommend and it was this love of books that led us to create a book club.

I always looked forward to their class. It included two other women: Aesuk and Natalia. Aesuk was an energetic middle-aged woman who tended to use the word "just" in every other sentence and spent her nights at every single concert she could possibly get tickets for (including: Sting, Lang Lang, and even the Flaming Lips!). She was once generous enough to invite me to join her to go see Taylor Swift knowing what a huge fan I was, but to my complete and utter dismay, I was not able to make it because I had friends in town. Natalia had graduated from university and was ethnically Korean, but had lived in Russia. She spoke Korean, Russian, and was improving her English. She preferred living in Korea, because she felt less discriminated against. It amused us all that she would always wipe her desk down with a wet-wipe before actually sitting down.

Somehow I felt closer to this class than my other classes; partially because it was all women and partially because the women in it were so open-minded and accepting of me and my crazy ways. There were some days we would talk about PMS, and Ji Hye as well as her new boy interest—who is now actually her hubby (!).

It was in their class, because they made me comfortable enough to do so, that I read one of the creative essays that I had written about an angel. I wasn't sure what to expect. I knew they would be supportive and listen intently as they always had when I was teaching them something, but I didn't think that they would tell me then as they were telling me that night in Hapjeong that I should really think about writing a book.

I have always wanted to write a book. After returning from Japan in 2003, having lived and taught there for three years, I moved back into my parent's house in California and was job searching and soul searching. It was perhaps one of the darker periods in my life, because I really had no idea what I wanted to do WITH my life. Not to mention I was dealing with reverse culture shock. I'd catch myself talking to myself in Japanese, bowing to strangers, and I would only really notice when I was out and about and people would give me weird looks. It was writing that saved me and helped me through this period—almost like an old friend would. It was writing that became like therapy. I began writing about my dating experiences in Japan and then in the U.S. What started out as a therapeutic, creative outlet has grown into a collection of creative essays chronicling my dating adventures as well as other thoughts on issues that became important to me. I have included some of these essays for your reading pleasure.

In 1994, Dave Levine and Mike Feinberg founded KIPP (Knowledge Is Power Program) Charter schools. They began their careers as teachers in Texas with the Teach for America program, but what was so amazing about their commitment to educating those who had less was the way in which they recruited fantastic teachers who could make a difference[1]. They would ask these teachers about what kind of legacy they wanted to leave behind. Up until then and after reading their story I had never fully thought about what kind of legacy I wanted to leave behind. I mean, it is a rather morbid thought. I ended up adding a little discussion on Legacy in my Career Development courses at Yonsei. Students like me, up until that point, had never thought about their own legacies, but found it to be a very powerful exercise: to think about it and figure out what it is they should leave behind.

In one of our classes at FLI after talking about Michael Sandel's *What is Justice?*[2] The discussion turned and Ji Hye began talking about her funeral:

"What if no one comes to my funeral? I worry about that," she confided.

"I don't think you need to worry about that for a long time," Jae-kyung chimed in in her usual positive way. After all, Ji Hye was just a senior at Yonsei at the time.

"You know, Ji Hye, it is not how many people who show up to your funeral that you should worry about. You should be more concerned about what you leave behind," I said, worried that she was focusing too much on what she had been told to focus on, rather than something that is much more significant.

More than a decade after writing my first creative essay and inspired by my students, I would have never dreamed that I would be embarking on another writing journey—this time for my students WITH my students and many other incredible humans who have helped make this book sparkle. I have been teaching on and off for more than a decade now both in Korea and in Japan, as well as in the United States. I have kept in touch WITH some of my students over the years and some have even gone as far as telling me that I have inspired them. Some have sought out my classes and even my humble advice. Most importantly though, I don't think *they* have realized to what extent *they* have inspired me and touched me. So it is this book, this journey, this whatever you may call it, that I will leave behind as both my legacy and my gift for my students—the Jae–kyungs, Ji Hyes, Natalias and Aesuks-- in order to express to the best of my abilities in the form of a book what I cannot verbalize: my deepest and most sincere gratitude to them for believing in me.

Why Korea?

This has got to be, by far, the most frequently asked question of all time in Korea, second only to: how old are you and do you have a boyfriend. It has never been a neat one answer question for me. It does require your full attention, as it is in and of itself another story.

"How come you never come and visit me in Seoul?" Katherine asked. I was enjoying living in sunny California at the time. Katherine was my former roommate from graduate school. We lived first in the dorms together and then as roommates in an apartment off campus in Cambridge, Massachusetts. However, I rarely saw her while we were in graduate school. She was incredibly generous with her time, which was spent on volunteer work with Africare (a non-profit organization), being president of the Korean Student Association, being involved in her church, and oh, grad school work in general.

She was born and raised in Korea, and she had an affinity for traveling. During her university days, she would take off spending summer and winter breaks to just travel by herself. This is how she was able to improve her English—not through rote memorization in the *hagwon* system, but through real, raw travel adventuring. A few years ago, she outdid herself and quit her highly esteemed job at the Seoul Metropolitan Government Office to travel around the world solo, covering 19 countries in 10 months. She is now working on her Ph.D. at The University of Pittsburgh.

Raised by a hard-working mother*, Katherine was likewise fiercely determined. She graduated at the top of her class at Kyunghee University in a major she chose only because her family members thought she could find a "good job" with it upon graduation. She made her mom and family proud afterwards working tirelessly for Samsung for several years before joining me at Harvard for grad school.

"How come you never come visit me in Seoul and you always go to Singapore?" she persisted. It was true that I spent my winters heading south for warmth like a bird, since I was quite averse to cold weather, even though winters were quite mild in California. The last thing I really wanted to do was spend a real winter in Seoul, but I had not seen Katherine since we graduated from Harvard in 2006 and it was then the winter of 2009.

"Let me see if I can route my ticket through Seoul this year and come see you for about three days." Katherine was ecstatic. She emailed back and asked me what I wanted to do while I was out in Seoul.

"*Jimjilbangs* and maybe teaching jobs at universities." I replied. The next thing I knew, Katherine had emailed the top 5 universities in Seoul alerting them of the dates I would be visiting. Within another 24 hours, my former boss and now very good friend, Herim, wrote back to Katherine with a job application attached. The following week, after having filled out the application, I had a phone interview and was offered a job as an English Instructor at Yonsei's Foreign Language Institute.

I thought it might be a good idea to visit the campus, check out where I would be living, meet Herim, and look around before making the final decision to move. The truth is, I had wanted to move to Korea for a while, but hadn't found the right opportunity. It was not because my life wasn't going well in California or anything. I had been working for a language company that provided ESL lessons to employees and their family members at Chevron. I was able to work from home, my commute was as easy as crossing my living room from my bedroom in the mornings. For the first time in my life, all of my books were snugly sitting on my Ikea bookshelf in the living room of my very own one-bedroom apartment that sat overlooking a golf course. I had my car from university days that my roommate had affectionately nicknamed Winnipeg (because the license plate was 3WPG925), I had a great gym, my dad was a short 15-minute drive away, and I had a group of close-knit friends from high school and university that I would hangout with on the weekends. Yet, something was not quite right: I felt complacent and not challenged. What better way to

---

* I have since spent many a *Chuseok* with Katherine's mom and her family. Her mom always makes sure to send me home with mountains of Tupperware full to the brim with my favorite *panchan* that I can barely carry home. Thank you *Omma, Sarang hae yo.*

beat that then move across the world, to a country I had never lived in before and with a language I had never studied?

"So, would you like to sign the contract? Have you decided?" Herim looked at me curiously.

"You had me at the walk…" I semi-joked in response, referring to *Jerry Maguire.*

I had walked from my future dorm accommodation to FLI along a tree-lined path that eventually led to a tree-lined street, which at the time, was covered with snow. It was truly magical, something out of a Korean drama. Actually, not far from there, Kim Tae-hee and Lee Byung-hun (who were playing students in the K-drama crime thriller *Iris*) met for the first time on Yonsei's Sinchon campus. My heart was beating a little bit faster than usual, as I was half-excited and half-nervous: *would I be a good teacher? Would I be able to adapt to Korean culture? Would I be able to make friends? Would I be happy there?* With all of those questions still swirling around in my mind, I returned to California and began wrapping things up in preparation for my move to Seoul in March 2010—thanks in part to Katherine.

SELF WORK:
What is *your* legacy? What would *you* like to leave behind? Write your thoughts below:

What I Love About Korea

1. Sometimes when a bus is crowded and you give up your seat to an *ajumma*, she will carry your heavy bag/groceries on her lap very insistently.
2. Food delivery: there are no additional fees, you can use your credit card, and your food comes quickly.
3. When you frequent a fruit store/grocery store enough, *ajummas* or *ajosshis* will give you freebies (the bones of a whole salmon fish, extra *panchan*, extra fruit to name a few I have received in the past).
4. You don't have to ever really wait for a doctor/dentist appointment. Not to mention the equipment is usually quite high-tech.

5. When you go to a hair salon, they give you coffee/tea/biscuits and you get a free head massage. And on the high end, you pay no more than USD$30!
6. At every restaurant, you get free *panchan* and you can order more at no extra cost!
7. When you get your nails done at a nail salon, they do a really good job, the color lasts for at least a week if not more and they even help you with your bag, coat, rings when you're done.
8. You can get glasses made within an hour, frames are inexpensive, and there are tons to choose from.
9. Customer service is fast/respectable/efficient. You never have to wait longer than one person, and if you are waiting, they will hustle to get another customer service representative to help you.
10. *Jjimjilbangs* have different rooms (sand room, charcoal room, steam room, and so much more) and you can eat really good Korean food there as well as lounge there for a very reasonable price. Check out Conan[3] at a *Jjimjilbang* with Steven Yeun[†] (from *The Walking Dead*[‡]):

11. No one will steal your stuff at a café if you leave it out on your table and go to the bathroom. Amazing.

What This Book Is And Isn't

Isn't

"What are you afraid of?" MK questioned, concerned, and wanting to help.

It was a valid question. I had wanted to write a book for as long as I can remember. I had started writing creative stories upon my return to the U.S. after my three-year stint in Japan. It was part creative, part cathartic,

† Korean-American actor who stars in *The Walking Dead*.

‡ American TV series about zombies that features Steven Yuen.

part accomplishment. It came at a time when I didn't know what I wanted to do with my life, was living at home with my parents, and getting rejected from jobs at the local supermarket and Starbucks. MK was a veteran writer. She had done the mecca of all writing jobs, in my humble opinion, and had completed her very own Ph.D. dissertation. She and I had met at Harvard as we were in the same program and had mutual friends, but we didn't fully become BFFs until Seoul: I had moved there for work and she for research. We naturally started spending a lot more time together.

"I am not a good writer, I don't use big SAT words or research," I lamented. "I am afraid of failure. What if nobody publishes the book or buys it for that matter?"

"Well, how are you gonna know, if you don't try?"

I stopped in my thought tracks with a screeching halt. It was true. *How was I going to know if I didn't at least try?*

"I have to be a role model for my students. That is what I am always telling them," I told MK as I thought out loud.

"Think of the books you like, right? Kaling's *Is Everybody Hanging Out Without Me and Other Concerns*, Sandberg's *Lean In*, Dunham's *I'm Not That Kind of Girl*...they weren't necessarily conventional books, right? People still bought them, right?" She had a point.

So what this book isn't is a book full of jargon, data, research, and other boring stuff. If that is what you would like to read, perhaps you can pick up a copy of *The Economist.* I usually get through the summary of the world debrief section, and then fall asleep immediately on the plane. At least I look smart though, clutching it on my lap, in a vain attempt to hide my other guilty pleasure: US Magazine.

Is

"Why would you think no one would buy your book? That would be impossible," John looked at me in disbelief. John headed up the Asia Leadership Trek, where I had applied to teach middle schoolers about leadership in January 2012 at a camp in Pohang.

I didn't know what to say. I was so emotionally and intellectually drained talking about my adaptive leadership challenge. We were taking an Acumen online course together, and, for the first and now second session, we had been self-analyzing why we were the very reason we could not overcome our challenges. My own adaptive leadership challenge was writing a book, *this* book. One of the questions in the activity asked, "If there was a security camera on you, what would it see you were doing?" I answered very matter-of-factly that it would show me checking Facebook, celebrity gossip on US Magazine and People's websites, and watching action movies on TV.[§] Another question asked, "What is a less noble way to explain what you are doing?" I answered immediately that I was being lazy.

"I guess I fear failure, because when I was working for that non-profit[**], I worked my ass off, and got burned, and for what?" I went on to explain, as John probed further.

"Sounds to me," as he eyed the "Speaking the Unspeakable" section on the white board he had just written, "You are just making excuses."

He was right, I should write. MK was right, John was right, my husband Edgar was right, everyone around me believed in me, and I understood why I was afraid, I had verbalized it time and time again. There was only one thing left to do: start typing (!).

So this book is an adaptive challenge: a recurring problem, avoidance, a gap between my reality and my aspirations. This is me confronting my fear of failure, and trying. So it isn't really a failure. This is me doing what I have always told my students to do: do what you love, drown out the other voices, and if the "haters are gonna hate," then, as the great Taylor Swift sings, "Shake it off."

And if I can help YOU accomplish what you have always wanted to do along the way, learn from my mistakes, be a better human-being, then I think I have done something great, created change in this world for the better: one human-being at a time.

Is there anything that you have always wanted to start doing? In my listening and speaking classes, for our integrated project, I usually have students watch this TED video by Matt Cutts:

[§] I'm not trying to make myself look good, but I thought I just had to point out the fact that since boarding school I never owned my own TV, because we weren't really allowed to watch TV. It was just over part of winter break (February 11-28th, 2015) when I had to move out of my on-campus apartment due to drilling downstairs that I became somewhat of a TV addict. Don't judge me.

[**] I talk about it in my TED Talk and later on in this book, but basically I worked for a non-profit in Cambridge, Massachusetts after I graduated with my master's from Harvard and was often verbally abused by the Development Director there.

If you watch the video, you will find out that Matt's life is seemingly very predictable and he wants to create change in his life, so he creates these 30-day challenges. He realizes that if he makes smaller changes during a 30-day period, the changes are more likely to be sustainable. Upon watching the video, my students have to complete a 10-day challenge of their own choice and then give a presentation on what they learned along the way. The goal is not necessarily to "successfully" complete all of the challenge(s) over the 10 days, but to learn something about yourself in the process.

One of the more meaningful and heart-breaking 10-day challenges I had students do during the spring semester of the Sewol Ship tragedy back in 2014, was think about ways they could honor the families who had lost a family member in the sinking. One student taught her friends how to swim, reasoning that if a lot of the high school students on the ship actually knew how to swim, they would still be alive today. Yet another student went out all over Seoul and tied a yellow ribbon on bridges so that we could remember those who passed away. One student even created his own post card, where he drew the heroes who had lost their lives saving others; he handed out copies he had made to me and the other students in our class after his final presentation, and just like that created change. Here is the postcard:

We were all extremely touched. The classroom fell silent. I'd like you to take a pause, a moment to remember the heroes represented in this postcard but also those who lost their lives, and those who lost their loved ones that day.

Reading With Vs At

You will probably not be surprised when I tell you that I have tried to structure the book in as WITH a way as much as possible. To that end, you, the reader, have tons of ways to interact WITH this book and thereby me. There are DOODLES/TAKEAWAYS/REFLECTION POINTS sections at the end of every chapter, but feel free to add your mark anywhere in the book. I have included QR codes, so if you get bored of reading you can watch a cool video. My all-time favorite parts (the inner educator in me is just screaming WITH joy right now!) are the SELF WORK sections scattered here and there throughout the book--I would love to see you put your two cents into what you've just read. Take this book to a café, on a date WITH yourself; go to the beach WITH this book, read it on the sand, and do your reflection there or wherever your heart takes you.

This is not a boring textbook, or a book you *have* to read in an AT way. This book is entirely for you to learn and discover as much WITH yourself as possible. If you need to skip around, feel free to do so. If you only want to read certain chapters first, and certain chapters later, feel free to do so. If you don't feel like reading and just feel like watching some videos, get out your QR reader and have a ball. No one is judging you. I promise.

As you are reading along, please feel free to write to me if you have any suggestions, comments, thoughts or anything else in between. I would love to hear from you and work WITH you!

SELF WORK:

So as Matt Cutt says, "What are you waiting for?"

Write down some thing or things you have always wanted to do/change:

What/who is preventing you from doing it?

In the next 10 days, start your very own 10-day challenge. Use the space provided to record how you spent your days. What did you learn about yourself? Was it difficult? Why?

Day 1

Day 2

Day 3

Day 4

Day 5

Day 6

Day 7

Day 8

Day 9

Day 10

What changed over the course of the 10 days? Could you foresee continuing this after the 10 days? Repeat (for another 10 days or more!) something you have always wanted to start. Some things that I have done on my 10-day challenges: paragliding, horseback riding, running in 5/10/15K races. Some students who love the idea actually try to keep it up even after the semester is over. Why not? If you can incorporate this new challenge into your daily schedule--even better—do it!

CAST OF CHARACTERS

(In Alphabetical Order By First Name/Nickname)

Amy (AKA Fran): We met teaching at an after school program for Korean students in the Bay Area in California. Her nickname became "Fran" because her mom misheard her call me "Friend" and thought my name was "Fran." We have been calling each other "Fran" ever since.

Carlos: Then Dean at CETYS University in Mexico.

Catrina: A good friend from college.

Charles: A friend I met through college buddies of mine.

Chris Anderson: TED Curator.

Chris P.: A former co-worker from Yonsei University and good friend.

Crystal: A former student of mine from Yonsei University. She first took my Career Development course, later co-headed a leadership seminar we created, and is currently working for a pharmaceutical company in Seoul.

Gabi: A former student of mine from Yonsei University.

Greg: A friend from boarding school.

Edgar: My hubby/soul-mate/love of my life.

Emilia: Finnish Sisu expert and friend.

Eugene: A friend introduced to me by Niko, and founder of kinlovgra.com

Herim Kim: Former Head Coordinator at the Foreign Language Institute (FLI) at Yonsei University, and one of my first friends I ever made in Korea.

Hugh: My college friend.

Ilkka: We met in Finland when he happened upon one of my workshops at Laurea University in 2015. We decided to start collaborating. We have Skyped each other in to workshops, created a podcast together (called The Happy Hour), engaged WITH each other's students, and so much more. I have since been back to Finland twice and been able to collaborate WITH him in person too, which has been amazing. We are constantly pushing the boundaries of what it means to collaborate cross-culturally and otherwise.

Izzy: Short for Isabelle. She was my former Chem teacher in boarding school and now one of my best friends/mentors.

Jae-kyung: A former FLI student and friend.

Ji Hye: A former FLI student and friend.

Jiwon: A former student of mine from Yonsei University.

Joanne: A college friend of mine from UCSD.

Katherine: A good friend and former roommate from grad school.

Katrina: A former Co-worker who used to work with me at a non-profit in Boston; now a good friend.

Kelly Stoetzel: TED Content Director.

Krystal: A former JC Education tutor.

Lusekelo: He was an exchange student who hailed from Tanzania, but was attending university in a small town called Steyr in Austria. He took my Cross-Cultural Communication course during the fall of 2013 at Yonsei University. He has since graduated from university and is currently back in Tanzania.

MK: One of my best friends from Harvard; MK stands for Min-Kyung

Minjeong: A former Yonsei student and friend. She wrote the foreword.

Miu: My sister's nickname. Her real name is Tisha.

Mr. Wood: Former Japanese High School teacher and mentor.

Mrs. Hughes: Former 2nd grade elementary school teacher.

Mrs. Hwang: Owner and founder of JC Education where I worked as a tutor in the Bay Area from 2003-2004.

Niko: Personal chef and founder of naturallyniko.com

Paul Pickowicz: A mentor of mine and former professor at UCSD.

Ping: One of my best friends from UCSD; her real name is Ann.

Ramu Damodaran: Then UNAI Deputy Director.

Roommate: One of my best friends from UCSD; a former roommate; her real name is Michelle.

Sean: Then TED AV/IT guy.

Seongju: A former student of mine from Yonsei University.

Shawna: My college friend Hugh's girlfriend; professor at University of Hawaii.

Tarah: A good friend of mine from my boarding school.

Tarja: I met her at the Cross-Cultural Business Conference I was invited to speak at by Lusekelo in Austria. Later, I would go on to meet Ilkka through her in Finland, and be invited by her to speak in Finland. We would become good friends.

WonJae: A friend from boarding school.

Ye Il: A former student of mine from Yonsei University.

THE WHAT

CHAPTER 0

THE BEGINNINGS OF WITH VS AT (WERE AT)

"If you don't have confidence in yourself, nobody else will."
~me

"How many cups of coffee have you had?!" Chris Anderson demanded, "You have too much energy!"

"This is how I teach and my students seem to really enjoy it," I stammered back, almost ready to cry.

"This will not come across on camera and people will not take your points seriously," he continued.

"Yes, it is also too long and cliché," Kelly chimed in. Sean worried about playing a song in the background. I had wanted to play Journey's *Don't Stop Believin'* as a message to people that life is a journey and you should never stop believing in yourself. Note to self: too cliché.

After doing a mock presentation in front of Chris Anderson (TED Curator), Kelly Stoetzel (TED Content Director), and Sean (AV/IT guy), this was the last thing I had expected given my blind confidence in both my slides and my content.

In 2012, TED decided that they would go on the road to 14 different countries around the world to seek out, in their words, "the young, talented and undiscovered" speakers for their annual TED conference in 2013. They only asked that you submit a 1-minute video as to why you thought you were worthy. I debated whether or not I should apply. I used TED all of the time in the classroom: it was inspiring, relatable, and did I mention inspiring? *Was I at the same level as the TED speakers I was sharing with my students?* Then one of my best friends from university, Ping, asked me what my motivation was for applying to audition. Was I interested in fame or fortune? Or did I think I had an important message to get out to the world? I thought about me on the red carpet, walking arm-in-arm with my tuxedo-clad hubby wearing a sparkly dress from Versace…and then I thought, *it was about the message who was I kidding? I know I have an important message, but what is it?*

With very little tech skills, I asked a good friend of mine and then co-worker also by the name of Chris (who used his old-school video camera) to film me in my office. Let's call him Chris P. so we can differentiate between my friend Chris and Chris Anderson. Between the two of us, we had absolutely no editing skills, so Chris P. just did 6 or 7 re-takes. It is actually not bad considering there was absolutely no editing involved. I use pictures that I have drawn to show how I would like to create global leaders who will change the world, and this is why I deserve to be on the TED stage. Check out the video here on vimeo.com:

I found out a few months later, via email, that I was one of the finalists chosen to speak for 6 minutes. I have to admit, I was nervous as hell but excited at the prospect of speaking on a TED stage, yet still the question plagued me: *what the hell was I going to talk about for 6 minutes?* I began thinking about the message that I wanted to get out there. It was how I taught. I never droned on and on lecture-style, but I preferred to not only teach WITH my students, but also learn WITH them. It made me sorely uncomfortable to be the center of attention. I always tried to put myself in my students' shoes: How would students get the most out of any given activity? How could students maximize their learning potential/growth? That was when WITH vs AT was born.

Chris Anderson continued, "There is something about WITH vs AT though. I have never seen that before. You should flush that out."

I was stunned. I had gone in cocky thinking, *I do this all the time. I can present in my sleep. I give my students feedback on their presentations all the time. I got this.* Things couldn't have been further from this. Oh and it was 11AM. The live filming would take place at 5PM. There would be a stage rehearsal at 4:30PM for those of us who had messed up big time.

I was also underprepared: I was not told that there was a rehearsal the day before, and was given very little information about the big day itself.

Sean was the most approachable of the three. I found him chatting with one of the Korean AV/IT guys in front of his MacBook Pro.

"Sean, fuuuuuuck, what am I going to do?"

"OK, tell me what you're thinking. Use me as a sounding board."

"Well, maybe I can tell 3 stories about WITH vs AT," I was wiping away tears at this point, hoping Sean wouldn't notice, lest I be taken less seriously.

"Great, everyone loves a story," Sean responded calmly and supportively. His brown curly hair seemed all over the place, much like my own presentation.

I went to the bathroom. It was quiet in there—I could hear my voice, my thoughts, and drown out the negativity I had just heard in the green room. I was alone in there. I put the toilet seat down and sat down. *OK, Kyla think. You can do this.* I wiped away my tears, pulled out a copy of the newspaper I had bought (I think I am the only person in all of Seoul who actually buys and reads paper newspapers in English). I used the side columns to draw 5 squares to represent my 5 slides. The first slide would be my intro, the following three would be my three stories, and then my final slide would be my conclusion. It was simple, maybe too simple, but better than over complicating things.

I had done a brief rehearsal for MK and she had liked the original 16-slide Power Point presentation. She asked me to call her if I needed anything, if I wanted her to come. I was allowed to invite 10 people, but decided to give all 10 of the invitations to my students, and make them part of my presentation. After all, a teacher is nothing without his/her students, right? I firmly believed this. I also thought it would be an incredible opportunity for them to see the other 17 TED@Seoul audition finalists. Although I couldn't see MK in person, I could at least call her. I decided to quickly go outside to call and update her.

"They hate me, I don't wanna be here…" I sobbed in response to MK's question of how things were going.

I was in downtown Kangnam, a place where Psy would make famous in his catchy song by the same name just two short months later in July. Men and women in suits were walking with purpose. They were important. They had places to go. In their busyness, they were taken aback by this girl who was sobbing on the phone, but only momentarily. They quickly went back to their busy lives, clutching their Starbucks coffees perhaps trying not to stare and be rude. I definitely did not fit in to the Kangnam scene.

"Kyla, there is a reason you are there. You have an important message. Go back up there. You belong there," she reasoned.

I took MK's advice, pulled myself together, and went back upstairs. Before heading to the auditorium, I was caught off guard by a reporter. She wanted to interview me for a KBS (Korean Broadcasting System) special documentary on TED. My eyes red and puffy, I told her I would be right back after I went to the bathroom really quickly. Again, in my sanctuary, I looked in the mirror: *Kyla, get it together. You can do it.*

The interview did miracles for my self-esteem and restored my self-confidence. Fortunately, I didn't know at the time, that they would end up cutting my entire interview, and showing a picture of my face for a brief second before the documentary began.

"So much better," Chris Anderson and Kelly said at different points after my stage rehearsal.

"Ask them what the ball is," Chris Anderson coached. He was referring to one of the AT balls I was going to throw AT the audience to illustrate my point of WITH vs AT.

The kind of AT balls he, Kelly, and Sean were hurling AT me. None of the three ever asked me how I felt, what I thought should/could be changed; instead they threw their ideas of what I had to change AT me. I felt like I was on some reality TV show for presenters. Before going up on stage, I recall being nervous, but honestly, I cannot recall what I said. By the time I got up on stage, I was so emotionally and psychologically stretched, my brain was almost too tired to be too nervous. Shortly after my presentation, I stayed long enough to watch the teenage archer who presented after me (and was one of four who ended up going on to the annual TED 2013 conference) shoot an arrow at a target using a homemade bow clear across the stage.

"Can I get you some coffee?" I asked the Korean AV/IT guy who had lent me his Macbook Pro to edit my slides. I felt I owed him a big one.

"Can I get a latte and your phone number?!" I don't think I owed him *that* much. I pretended I hadn't heard the last request and told him I would be back with his latte.

I almost ran out of that auditorium. Breathing in the Kangnam air never felt better: I still did not fit in or belong, but somehow, there was a sense of relief that I had accomplished what I had come to do. What MK had told me to do. What I had wanted to do. But more importantly, I had been a role model for my students, and they had in turn inspired me: during the intermission, Chris Anderson and Kelly had invited audience members to get up on stage to answer one of two questions: 1) What can Seoul learn from the world? 2) What can the world learn from Seoul? Three of my ten students had gotten up on stage and answered the questions in English, when a lot of other audience members had defaulted and responded in their native Korean.

When people ask me about TED and what it was like on stage, I say this, "My moment was not when I was on stage. It was when my three students were on stage, speaking in English about changing the world."

Here is a picture of one of my students, Jiwon, talking about how Seoul can learn about education reform from the rest of the world. I show this picture to my students every single semester to inspire them and I tell them:

"This is what I wish for you: The confidence to get up in front of almost 500 people, and present in English. You can do it."

And this is what I wish for you, too.

Jiwon on the TED@Seoul stage | Seoul, South Korea | May 2012

Here is my TED Talk on WITH vs AT where our story truly begins; I talk about the importance of communicating WITH people instead of AT them. I highly encourage you to check it out so you can get a deeper understanding of why this book is so important and how it came about:

Elevator Pitch

As urban legend would have it, there was a salesperson who was desperate to sell an idea to a CEO. Here's how the conversation went:

> SALESPERSON: I have this great idea.
>
> CEO: I don't have a lot of time. If you can convince me by the time I get to my office on the top floor of this building, I'll see what I can do.

The rest, well, is urban legend history. Out of this story, the elevator pitch was born. I am not sure if I made this up or someone told me about it, but either way, I have always taken to the idea. I have even had to do some real elevator pitches myself, not actually in an elevator, but when high-powered people are pressed for time. I even do this exercise with my students too. I have them walk in pairs (taking turns being CEO/themselves) down the corridor. By the time they reach the end of the corridor, they have to convince their partner/CEO why he/she should hire them. So, here's my own elevator pitch about WITH vs AT.

> ME: I came up with this style of communication WITH, two-way communication rather than AT just lecturing one-way at someone.
>
> CEO: Oh? Tell me more. (He/she is not that interested at this point. Yikes, we are on the 5th floor already…)
>
> ME: Well, I started noticing not just at the university where I was teaching in Korea, but at conferences all over the world, where I spoke, that no one was paying attention to what the speakers were saying. The audience was distracted on their device of choice.
>
> CEO: Why does this matter?
>
> ME: Well, it matters in how we communicate successfully WITH people. If we can fundamentally change the way we communicate and interact WITH others, then we can create substantial positive change in our lives.
>
> CEO: So what have you done about this?
>
> ME: In 2012 I gave a TED Talk on this and I think it can impact so many different facets of our lives, not just in education but in relationships, love, work, and of course fundamentally bring awareness of how we communicate WITH others. I'm so passionate about it I decided to write a book about it.
>
> CEO: Ok, send me a copy…and a link to your TED Talk. (This is the best-case scenario. I have thought about how this could also end in the CEO leaving without a word and the elevator doors closing in my face.)

SELF WORK:
Create your own elevator pitch. Practice with a friend. Walk and talk with your pretend CEO for 2 minutes and convince your pretend CEO why he/she should hire you.

Doodles/Takeaways/Reflection Points

THE WHY

CHAPTER 1

EDUCATION (LEARNING + TEACHING WITH)

"A teacher is only as good as his/her students." ~me

I am an accidental educator. When I was young, as in elementary school age, I despised my teachers. Not because they were necessarily bad, but because they disciplined me and didn't let me get away with inappropriate behavior. Like the time my 2nd grade teacher, Mrs. Hughes called my mom and told her that I was throwing my lunches away. Up until that point, I had thought Mrs. Hughes was just a regular teacher. After she cared to tell my mom and voice her concern, I realized she was going above and beyond her teaching duties. Even though at the time I totally resented her for doing so.

I would scrunch my ham, cheese, lettuce on un-toasted white bread sandwiches in foil, and throw them in the trashcan or, in British speak, bin (I went to British schools in Hong Kong until I was 14 years old). I didn't have the heart to tell my mom (who had painstakingly put them together) that I did not like them at all. Needless to say, I got in serious trouble with my mom when she found out, but don't worry, all is well that ends well, because once *Popo* ("maternal grandma" in Cantonese) moved in with us and my sister introduced the thermos flask, we were able to start eating lasagna, *char siu* ("roasted pork" in Cantonese) with rice, and lots more scrumptious hot lunches.

It wasn't until boarding school, in California, where I started appreciating the awesome teachers I had. Take Mr. Wood, my Japanese teacher, for example: A meticulous Caucasian man who knew if your stroke order was incorrect (even though you tried to erase it) and he would dock points. He was one of my favorites. I didn't realize it though until I got into some serious trouble (getting caught drinking off campus*); I felt like I had letdown not only my parents, but faculty members like Mr. Wood who were like surrogate parents to me.

Shortly after the incident, Mr. Wood left me a small wooden vase filled with fragrant tuberoses and a card. I can't remember exactly what was written in the card, but I remember that somehow it made me feel that everything was going to be alright, and that I would be alright, and that he wasn't judging me for that one incident.

Science and math were not my forte. I remember struggling to understand pollination in flowers in my freshman bio class. Mr. Denison (my high school bio teacher) or Mr. D as we affectionately called him promptly took me outside, showed me some flowers that were blooming, and I understood so much better than I could have ever understood from the thick textbook that awaited me in class. *So awesome.* I didn't realize it then, but this would play a huge part in why I would take my own students outside for class at Yonsei.

Then there was Izzy (Isabelle) who was my AP Chem teacher. She would invite my friend Rita and I over to her place on campus to watch *Friends*. Perhaps this would foreshadow that years later, we would become best friends in the Bay Area, going as far as selling our own hand-crafted jewelry on Telegraph Avenue in Berkeley (!). Today, she is launching her very own hand-made granola business, and still very much inspiring me.

Classes were small: there were usually about 10-12 students in one class, which meant you couldn't hide if you hadn't done the homework or you didn't know the answer. You had to participate. Participating was worth about 1/3 of your entire grade. My first semester, I received mostly Bs and Cs due to my shyness. Yes, I was shy. My father was so concerned, he soon enrolled me in an Acting Workshop class. 15-year-old Kyla was mortified. I could barely imagine my shy self up on stage, but it ended up being a surprisingly fun class and a nice reprieve from the other academic classes I was taking my sophomore year. You may be even more surprised to note that at the end of my freshman year and then again my sophomore year, I won the speech competition for my entire year and had to give my speech in front of the entire school (!). Pretty cool.

Perhaps it was foreshadowing things to come?

In January 2017, I went back more than 20 years after I had graduated to do some workshops with sophomore students and I even got to speak in front of the entire school. During my talk, I gave Mr. Wood a notebook and inscribed a little note on the inside thanking him for believing in me. I

---

* Going to a big public school it wouldn't be a big deal, but because my boarding school consisted of roughly 250 students only, everyone knew everyone's business (!).

found the card that he had given me with the vase of tuberoses, and read part of the card in front of the whole school, fighting back tears as I did. That night, we caught up (as if no time had passed) over dinner and I was happy to learn he had since gotten married, had 2 kids, and his daughter was a freshman at my boarding school. The highlight of the night was showing him a draft of my book and having him read the part that featured him. He laughed out loud. After dinner it was pouring cats and dogs. In the car on the drive back to where I was staying in Carpinteria, I asked Mr. Wood for some marriage advice. He quoted a song from Wilson Philipps inadvertently, saying that when things get tough just "Hold on for one more day." How appropriate given the song came out in 1990 shortly before we had first met in 1992. He escorted me to the door, holding a large golf umbrella over my head. *What a great teacher, father, and man*, I thought.

When I teach, I channel all of these experiences. I think about the Mr. Woods of my boarding school, and how they were really on my side both personally and academically. They wanted me to succeed. I think of the Mrs. Hugheses of my elementary school, who used tough love to get us unruly kids on the right path. I try to be the best version of the best educators I have had throughout my life, and I teach how I would have liked to be taught.

I think when people think about education, they think about a classroom, books, homework, assignments, and a school, but actually so much of *real* education happens outside of this realm. Those moments where you get an encouraging note with a vase of flowers or your mom receives a phone call from your teacher about that sandwich you haven't been eating.

Here I want you to pause and think about education with a wider lens: think about each and every moment you have ever been taught something, whether it is a parent teaching a child how to tie his/her shoe laces, whether it is a CEO teaching his/her manager to write a report, whether it is a child teaching a parent how to use Facebook, or a manager teaching his/her CEO how to use a new computer program. Whatever the industry, whatever the scenario, education is truly ubiquitous. We cannot escape it. Some of us have better access to it than others, some of us take advantage of it more than others, some of us recognized it more than others. Some of us just detest it and can't wait to graduate, while others live for school and wish they could have just one more year. Whatever the case, we are constantly learning, therefore, we constantly need "educators" in our lives.

What I want you to think about is when you teach someone that next thing (whether it is your boss, co-worker, classmate, student, whomever) whether you are teaching Quantum Physics or merely giving directions how to get somewhere, think about doing it WITH instead of AT. Think about those true moments of WITH vs AT teaching where about the subject necessarily, but about the delivery and how much you truly care about the well-being of that person/people.

Only Teachers Can Teach

Let me tell you, I have met plenty of so-called "teachers" and "professors" who cannot teach to save their lives. Similar to any other profession, there are people who are amazingly talented, naturally gifted, average, below average—you get the drift. The profession of teaching is no different. What I want people to understand though is you cannot separate yourself from being a teacher just because you are not in a classroom. If you have ever taught anybody anything in your life, that was a teaching moment, you were a teacher.

Actually, think back to a moment when you did teach someone something. I want you to close your eyes and try to remember what you did, what you said, what was the interaction like between you and that other person. Ask yourself these questions: Did I ask that person any questions? Did I check that person's body language to see whether he/she was comfortable and understood what I was saying? Did I basically lecture at this person? If your answers were No, No, Yes, then here we should pause and evaluate what happened. You were teaching AT someone. There are no two ways about it.

Let's take feedback for example. This is more or less universal. Feedback happens regularly, at companies, in schools, in all kinds of organizations. We are always looking for feedback to improve ourselves or others. My co-workers and I often commiserate that in no other profession are we constantly being evaluated. At Yonsei, students created an unofficial website where they can basically log in and evaluate us real time using their smartphones (!). *Pretty intimidating.* Feedback is constant, and with today's technology it is actually easier to access it than ever before. We can always learn though and become better if the feedback is constructive, right?

In my listening and speaking classes, students have to give presentations in English. Now that is scary for them. I have tried various forms of feedback over the course of the 6 years I have been teaching, but I have found that individual feedback is the most constructive. Students sit down next to me, nervous, sometimes shaking a leg or rubbing their hands together, looking away. They want to know, but at the same time, they don't. In most cases, they fear the worst. I think we can all empathize with how they feel. We have all been on the other side of the fence and been evaluated.

Students expect that, right away, I will rattle off something they need to change. They expect that I will do all the talking and then they will just sit there quietly. Actually, I do the exact opposite. I first ask them, "How do *you* think your presentation went?" It usually takes them back a few seconds to process that 1) I am actually asking them a question, rather than giving them feedback; 2) They have to think, rather than just receive information; 3) They have to be objective about themselves. In short, their evaluation is being done WITH them.

Be comfortable with the pauses and silences. It is ok. They will eventually respond.

Then I ask, "What do you think you would do differently if you had to do the same presentation tomorrow?" By now, they are a little more used to responding and being more objective about themselves. You will be surprised that 9 times out of 10, they get everything that they should have improved on. What about the other 1 out of 10? Well, mostly they were so super nervous that they blanked out and have absolutely no recollection of what happened, what they said, or anything for that matter. I get it--that happened to me on the TED stage.

How To Teach (Creatively) With (Not At) Students: Or What I've Learned Teaching With Yonsei Students

These were in the form of post-it notes stuck to my bathroom door (when I used to live on campus in a tiny yet cozy studio) as reminders to stay true to my teaching philosophy. Remember to think of teaching broadly, and in the same vein, think of the classroom broadly too. The classroom can be thought of as a home, office space, café or anywhere else you frequent on a regular basis. The learner can be anyone from your friend, family member to a co-worker. The more broadly you think of teaching, the more creative you will be, and therefore the more WITH you can teach.

1. Create communities not classrooms

> I would say that I work just as hard to create a sense of community in the classroom as I do on teaching. Why should this even matter you ask? Well, if students feel comfortable in a fun, safe, non-threating environment, they are more likely to show up to class every single time, they are more likely to participate actively, they are more

likely to be relaxed, and they are more likely to help and support each other rather than compete against each other. Get to know your students, what they like, dislike; this will help focus your lessons more. By the end of the third week of each semester, I will have memorized all of my students' names. It's the little things. Students will notice the effort, and give back in the form of hard work, attendance, participation and much, much more.

2. Only 2/3 of learning takes place in the classroom

I have my sister to credit with this one. When I was struggling at Harvard in grad school, my sister said this to me. It was exactly what I needed to hear and prompted me to seek more learning and out-of-the-box learning experiences. At Yonsei, I would take full advantage of the forest or the amphitheater often holding classes outside to give students a different perspective other than the one from inside a white-walled classroom. What better way to learn about the 5 senses, than to actually use them in the forest and then write them down? Students also bond as we walk to the forest, because they feel a lot more comfortable since it is not a structured environment.

3. Create Global Leaders not Students

This may seem like a minute difference, but it actually has huge ramifications, in my humble opinion. In the 1960s, Robert Rosenthal and Lenore Jacobson (two psychologists) conducted an amazing experiment at an elementary school in San Francisco. The two rigged an IQ test, choosing random students as "academic bloomers." The results were shocking: the students who were labeled "academic bloomers" ended up outscoring their peers by 10-15 IQ points upon taking the same IQ test again a year later. Only 50% of the non-academic bloomers improved their score by 10 points[1]. In a way, what you label your students is a self-fulfilling prophecy—very scary.

4. Think Self Work Over Homework

Kind of like in this book, you are given self work—work to improve yourself. Give students work to not just enforce an activity but something that will change their lives for the better. I think homework is often given just to give busy work. Nobody *really* wants to do it (at the student level) and nobody *really* wants to grade it (at the teacher level). But what if in each and every self work assignment you gave, you actually did it too, and it inspired you when you saw the self-work that your students created? Thus, creating a virtuous cycle of inspiration (!).

5. Create Content that Matters

At a recent book fair, where the usual suspects of publishers had tons of shiny ESL textbooks galore, I thought: I really don't want students to listen to some boring listening activity on something they don't really care about and fill in the blanks about it, etc. I think it is fine to photocopy some stuff out of textbooks, but why not create your own content? You know your own students better than the textbook publishers, right? The other thing is that you can create content that matters. In my World Issues class, we talk about human trafficking, and I come up with a role-play activity involving a broker and a human trafficking victim, not telling students what it is all about. They then have to guess what they were role-playing about. I can tell you this much: they aren't going to have that in any textbooks! Here is another activity inspired by a TED Talk where students have to create their own condom packages: Here's a screenshot of my blog from spring semester 2013 with one of the condom wrappers designed by one of my students and a response from Amy Lockwood (the TED speaker). So cool she actually responded to my email!

6. Build Creative Confidence

> Start backwards. I know it sounds weird, but think about the lesson you are going to do. Think about the purpose. What do you want students to get out of it? Then work backwards. For every point you want to make or emphasize, think of a creative activity that you can use to help students learn by doing. Not only will they retain it more, have more fun, but you will also get to hone in on your creative skills and the students' creative skills. Oh and lose the creative myth that only artists and designer types can be creative. Teachers and anyone for that matter can be just as creative if not more.

7. Be Yourself + Channel Your Inner Child

> No matter what age group you are teaching, I am telling you, every student has an inner child. An inner child whose creativity, critical thinking skills need to be drawn out. You can do that and more with your students if you also let go of the "teacher" persona and channel your own inner child. When I first started at Yonsei, I was so stressed. Not because of the workload nor because it was my first time teaching at a university per se, but because I was so caught up with the idea that professors had to be a certain way, teach a certain way, look a certain way, and so on and so forth. Once I let go and embraced my inner child, the sky was really the limit. I was less stressed, the students were

less stressed, because they can really feel your stress. It was so much more productive.

8. Make Students Cry (!)

This sounds like it is going to be about corporal punishment, shaming, blaming, failing, pointing out mistakes, but wait a second, it is actually about touching your students so much so that they begin to cry. Whenever I give students one-on-one feedback about their presentations, it is not just about their score or their grade, but it is about what they have learned about themselves in the process, and how they can improve themselves to be the best versions of themselves. Moreover, it is getting them to see the big picture: what does having confidence in oneself have to do with life after graduation? A LOT. Think about a job interview, a chance meeting with a CEO, a first date, a blind date, a salary negotiation, and the list continues. If you don't have confidence in yourself, then others will not have confidence in you. I often tell myself this and my students as well.

The Relationship Between Motivation, Success and Happiness

It came to me as every semester there were inevitably some co-workers who would always ask, "Oh, do you not have a full class this semester?" or "It's a Friday afternoon, do you have less students coming to class today?" I never told them exactly how many students I did or didn't have, as I didn't want to make them feel bad, but what I started noticing was that I always (more or less) had full attendance in all of my classes from the beginning of the semester until the end. I began hypothesizing: if they are generally happy in my classes, they would then want to come, right? Right. I had to prove it though.

During the fall of 2015, I asked 100 students (anonymously) several questions about happiness as it is related to attendance, motivation, success. The majority said either "YES" or "MAYBE" to most of the questions, but the interesting thing was I then asked how happy they were on a scale of 1-10 (10 being the highest) in my class versus their other classes and generally they were at a 6 in their other classes and a 9 in mine. *Pretty interesting.*

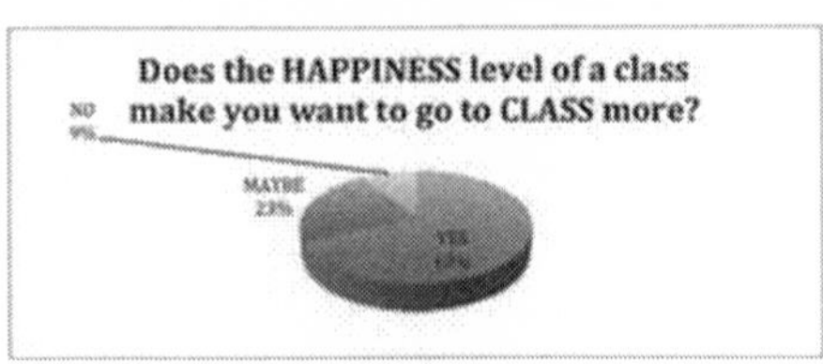

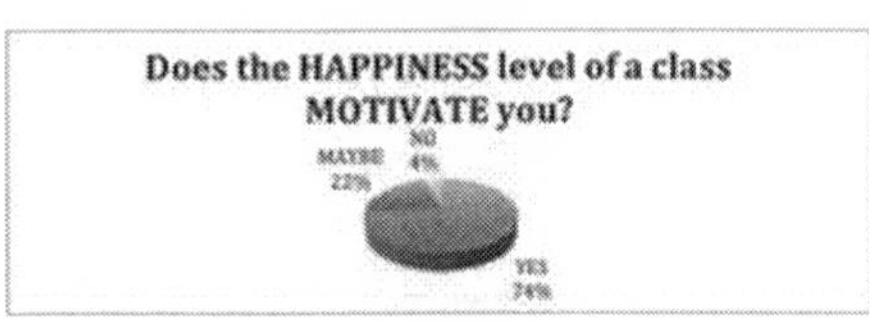

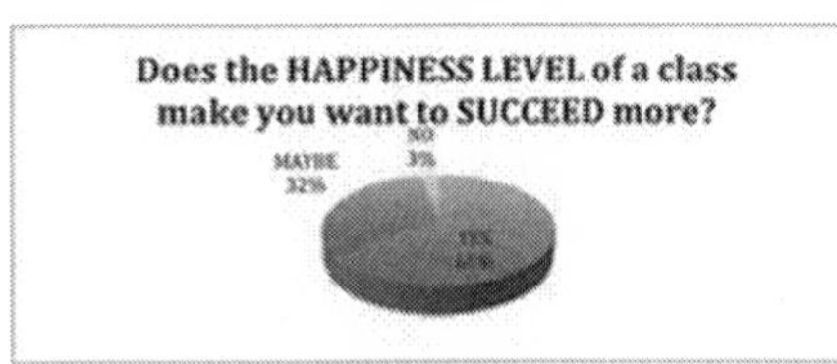

SELF WORK:
Answer the same 3 questions for yourself:

1. Would the Happiness level of a class/company make you want to go to class/work more?
2. Would the Happiness level of a class/company motivate you?
3. Would the Happiness level of a class/company make you want to succeed more?

It's Not About You: Teaching With Goes A Long Way

Somehow people who give feedback feel entitled to give it AT people. Often, they assume that because they have had more experience, they are older, hold a more senior position, they are of a certain gender, whatever the case, and they throw feedback AT others. What they fail to realize is it is actually NOT about them only. It is also about the other person on the receiving end. From my TED experience, you might have already gathered that Chris Anderson was not giving me feedback WITH, but rather AT. He did not *once* ask me my opinion on how I thought I could improve my presentation. Although he and the TED crew did do something WITH: that is during the intermission, they shared the stage WITH audience goers. What a neat opportunity for many of the audience who were young and eager to learn.

So often ego is tied up in learning. This attitude of I-know-more-than-you, therefore you have to shut up and listen to me. Just look at the direction in which lecture hall seats are facing. They are all facing the same direction, towards one point, where one person or a few key people will stand and deliver an AT lecture to hundreds of others. One of my main frustrations during my last semester at Yonsei, fall of 2016, was making my 150-person lecture hall for my Happiness Workshop class (which had grown from 40 the previous semester) more interactive, more WITH. I totally wish I could have moved the seats.

So I moved classrooms instead. I moved the class to a classroom where I could move the chairs and tables. This simple act changed everything. Students were more interactive, they sat closer to each other, and became closer emotionally.

In the old days, back before the days of the Internet, this AT style of learning could kind of be justified—somewhat. You would have a super old person who knew a lot about a certain subject lecture away to a captive and sometimes captivated audience. Now, we can't do that anymore, because most universities in the developed world are equipped with free Wi-Fi which basically means students can look up whatever they want on their own in between checking their FB messenger and FB walls. In a way, the playing fields have been leveled. Well, professors still hold PhDs and spend tons of years sequestered in some musty smelling library akin to one featured in Harry Potter, or CEOs have years of experience yelling AT people, right? Wrong. We should never assume we know more than others. Period.

How do we make sure that we don't become old ranty know-it-alls? Share your "stage" WITH someone or many people:

- Bring in some experts in other fields, industries, and expertise—think Taylor Swift sharing her stage with different artists such that she had to learn songs outside her comfort zone such as *Frozen* and *Can't Feel My Face.* Make professional development a priority for your organization/company/university/etc.
- Let your students/employees/co-workers share their talents. You know, you are not the only one who knows a thing or two. Perhaps have a brown bag lunch session where a different person leads it each time with a different topic

- Encourage multi-generational/cross-departmental/cross-cultural collaboration both internally and externally. I cannot tell you enough how much I have learned and grown from working with my Finnish collaborator, Ilkka†
- Support spaces/places/ideas to work together rather than individually (kind of related to the previous bullet point)
- Get creative with feedback, such that people have multiple ways to give you feedback (online, FB, messenger apps, chats, videos, paper, post-it notes). The more ways there are, the more people will feel free to

The Greatest "Gifts" To Teaching With: Failure and Mistakes

Two words that every learner tries often in vain to avoid are failure and mistakes. However, avoidance is not the path to take here, but rather facing these two words head on and letting learners know it is ok to make mistakes and fail. In some of my ESP (English for Specific Purposes) courses at Yonsei, we did these exercises to work through failure and mistakes. Students often told me after completing the exercises that it was their very first time to talk about failure and mistakes so openly. They had never thought about it before. Whoa.

During the fall semester of 2017, I ended up teaching two courses on Public Speaking at George Mason University (Korea). They called it COMM100. As had been my experience at Yonsei, most students were concerned about getting an A+. Some would become angry or upset whenever I asked them what *they* thought *they* could improve on, using the WITH paradigm of giving feedback. However, there was one student in all of my career teaching in Korea, who actually made an appointment to come see me during my office hours and ask me what she could do to improve—not for her grade, but for herself. She was already a top-performer and had scored an A+ on every single assignment up until that point.

---

† I will talk more about him later on in the book, but we met in Finland when he happened upon one of my workshops at Laurea University. We decided to start collaborating. We have Skyped each other in to workshops, created a podcast together (called The Happy Hour), engaged WITH each other's students, and so much more. I have since been back to Finland twice and been able to collaborate WITH him in person too, which has been amazing.

As my mind raced to attempt to even find one thing she needed to improve on for her next speech, I thought about how awesome it would be if every single learning environment, work environment, home environment, living environment embraced failure and mistakes such that every single person could feel free to ask, "How can I improve? How can I be better? For me."

Here is an essay I wrote about the "F word" and then actually ended up printing and giving out to students to read, because I was deeply troubled by their attitude toward failure.

(May 2014)

Kyla Mitsunaga

5/1/14

What Are We Really Afraid of?

"Our greatest fear is not that we are inadequate, but that we are powerful beyond all measure."

~Marianne Williamson

This quote is on my door and greets me every time I leave and return to my home. The truth is I have many fears: I fear failure, rejection, confrontation, my mom when she's angry, having no students sign up for my classes, cockroaches, growing old, not having enough money, and the list goes on. After having read about 20 paragraphs on Fear written by my audacious students, I was inspired to write my own thoughts on Fear. Furthermore, what struck me about the paragraphs was that there were some commonalities: most fears stemmed from childhood, many were psychological, and all of the writers had some extremely thoughtful ways to overcome their fears. Then I began thinking. Perhaps the important thing is not that we FEAR, but WHAT we fear that can make all of the difference. For instance, does anyone ever say they fear success? I fear becoming the greatest president that ever lived? I fear changing the world? No, hardly ever.

3 days before my 36th birthday, I wrote this paragraph on one of two F words that come up time and time again. The card with the Marianne Williamson quote on it was given to me by one of my best friends from grad school. She had overcome being diagnosed with a mild form of MS with this logic: Rather than ask, "Why me?" in a pitiful-poor-me-kind-of-way, think, "I was chosen because I am strong enough to deal with this." This same friend turned me on to a job listing she thought would be perfect for me in the non-profit sector in Cambridge, Massachusetts and I applied and was hired. 9 months into the job, I was very much facing my biggest F word:

FAILURE.

The Development Director, a ballsy no-bull-shit hunch back of a middle-aged woman had come to our non-profit from Harvard. She had brought with her a male deputy who was always at her side and beck and call. At first, she liked me. I was her go-to-girl. Then slowly, and painfully, as she peeled away what she called "smoke screens" she realized that the non-profit was not what she had thought it was and that it was going to be an epic failure. Yes, she would tell us this to our faces during meetings when my awesome visionary boss/founder was away on business trips.

During the winter of 2007, I was tasked with getting the board-meeting docket to print and getting it back to the office. It was just months away from the board meeting I was put in charge of planning-- the board meeting that was happening in New York, the board meeting that included government officials and other heavy hitters, the board meeting that the Development Director did not want to help me plan nor deal with, so she had her deputy work with me on planning it. That night, there was heavy snow, and by the time the founder had OKed everything, it was close to midnight. I had missed my then boyfriend's saxophone performance, and had no car to get all of the Kinko's boxes back to the office. It was then that I called Katrina, a co-worker and friend, and it was then, both of us crying, I finally admitted to myself that it was time to leave this job. And that dreaded F word popped into my blurry, exhausted head.

I think we have all been there. It doesn't have to be a job. It doesn't have to be a relationship. Whatever it is, we have all faced Failure on a micro or macro level. It is how we address or do not address it that matters more than the fear itself. For me, it took 5 years before I could go back to the Massachusetts area or even publicly speak about it. It made me doubt myself, my direction in life; it shook me to my very core. I mean, this was the first time since graduating that I had really "failed."

That same friend from grad school, throughout all of this chaos in my life, was my rock. Even now, whenever Failure raises its ugly head and pops back into my life, I recall some invaluable advice she gave me: "You know, what if failure wasn't really failure? What if failure was not trying something? Since you have already tried and you know that this job isn't for you, it's not really a failure is it?" I have used this same advice as foundation to create some new activities for students to help them understand failure better. You'll find one at the end of this chapter.

Students in Korea are under an immense amount of pressure. They are also amongst the unhappiest when compared to their OECD peers, and suicide is the leading cause of death amongst Koreans in their 20s. Over the years, not at first, but more and more students have done midterm or final presentations on how the education system in Korea needs to change when asked if they could change one thing about Korea what would they change and why. It is no secret. I bring this up, not because I want to criticize Korea or Koreans-let it be known-I love Korea and Koreans. I bring this up, because I worry about my students. Call it maternal instinct or what have you, but I do worry.

This semester, I tried for the first time to address some of these issues.

The first time I have ever addressed suicide in class, I decided to use a back-door approach. Rather than come out and say, "OK guys, today's topic is SUICIDE!" I thought, why don't we talk about LOVE and SELF-LOVE instead? As in most of my classes, there are hands-on activities, speaking activities where students go around and discuss different topics in English. One of the final questions that they have to answer is: if people loved themselves more, do you think they would try to kill themselves? Another question asks: What is the leading cause of death amongst Koreans in their 20s? Surprisingly, only about 50% of the students guessed correctly. The lesson went surprisingly well, although it hit home to some students in that a close friend of theirs or a friend of a friend of theirs had actually committed suicide.

Another activity I tried for the first time was asking students to talk about three times they have "failed" in their lives. More often than not, students will bring up the university entrance exam. When I first started at Yonsei in 2010, students would rarely mention it, but if they did, it would come up in terms of how they had failed it once.

Now more and more, I hear students talk about how they have taken it twice or even three times. Not to say that it makes you any less for having taken it more than once, but what does it say about a society that only values people from top universities like Yonsei? Are you any less smart if you graduate from a non-elite university? Does it make sense to devote an entire year of your life to studying for a test-not just the university entrance exam-but countless others: the law exam, the government exam, and other exams that are notorious for making test-takers waste away in koshi-wons (a tiny room used for studying where students will often live for a few months so they can focus on studying) for year upon year after "failing" the exams?

The light bulb moment (for a small handful of students) comes when I tell the students the story of my grad school friend and the advice she gave me. Some of the students' eyes sparkle. Those are the students you know have made that switch in their head to FAILURE = NOT TRYING, rather than FAILURE=FAILURE. I realize that the rest of the students will go back into their heads and compete, compete, compete and then beat themselves up when they do "FAIL," but for the few students whose definitions of "FAILURE" have changed, I am grateful. I am grateful because they will not go through their 20s the way I "failed" to.

More recently I even added a redefining failure activity, where students create their own definitions of failure. 2/3 are positive and 1/3 are negative. The students also have to come up with an improv skit about Failure. One of the groups used military service as a theme. One of the students Seongju didn't want to leave his girlfriend and complete his mandatory 21-month military service, so he kicked a chair in anger and ended up breaking his leg. Since he broke his leg, he didn't have to go in the end. He was then reunited with his girlfriend.

As I was watching in the back, half giggling, half recalling my own past, I thought of my own experience in non-profit. Perhaps if I had never "failed" or "broken my leg" in non-profit, it would have never led me to teaching, which I absolutely love. Redefining failure also helped me to reframe what I wanted in life. I had always thought *that I wanted to help people and that the only way I could go about doing that would be in the non-profit sector. Going into teaching, I realized I was still helping people-- I was helping them learn. As I approach my 36th birthday, the greatest gift I could ever give myself is changing my perception of fear, such that I embrace rather than fear greatness over weakness, successes over failures, gains over losses, and begin truly valuing how powerful I really am.*

SELF WORK: Here is the activity we did in class. Students find this activity extremely useful because they learn to not only talk about failure but also define it for themselves, as opposed to having society define it for them. Why don't you try answering these questions below as well:

1. When you hear the word FAILURE what do you think of? Why?

2. Create your own definition of failure.

3. What would you do if you were not afraid of failure? Why?

4. Why do you think so many people are afraid of failure?

5. What is the relationship between TRYING AND FAILING? Why?

Kyla Mitsunaga

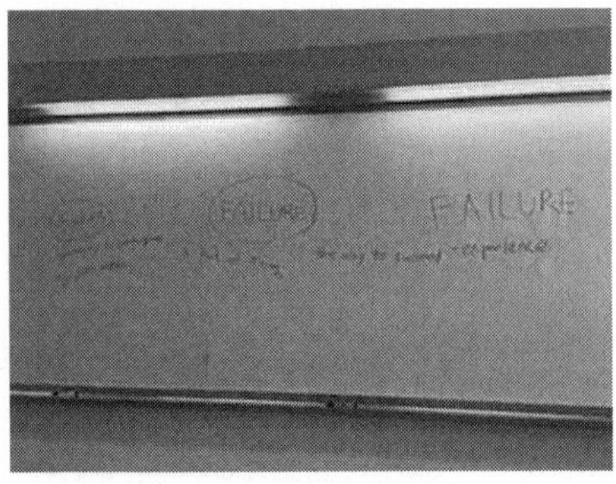

Yonsei Career Development Course: Students Redefined Failure | Seoul, South Korea | Spring 2015

Doodles/Takeaways/Reflection Points

MORE WHY

CHAPTER 1.5

CREATING CHANGE (IN LEARNING WITH OTHERS)

A friend: Why do you think you can change the world?
Me: It would stress me out not to do what I can to help.

Workshops

I started giving workshops at first to challenge myself: I loved teaching in the classroom at Yonsei, but I wasn't quite sure how people outside of Korea would take me and my different WITH-style of teaching.

So, when an invitation came to speak in Austria from a former student of mine, I jumped at the chance to push through my fears of public speaking, speaking outside of Korea, speaking to a different kind of audience, and trying new things.

It all began because one student believed in me. Lusekelo was an exchange student who hailed from Tanzania, but was attending university in a small Austrian town called Steyr. He took my Cross-Cultural Communication course during the fall of 2013 and would walk into class every week beaming. One day, after class, we grabbed coffee:

"Lusekelo, you are always so happy, and you smile so much. It is great having you in class," I said as I looked at him curiously.

"Well, you know, in Tanzania, we do not have a word for depression…"

I usually ask students to keep in touch and they nod their heads, but nothing ever comes of it. Lusekelo was different. He and I shared a love of 1980s music videos, so our email exchange began with these videos. We would email each other our favorite music videos from the '80s and kept in touch even after he went back to Austria.

In March 2014, instead of the usual music video, Lusekelo's email contained a different and surprising note: he had recommended me to speak at his university's Cross-Cultural Business Conference that May. *What do I know about business let alone Cross-Cultural Business? What will I speak about? That was super nice of him to recommend me, but what?! And where is the '80s music video?*

Saying "yes" to that opportunity was the best decision I ever made. A friend from grad school recently recommended Shonda Rhimes' book *A Year of Yes.* Rhimes talks about how her sister had called her out saying that she never said "yes" to anything, so she decided to prove her wrong and set out on a year-long "yes" journey. She even has a TED Talk recounting her "yes" journey and everything she learned along the way (because there is a TED Talk for everything now):

But I digress. I eventually applied in a cold sweat late at night in my bed (as I did most things that were particularly scary/challenging) and thought that the intersection of what I taught and cross-cultural business was global leadership. I encouraged each and every one of my students to be a global leader in everything I did in the classroom, why not bring this method to Austria? One thing led to another and I actually ended up holding a joint workshop (in addition to my own on global leadership) with Ramu Damodaran (then UNAI Deputy Director) on Global Citizenship through Education for the other participants and big wigs at the university. It was insane, but I bring this up because in that workshop session, I met some key people: Carlos (then Dean at CETYS University in Mexico) who asked me to speak at his university and Tarja (a lecturer from Finland) who also invited me to speak at her university. And I said "yes" to both. Shonda Rhimes would have been proud.

How To Not Bore Your Students To Death (!) (The Title Of My TESOL Workshops In Daegu, Korea, Bangkok, Thailand, And Macau, Macau)

The word lecture comes from the Latin word *lectura* meaning to read. This idea came about in the context of universities which began in 1044 in western Europe. Ok, it makes sense that back in the day, you sat in a class, where you were read to, and you listened to your professor lecture on the classics, philosophy, different theories. It was all so fanciful and intellectual. Fast forward to the 21st century: an age where smart phones have made the average attention span a mere 8 seconds—shorter than that of goldfish[1], laptops on which students are supposedly taking notes are just another excuse for students to play computer games, chat with their friends online, and do anything but take notes. In Korea, Kakaotalk has signaled the death of the attention span. Students often carry 2-3 spare batteries around with them in the hopes that the batteries will last them a full day. One student of mine did a 10-day challenge where he tried not to use Kakaotalk for 10 days, because he had fallen whilst Kakaotalking and hurt his head quite badly. Kakaotalk kills brain cells, I swear.

In May 2014, I actually ended up speaking at and attending that Cross-Cultural Business conference in Steyr, Austria at the University of Applied Sciences, Upper Austria—thanks to Lusekelo. It was the first conference I had attended in a long while. Needless to say, I was a bit intimidated and felt a bit out of my depth. However, I pulled myself together, and thought I couldn't miss out an opportunity like this and decided to see how Austrian students, Europeans, and others invited to the conference would take to my WITH style of teaching. I also got to co-host a workshop on Global Citizenship through Education with Ramu Damadoran (then Deputy Director, United Nations Academic Impact UNAI))!

In conference buddies, I found a group of awesome Finnish female professors to hangout with. Having never been to Scandinavia (at that point in my life), but having read and researched gender equality and gender empowerment, I knew that they were among the top in the world. I had so many questions for these women, and of course, they answered all of the questions frankly and matter-of-factly. They had just as many questions about South Korea, North Korea, and what it was like to teach at a university in South Korea. I became quite close with Tarja, one of the three Finnish women. She was a mother of three, lived outside Helsinki in a house in the woods, where she would take long walks with her dog and sometimes pick blueberries for her smoothie when she wasn't prepping or teaching. Tarja would later invite me to do some workshops on Global leadership and Happiness in her class and I would have never predicted that I would serendipitously meet another lecturer named Ilkka who would become an amazing collaborator, and in subsequent visits back to Finland, Tarja would invite me over to her house, introduce me to her family, and collaborate WITH Ilkka as well (!).

I decided to attend some of the other workshops while I was there, hoping I would learn some presentation tips. Sitting at the back of the room, I was stunned to see people seemingly hiding: they were hiding behind their laptops, smart phones, chat sessions, pretending to take notes.

Ok, so I expected this of my Kakaotalk-addicted adolescent students in Korea, but not from *these* participants. Some of them were university students, but the other participants? Surely you could commiserate knowing that you wouldn't want others in your audience not really paying attention? Surely you could tear your eyes away from your devices for an hour to pay attention during the entire workshop? But were they purely to blame? Wasn't it the speaker's job to also be as engaging and interactive as possible? And to lecture WITH the audience rather than AT them?

I finally found my vindication in the form of an article published in the *Proceedings of the National Academy of Sciences.* Scott Freeman from the University of Washington looked at 225 undergraduate STEM programs across the U.S. According to the study, students who attended lectures where they were taught AT rather than WITH were 1.5 times more likely to fail. It doesn't seem like a big deal, but that is the difference between a B- and a B. A whopping 6% difference! Check out the full article here:

Furthermore, when you look at retention rates, audio is 5%, visual is 10% and kinesthetic or learning by doing is a whopping 75%[2]. During my TESOL workshops and all my workshops for that matter, I have participants volunteer and be my human PPT. They each hold pieces of paper that make up my entire PPT. To illustrate this point, I have participants hold 5%, 10%, and 75% respectively. Why just have a boring PPT? I have come to realize that most people, just use their PPT screen in place of their PPT script. Why did we have to come and sit through your boring presentation/workshop anyways? We could have just read it ourselves at home in our pajamas. Probably would have retained more information that way anyways.

It was then that I realized the word "workshop" was just another word for "lecture" and there was absolutely no WITH learning/communicating going on whatsoever.

Macau TESOL Conference: "How To Not Bore Your Students" Workshop | University Of Macau | February 1, 2015

The Pleacher Plab

When was the last time you got to experiment and try something out at a workshop let alone get out of your seat to stretch from boredom? Imagine going to a conference alone, where you don't know anyone. If you are not interacting with the other participants in your workshop or someone else's presentation, then chances are the only other opportunity you will have to be social is during lunch breaks. I swear to you, it is like trying to decide where to sit during middle school lunch break: do you sit with the cool presenters who know all the theories about everything and can talk you under the table, or do you sit with the shy participants who had just enough courage to sign up for the conference let alone come. Who wants to deal with that?

Bring in the PLEACHER PLAB experience. Before hopping over to Bangkok and Macau to present at two respective TESOL conferences in 2015, I happened to catch up with a dear Korean friend of mine. She has been working in museum management for almost the entirety of her career and is completely knowledgeable on contemporary art: something I have absolutely no idea about and to be honest, I feel rather sheepish admitting this but I often don't understand it at all. Anyways, on a rather cold January afternoon in Seoul, we got together at the new Contemporary Art Museum in *Samcheongdong*. At the counter, there were the usual brochures I didn't understand in Korean, and then my eye caught a playful foldable pamphlet for children that revealed a fun game in the middle.

I quickly grabbed it and played around with it while my friend looked on at me and giggled. *Why can't adults play? When was the last time you actually play played? And not just a sport?* Inspired by this pamphlet, I wanted to create an actual learning experience for adults, where in this workshop they could play WITH each other, learn WITH each other, and have fun WITH each other. No more sitting down and pretending to take notes on some device. Thus the PLEACHER PLAB was born. I used PLAY+TEACHER and PLAY+LAB. The results were interesting and astounding all at the same time: In Bangkok, participants who came earlier than the actual start time looked nervous. I told them to look around at the posters I had put up all around the room, but they preferred to just sit down and wait for the workshop to begin. I had the chairs arranged in two rows facing each other, so the participants had to face each other and talk to one another too, but before the workshop began, they barely made eye contact with each other. When asked to take a crayon and draw something that makes them happy on the post-it note they were given, they did so quietly, yet nervously. When asked to present an activity they brainstormed with their partner to make as many students in their classrooms as happy as possible, only one pair volunteered.

Having said all of that, during the workshop, participants were interacting, engaging, getting to know each other, and having fun (!). They were brainstorming, learning by doing, talking, there was absolutely no passive learning. They were able to experiment, discuss ideas just as scientists do in labs. Is it really that different in classrooms, workshops, presentations, even if you aren't teaching science? Why don't we blow up ideas?

Here is a testimonial from one of the participants from my Pleacher Plab workshops:

"As an educator myself, I quickly felt Kyla's passion for teaching and sharing her knowledge with others. During the workshop, we got a feel for her classes at Yonsei, and how she incorporated socially relevant materials to help develop the critical minds of her students. The students' video project on human trafficking was an eye-opening experience for many of us in the audience for several reasons. First, the project was not limited to the four corners of the classroom. The students were actually out there on the streets working on their projects. Second, Kyla was right there WITH them. She did not just give them instructions and then leave them to do their own work. Third, we could tell from the video that the students had fun doing it, and that they would be better global leaders after they were finished. Although the idea of thinking outside the box is an old one, many teachers still often run out of ideas of how to extend learning outside the classroom. This workshop not only gave me practical ideas, but also forever inspired me to reflect on my approach to teaching and working WITH my students."

~Teri (2014 KOTESOL National Conference Participant)

SELF WORK:
If you could create the most awesome WITH workshop/class what would it look like? Draw your ideas below.

The Happiness Workshop: Where The Happiness Began

In August 2014, Carlos (whom I had met in Austria at the workshop I gave with Ramu) invited me to create workshops for incoming freshman during orientation week to get them motivated about volunteering and giving back to the community, something that was very much inline with his university's mission/core values. I thought to myself: *Hmmm…I could get up there and give a totally boring power-point lecture (even though I never used power-point in my regular teaching) on the reasons students should volunteer or I could do some more research and do what I like to call a back-door approach: trick students into doing something by making them have so much fun along the way, they end up loving something they think might initially sound boring or terse.* I did a bunch of research and the end result was really that everything boiled down to this: if you make others happy, you become happier. That's it. Drum roll please…the happiness workshop was born. Thus far, I have delivered the happiness workshop to people in Finland, Norway, Macau, Thailand, Cambodia, Hawaii, California, Italy, India, Malaysia and most recently I even created a freshman seminar class at Yonsei called The Happiness Workshop. *Best decision ever.* Just ask Kony, one of my students in that freshman seminar class:

One of the main projects that comes out of this workshop is students get to try to make as many people on/off campus as happy as possible. I call it the Happy Yonsei project or the Happy ______ project for whatever institution I am at. It is the hands-on/fun/social experimental part of The Happiness Workshop. I love it.

STRANGER DANGER?

(Fall 2016 Semester)

"You know, The Happy Yonsei video project was fascinating to me..." Ye Il, one of my freshman students said nervously. I was wondering what he would say next.*

"Why?"

"Well, because it taught us how to interact with strangers. Usually we Koreans do not interact with strangers at all, just people we know. While making this video, we had to talk to strangers, but also in a way, teach them without teaching them." He went on to use an analogy about how most teachers point to the treasure. However, it is those rare teachers who actually lead you rather than point to

---

* He starred in a TV program called *Torondaejeop,* (Debate Showdown).You can find him speaking on TV here: https://youtu.be/i-droa3FaAo. What a badass!

the actual treasure directly.

"Students don't like to be told that they are learning something. They kind of get defensive or they don't pay attention, but if you teach them without teaching them, then that is when true learning happens." I was stunned. I had never thought that The Happy Yonsei video projects would be a catalyst to push students to talk to and engage WITH strangers. My original vision for the project was almost naïve and oversimplified: make others around you happy, so that you will then be happier. I would have never imagined two years later that I'd be having this kind of conversation with Ye Il who was incidentally an education major.

In another Whatsapp call the following day with Aamirah†*, a young Muslim woman from London, she added, "It's about the process. Your workshop and the videos help people overcome social norms, fear of rejection, they help them reach out to others, and you are doing all of that in*

† Aamirah was assigned to help me at the Global WINConference in Rome in September 2016. She helped me moderate the Young Leader Forum; we got along so famously, she requested to change with another volunteer so she could assist me in my own Happiness Workshop later that week. In her early 20s, she was definitely already a force to be reckoned with and one of the youngest participants at the conference.

your own daily life. You're just cracking on and doing it."

I loved the British "cracking on" expression. I did feel warm and fuzzy after hearing that she also felt the same way Ye Il did. I then shared the story of how I had been challenged to create a selfie video answering a question I had posed to students for a self work assignment: What if you had no fear, what would you do? Last semester, a student came up to me in the elevator:

"Do you speak Korean, Kyla?"

"A little..." I responded sheepishly, avoiding eye contact.

"Can you speak a little now? I want to hear you speak Korean."

Of course, like any self-respecting adult, I ran out of the elevator like a kid, screaming, "I'm shy!" That night, I went home and reflected on my behavior. I always tell my students in class, "Push through fear! Don't be afraid of failure! You can do it!" But yet, I am also afraid. What a hypocrite I am! So the following morning, I decided to create my very first selfie video in Korean and filmed it on my walk to work. I posted it on FB and had students do the same after sharing the story I just mentioned with them. They seemed touched.

Here is that video where I basically introduce myself in simple Korean:

Later on I ran into a student who had already watched the video:

"Kyla, I watched your video..."

"Oh, what did you think?" Please don't hate it. Please don't judge my Korean or me.

"You know, I had like a tear coming out of my eye. It made me feel very touched that you would do that for us." I think she liked it. Phew.

"Oh, really?! Thank you so much for watching it and saying that. You know, sometimes we are our biggest critics. And even though something may seem scary or terrifying, we should try to just push through our fear and do it, right?"

"Yes, thank you. Hope you enjoy your dinner." And with that, she was on her way.

Later I shared the same story with Ilkka's MBA class, where I Skyped in for just 10 minutes. One of his students asked, "How can we get to know ourselves better?" I responded by sharing this story and how the more you know yourself, the better you can communicate and help others around you.

Ok, back to Ye Il. He continued, "There is something different in your classes with creativity. Most classes do not use creativity or think about being creative, because most professors think that it would not be efficient. However, in your classes, efficiency is not sacrificed for creativity." Mind blown again. I mean, I know I can be disorganized and not the most efficient educator on any given day, but to be told by a Korean person- a student no less- that I was actually efficient, I would have never seen this day coming.

"Also, we are a homogeneous society. We do not know how to interact with strangers because we have never had to."

"What about the young generation like your generation though? Aren't they more open-minded?" He drew a map of Korea for me, and showed me the various places he had lived outside of Seoul. There was one particular place he had lived called Beolgyo (Southeast of Korea), which had a population of 50,000 people and apparently there was just one foreigner." I asked the police station, and they confirmed that there was only one registered foreigner living in Beolgyo. So you see, outside of Seoul, even young people are not used to foreigners, strangers, and even if there are strangers around, we do not know how to interact with them. We would not expect them to necessarily be kind to us like how strangers were kind to us in our video." Ye Il's team decided to go with the theme of awkwardness inspired by Wassily Kandinsky who was a famous Russian artist (1866-1944) known for his awkward nature. And boy did they go for it: they used a drone, 3D printer, and spread as much awkward happiness as they could around campus.

The following day, after this awesome office visit from Ye Il, I received an email from Izzy recommending that I check out NPR's "How I built this" podcast series[3]. I happened upon the one by Joe Gebbia (one of the AirBnB founders) from October 2016. Something he said caught my attention. He was talking about how early on, when he and his business partner Brian were trying to pitch the idea of AirBnB, nobody was buying it. It sounded absurd to them: let random strangers stay in your apartment?! He talked about how we were always taught as children, that strangers are full of danger: stranger danger.

It made me think back to my childhood in Hong Kong. It was a busy weekend day by the Star Ferry Terminal on the Hong Kong side. Back when the Star Ferry was 60 cents (HKD). My mom, sister, and I had come back from Kowloon, when in a split second I let go of my mom's hand, and was lost, gone. I don't really remember exactly what happened following that split second, but even until today, my mom can recall with complete clarity the events that followed.

My sister and my mom made their way to the nearest police station after trying to look for me to no avail. Meanwhile, I was found by a kind man who bought me a pack of Kleenex, because I was crying so much. He led me to the police station and there I was reunited with my mom and sister. Mind you, this was in an era of no cell phones, so there was no way we could have called each other directly. My mom was so grateful to this stranger that she wanted to give him some money, but he politely refused and went on his way. I can't imagine what my mom must have been going through during the time she thought I was lost. At the time, I didn't think too much about it or too deeply about any of it. I was just happy to be reunited with my mom and my sister, and I was hoping that I wouldn't get scolded for letting go of my mom's hand. As an adult who has studied human trafficking and read horror stories of modern day slavery, I am also eternally grateful. I think to this day, my family owes this complete stranger a debt of gratitude.

In his TED Talk, Gebbia shares a story of how one guest in Uruguay suffered a heart attack, and his host actually drove him to the hospital and waited for him in the waiting room. He goes on to say, how out of the 123 million nights that AirBnB has hosted, only a fraction have had negative experiences[4]. What if we weren't skeptical about strangers? What if we actually trusted them to be good? What then? Would the sharing economy continue to grow and outdo that of the regular economy? What about our happiness level? Would we be able to not only trust strangers, but also be open to their kindness? What if we worked WITH strangers instead of AT them?

Here are the things that I have learned about happiness along the way:

1. It doesn't take a lot

   Students/participants are often so shocked at how happy they are after my Happiness Workshop. They then realize that in turn giving just a little bit of time, effort, roses, high-fives can go a really LONG way in the day of someone who may just need a bit of happiness. Oh and watching the smile on not just the recipient's face but also the giver's face is priceless.

2. It's not about material things

   Somewhat related to the first point, we often think that if we just buy that new dress, or that new car, or new house that we will be happier, well, actually research shows that we won't and these video projects prove the same.

3. Human interaction is everything

   In this day and age of I-never-look-away-from-my-device, people need human touch, interaction more than ever. In fact, in the longest study on happiness ever done, over 75 years, researchers found that participants (regardless of socioeconomic status) were happier and lived longer because of their relationships. Check out the TED Talk:

4. Family is the backbone

   No matter where I go, no matter which culture or country, participants always talk about their family and how their family makes them happy. It is no surprise that according to UNICEF, Dutch children are the happiest in the world. And why? Because they treasure their time with their dads in particular[5].

5. It is timeless, ageless, raceless, whatever else –less

   Regardless of who you are, how old you are, where you live, where you come from, it is our common bond: what we all want to achieve, what we all strive for, and yet it is often what lacks in our daily lives because we are so busy worrying about other things.

6. It is holistic

   You can't truly be happy unless you are balanced physically, emotionally, psychologically, spiritually, cognitively, diet/nutrition (not losing weight diet, but what you eat diet), and have healthy relationships.

SELF WORK:
Create your own Happy _____ project (!) where you have to try to make as many people around you as happy as possible. Jot down your ideas below:

SELF WORK:
What is the relationship between EDUCATION + WITH vs AT?

Doodles/Takeaways/Reflection Points

THE HOW

CHAPTER 2

ADVICE (HOW TO LIVE A WITH LIFESTYLE)

"Feel free to take or leave my advice. I am not going to tell you what *to do, but hopefully, you can learn ~~from~~* WITH *my mistakes." ~me (to students or anyone who will listen)*

Students often come and ask me for advice. If you read the foreword (no judgments if you skipped it), like Minjeong wrote in the foreword, she was one of the first students who ever came to visit me during office hours, and she expected someone to sit down and tell her exactly what she should do. As you can imagine, she was surprised when I did the opposite. I listened, listened some more, and then asked HER questions so she could get to the answers WITHin her. That is the true way to learn. This chapter is no different. Take what you would like, leave what you would like, and make it your own.

Make More (Seeming) Mistakes

I was a mistake. Don't get me wrong. I don't harbor any ill will or ill feelings towards my parents. In fact, they always treated me as if I wasn't a mistake. I actually didn't find out until I was an adult and truly able to grasp that my parents had not wanted to really have a second child. But imagine if I had never been born? If my parents' "mistake" had never been made?

It makes me think about other mistakes: the post-it note and the chocolate chip cookie. Imagine if they had never been created by mistake. What would we write our memos on? We would actually have to cut out pieces of paper, get a piece of scotch tape, and stick it on someone's desk. What would we eat with milk?

Let's begin with post-it notes. Everyone knows what a post-it note is now, but back in 1968 Spencer Silver, a scientist at stationery company 3M, created a revolutionary adhesive. Something that could be used to bond enough for something to stick, but also light enough, so it could be attached. There was one glitch: he had no idea what to do with this amazing creation he had. Enter Arthur Fry. Fry attended a seminar given by Silver on this creation. One night while singing in his church choir, he had an epiphany: he had always had trouble marking the pages of his hymnbook with little bits of paper that would fly out. What if he could use Silver's adhesive material on one side of a piece of paper? Thus, the post-it note was born.

Who doesn't love chocolate chip cookies? It is as much of an American dessert staple as the yellow cake with chocolate frosting. But what if chocolate chip cookies had never been mistakenly invented? I shudder to think. In 1930, Ruth Wakefield was trying to bake a batch of chocolate cookies. She ran out of her baker's chocolate, so instead used what she already had in her pantry which were Nestle chocolate chunks; she believed they would then melt like the baker's chocolate, but they never did. Thus, the chocolate chip cookie was born.

It's not just classic creations with the likes of the chocolate chip cookie or the post-it note, it is also famous people we know. Take Stephen King for example. At a new Starbucks on Yonsei Sinchon Campus, I sat and caught up with my then office buddy, Duane. I told him of my plans to write a book. I was surprised to hear that he had written science fiction in the past and even published one of his pieces.

"I am afraid to write. I am afraid no one will read my book," I lamented. I figured the more people I voiced my insecurities to, somehow they would just magically disappear. "You do know about Stephen King and all of his rejection letters, right? He would hang his rejection letters on the wall with a single nail, and one day, there were just so many rejection letters that the nail fell!" I was stunned. I mean, the great Stephen King? I remember reading *IT* for the first time as a teenager and being so engrossed in the details of the horror, but wanting to read more, instead of being turned off. That's just it. We always think that people are immediately successful or popular or whatever. We don't think that they actually had to be rejected many times, be turned down as many times before they eventually got famous. Incidentally, King's first book *Carrie* was saved from the trash by his wife, and ended up earning him USD$400,000 later.

At a hotel overlooking the ocean, I was brunching with Shawna[*] and MK in Honolulu in February 2017. Shawna had recently published *Green Island*[1], a Taiwanese historical novel, which had taken her almost a decade to

---

[*] I had met Shawna through my friend Hugh who was a college buddy of mine; Shawna and Hugh had met in the Bay Area and had been dating for several years.

write. Hugh had told me that she saved all of her rejection letters from past publishers in a binder she called her "Rejection Binder." Upon my request, she brought it with her to brunch.

"I show this to my students at U of H," she said as MK and I flipped through the binder. She was referring to her Creative Writing students. She was a professor in the Creative Writing Department at the University of Hawaii.

"And how do they react to it?" MK asked.

"I think it gives them hope." She said wistfully and humbly. She was one of the most humble yet accomplished people I have ever encountered. *Green Island* was a number 1 best seller in Singapore; oh and she had been approached by a famous movie director to turn her book into a T.V. series recently. She was my book shero (she + hero).

"You're a great teacher." I chimed in.

I felt a bit sheepish asking her if she would mind looking over the second draft of this book. Of course, she generously agreed, making sure if it was ok with me. MK and I walked away from brunch in awe of Shawna's perseverance through rejection, but also her deep humility in the face of her recent success. *What a badass.*

Making mistakes is another AT concept. Again, like fear, failure, and risk we are told from a young age to steer clear or avoid mistakes and its AT siblings. I say, turn making mistakes into a WITH concept and go out there *with* your chin up and make as many mistakes as you possibly can. Remember: the key is not in making the mistake, but in learning WITH that mistake, so you don't make the same one again.

Do Stuff That Scares You (A Little Bit) On A Regular Basis

After I turned 38, on May 3rd 2016, I made a promise to celebrate myself everyday, instead of just on my birthday once a year. I promised myself that I would celebrate myself by recording a selfie video every single day for a year†. In doing so, I would:

---

† Ok, so I wasn't able to do it everyday, but I did make about 60 or so. Not bad. Also, created my very own YouTube channel:

 (Check it out!!)

1. Put myself out there
2. Challenge myself
3. Work on improving my tech skills
4. Be my authentic self
5. Share my daily epiphanies
6. Do something (a bit) scary every day
7. Create/Be creative
8. Every day would be more memorable
9. Be vulnerable
10. Be unedited/imperfect

On May 12th, a week later, I wrote and sang my first song (dedicated to my hubby):

Even though I was super nervous to put myself wayyyyy out there in the YouTube universe, and even though tech stuff kind of scared me, I was still able to create some videos. Yes, it did scare me, just a little bit. Was it a good scary? Hell yes! Challenge yourself to be better than you were yesterday by scaring yourself just a little bit—the good kind of scary. You can do it.

Get A Mentor

Mentors are invaluable human-beings in our lives. They guide us, teach us, make us better human-beings, and if they are that good, you don't even feel as if you have been mentored.

I just spent a lovely afternoon with a good friend and former co-worker, Chris P. Our story of friendship began at Yonsei, where he would give me advice whenever I would freak out about something that happened with my students or my teaching. We would walk along the tree-lined path from our dorm (*muak haksa*) to class. Chris would often tell me, "You know, just be honest with your students. I am really honest with mine, I tell them exactly what is going on. I am very transparent you know." Chris was a formidable educator: he would create his own textbooks down to choosing art work for each page, he would go through a lot of effort/work to help mentor and guide his own students both inside and outside of the classroom, he took creativity and critical thinking lessons to new heights, and as a trained lawyer, he was extremely meticulous. I have learned so much WITH him and continue to do so as now he is a very good friend. *Now that's a mentor.*

My first job in Korea was at the Foreign Language Institute (FLI) at Yonsei. I took that same walk (that I would take many a time with Chris P. in the future), and decided by the time I had walked to FLI that I wanted to work on that campus. Something I didn't mention though is that the woman who greeted me on the other end, the Head Coordinator Herim was absolutely a dream to work WITH. She was positive, happy, kind, thoughtful, generous, and wanted the best for both her employees and the organization itself. I think a real mentor truly helps to push you to be the best version of yourself, and Herim really went out of her way to do that. Knowing that I had outgrown FLI and needed a new challenge, she called the College English Department almost everyday for a week to see if there were any vacancies (since they don't publicly announce job openings). A few weeks into my new position at the College English Department, Herim invited me out for lunch and presented me with a ring that she had her friend Wooa make for me. It was inscribed with *COME PRIMA* ("New Beginnings" in Italian). She also has a similar ring that Wooa had made for her too. *Now that's a mentor.*

Me + Herim celebrating her birthday | FLI Seoul, South Korea | February 2011

The ring that Herim had given me inscribed with *COME PRIMA* ("New Beginnings" in Italian) | Global WINConference in Rome, Italy | September 2016

Me + Chris P | My apartment in Songdo, South Korea | Fall 2015

Lee (Paul's wife), me, and Paul | South Korea | Fall 2011

In undergrad, I approached Professor Paul Pickowicz to be a supervisor on this independent research project I was doing on The Great

Leap Forward as a sophomore. Paul and I soon developed a mentor/mentee relationship, but later it grew and blossomed into a father/daughter relationship. I would have never predicted that after graduating from UCSD, he would invite me to attend one of his workshops in Beijing at a Harvard conference, and tell me that he wished his daughter would grow up to be like me. More recently, he has welcomed me and Edgar (my husband) into his home in San Diego: Edgar and I have had the pleasure of cooking at his house for him and his wife (Lee), and Lee has made us paella on more than one occasion. Sometimes you just don't know where a mentor/mentee relationship will take you, but if you're open, the sky is really the limit. A few years ago, he came to Korea with Lee. While hanging out in *Samcheongdong*, he remarked, "Kyla, you have a white hair. Hang on…ok I got it. It's gone now." *Now, that's a mentor.*

Don't Be Judgy

Malcolm Gladwell talks about "thin-slicing" in his book *Blink*. I remember reading about it and thinking *that is so cool.* We should all actually listen to our intuition or gut more. Well, I certainly listen to my gut or as I like to call it my belly, whenever I am hungry. There is a caveat though, Gladwell warns. Sometimes, we do tend to let our biases get the best of us. An example he uses is when we see a Black man walking with a hoodie or in baggy jeans, we tend to quicken our pace, cross the street. I have done the same myself when in the U.S., especially walking at night. I am sure we have all done it.

In my Cross-Cultural Communication course at Yonsei, we'd have weekly discussions with students at Waseda University in Tokyo. Part of the training that I try to instill before we actually begin chatting with our counterparts in Japan is that yes, there are stereotypes of Japanese people (they are super polite, they eat sushi, etc.), but we should try not to generalize an entire nation of people, right? In the textbook that Waseda created for this course, there is a chapter on how *not* to do this. Usually when we encounter a new situation we do the following: Describe, Interpret, Evaluate (D.I.E.)‡. What is actually better is to Observe, Describe, Interpret, Suspend (evaluation)§. An example we use in class is two guys walking closely together. I have two male students volunteer and have them walk into the classroom together holding hands. Everyone

‡ Developed by Janet and Milton Bennett in 1975.

§ Proposed by Stella Ting-Toomey in *Communicating Across Cultures* in 2012.

immediately giggles and laughs, and yells out, "GAY!" We discuss how calling them "GAY" would be the D.I.E. method, but if we were to suspend our evaluations/ethnocentric judgments, those two could be friends, brothers, classmates, etc. In India, for example, it is quite common to see two heterosexual men holding hands.

When I was in boarding school, my best friend Tarah was Jewish. During our shorter school holidays, I would often hangout with her and her family. There was one particular scene that stood out in my mind when I feel like I was prematurely thin-sliced (still happens). I was sitting down and eating with Tarah and her parents. There were other Caucasian people at the table, whom we didn't really know, but I think we had to share the table with them. I can't recall why. At any rate, one of them leans across me to Tarah's mom and asks, "Can she speak English?" Tarah's mom looked at this person straight in the eye, and retorted, "Why don't you ask her yourself?!" It was the best response I could have ever thought up. I was grateful for her that day for saying what I couldn't say for myself.

In Korea, most people think I am Korean. It works for me. People feel comfortable with me immediately, I get to learn Korean faster (no one speaks English to me), I don't get stared at, I can blend in relatively easier (than my obviously foreign counterparts). I also *look* young. This does not always work for me. People don't take me seriously, my students often think I am the TA, other professors probably do too, when I go to conferences as a speaker people often assume I am a student/participant. The list goes on. OK, so bottom line: Don't be judgy.

Do Compare Yourself With Yourself (And Not With Others)

At the beginning of every semester, this is what I ask students in the context of their grades. I usually grab a pencil case, water bottle or whatever I can find on a student's desk, and grab another one that looks completely different. I ask the students: "Are these two things exactly the same?" They all yell, "NO!" Then I go on to explain, "If I were to compare these two completely different things, it wouldn't be fair, right? Why? It is not a fair comparison. There is no base line in which to compare. Just as much as there is no one out there in the world quite like you, so you cannot compare yourself with other students. This is why I don't. I compare how you were from the beginning of the semester, today and by the end of the semester in a few months. You will improve, but only if you compare yourself with yourself."

There is also data that proves this. When I was living at home during my "dark ages" after college trying to figure out what I wanted to do with my life, I happened upon a book called *Get Out of Your Own Way*[2]. At the time, I remember thinking: *Oh my God. This whole time I have been blaming other people or my situations for what it was that I was feeling, for my "dark ages," for everything. When really, it was all along me. It was my attitude, my take on what was going on. I had to get out of my own way.* Robert Cooper also wrote another book that I recently started reading called *The Other 90%*. In this book, there was a chapter about how athletes who wanted to better their own time, actually did, because they compared themselves WITH themselves—not other athletes. Those who wanted to better another athletes' time, actually performed worse. The reason behind this is when you try to compare yourself with someone else, there is an increase in negative stress hormones being released in your brain and you actually end up performing worse as a result[3]. This blew my mind in my mid-20s. It should blow your mind too, so get off Facebook and stop comparing your life with others.

When I was in first grade in elementary school, I was about to run in my first 100m-dash race. I had my hair tied in two braids. My mom gave me this advice before I went to go and line up, "Remember Kyla, don't look left or right at the other kids. Just look straight." As an adult, I asked my mom if she meant her advice to be a life metaphor, but she just laughed and said "no." During some of my classes, I have students do two similar walking races where in the first one they walk looking at each other, and then in the second one they look straight ahead. At the end of the "races" when asked which one they thought they were able to walk faster in, they all remark how they were able to walk faster in the latter one because they were just focused on themselves rather than worrying about what others were doing. Thanks mom.

Seek Inspiration Internally First And Then Externally In Places You Would Least Expect To

For our first Christmas together away from our families, Edgar bought me a wooden corkboard so I could pin up all of my photos (College style). I had actually accidentally printed a bunch of photos (by a bunch I mean several 100!) of us back when we first dated and whatever else I had in my iPhone at the time. One of the photos captured me on the TED stage. I made a decided effort to pin that photo up on my corkboard, which I look at almost daily. Believe you me, I am by no means a narcissist, but I just simply wanted to re-inspire myself on a daily basis WITH myself. Why not, right? Similar to the previous piece of advice about comparing yourself WITH yourself, we should also seek to inspire ourselves as well.

Sometimes at night, when I don't feel like reading the books I keep piled up on my bedside table in the hopes that one day I will eventually read all of them (!), I open up my orange colored journal. (Orange is one of my favorite colors.) I read about happier times or sadder times, and I am re-inspired at something I thought or an epiphany I had or perhaps I have new advice for myself. If you don't already, I encourage you to start a journal. It is not only a time capsule of your life, thoughts, reflections, inspirations, but a place you can go to –your own book of life if you will in times of _____ (fill in the blank).

In May of 2015, I spent my birthday in Helsinki, Finland, seeking external inspiration. I had been invited by a woman I had met at a conference in Steyr, Austria two years prior. Tarja was teaching at Laurea University of Applied Sciences. She and I had kept in touch and she had invited me to teach her course on Inter-Cultural Communications for a week during International Week, where they invited lecturers from around the globe to do just that, as well as host lectures. Tarja was looking for inspiration from me, and I was also looking for inspiration from her in this new completely foreign environment.

Did you know that for every 1 Finnish person there are 15,000 trees? Crazy. What a different world from the concrete jungle that is Seoul. Later on through Tarja, I met Ilkka who was also inspired by my crazy style of teaching and we became friends. He invited me to talk to a few of his students about "life" (my favorite thing to talk about, really), and we ended up chatting, I showed them videos of my students' work at Yonsei, and Ilkka asked me for advice on his talk that he would be giving at the very same conference in Steyr, Austria where I had met Tarja. In the fall of 2015, Tarja and I ended up collaborating on having our students work together on a fundraising project for The Red Nose Day Campaign. See how one inspiration point can cause so many others?

Be Authentic. Be Yourself.

In late January 2016, Ilkka sent me an email asking if we could have a Skype call in order to figure out ways in which we could collaborate. I must admit, I was a bit nervous. What would we talk about? How could we collaborate? Would it be awkward? My nerves were assuaged, as soon as we began talking. Ilkka was as enthusiastic and as excited as I remember him being when we first talked about collaborating back in Finland.

We got on the topic of being authentic in reference to Ilkka's first selfie video he had made for my students at Yonsei. It was him just walking and talking very casually, as if he was having a conversation with a friend. It was very raw. There was no editing. I was inspired by this selfie video, and also wanted to try, but I had never actually self-filmed before. I wasn't sure where I should film, what I should say, would I look like an idiot, would it be good enough, and the list continues. At any rate, I finally filmed one. Here it is:

After watching my video together on Skype, Ilkka and I talked about this obsession of wanting to appear perfect amongst Millennials, especially our students. This is fueled by Facebook: that perfect selfie, vacay shot, having fun with friends, I mean nobody posts pictures of themselves crying or depressed, right? But what if we are all just missing the mark? It isn't about being perfect. It is about being authentic—being your best self. At times, it may seem like the last thing you want to be, but there is no one out there quite like you, right?

SELF WORK:
List the three tasks here:
1.
2.
3.

Please do try the three tasks I list in my first selfie video. Write your thoughts below:

Exercise To Exercise Your Mind

My last year or so at Yonsei, I tried to push my students to exercise. I was worried that all they were doing were sedentary tasks: sitting and studying/kakaotalk messaging. I would sometimes see students play basketball or soccer outside, but it was inevitably groups of male students. It was rare to see female students exercising. If they did exercise, they would do so late at night.

Beyond the physical benefits of exercise (of which there are many!), I thoroughly enjoy the mental benefits of exercise. While I swim, my mind is clear, I can think through problems/issues, I am not distracted by anything, I am alone WITH my thoughts. Edgar often says I am a calmer person after I swim. I really think it is because water has always helped to balance me out, whether it's in the form of sailing, boogie-boarding, swimming, I love being in water or close to it.

Recently, I have come up with something Edgar terms pool-piphanies: A play on the word epiphany. My mind is often so clear while I am swimming, I have these amazing ideas just come to me in the form of pool-piphanies. Check out my video here where I talk about pool-piphanies:

Here are some additional benefits of exercising (Just 5 of more than 45!):

- Stress + Anxiety Reduction
- Improvement in Brain Cognition
- Happy Chemicals Released
- More Creativity
- Brain Power
- And so much more!

Find Your Happy Place

Every semester, I always ask students to draw their hobbies on a card. Every semester I am amazed at what students call "hobbies": sleeping, computer games, lying in bed looking at their phones. Ping[**], Roommate[††] and I decided to go back to UCSD for our own 20-year reunion. We went to the beach with Roommate's kids, went back to our old haunts. While we were at UCSD, yes, we studied, but we also had hobbies that allowed us to bring balance to the studying. Find yourself a hobby that doesn't include being indoors. Here's a video I made during our 20-year reunion at the same beach where I used to boogie board while at UCSD where I talk about the importance of finding your own happy place:

Journal Your Journey

Students often tell me they are too busy to have time for themselves. Even five minutes at the end of the day is all you need to write down some thoughts, reflections, what you are grateful for, draw, and anything else that will help you remember your journey. Every night, I write down 10 things I am grateful for. It really doesn't take that much time and helps me be mindful before I go to bed.

Fly Business (Class) Like A _____<-- Insert Your Own Adjective (!) Boss

I am a heavy drinker—of water. Most of my friends who know this about me make fun of me. The days I used to fly on United Business class (thanks to the free upgrades before they changed the way you earn miles) between Seoul and Boston to see Edgar, I began observing how the men interacted

---

[**] Ping and Roommate were my 2 besties from college. Somehow we ended up calling ourselves "Ling Cult" (not because we were in a cult per se, but just for fun) and we nicknamed ourselves Ping (Ann), Ming (Michelle/Roommate), and Ling (me). I called Michelle "Roommate," because we actually lived in the same room for 2 years in a row and yes, we are still friends!

[††] Ibid.

with the not-so-nice flight attendants. Oh, and how I was usually the only female, not to mention Asian female (who looked young-ish—it's because I don't wear makeup).

One particular incident struck me: I usually ask one of the flight attendants to fill up my water bottle for me, so that I have enough liquids to sustain me through the long-ass flight, and so I don't waste countless plastic cups. My water bottle is about 24 oz. (710 ml). This amount in addition to the meal service drinks, and the intermittent water bottles they hand out, is usually enough.

So, this is how I ask a flight attendant if he/she can fill up my water bottle: "Would you mind, possibly, filling up my water bottle please?" And since you cannot see my face, I have this look on my face of half shame, half shyness, and half expecting to get yelled at like a child. My seatmate once, a guy who worked for Apple, noticed I had done that and wanted to do the same.

So, this is how HE asked a flight attendant if he/she could fill up his water bottle:

"Can you fill this up?" And mind you, there was no look of distress at all on his face. I checked. He didn't over think it, put himself down—the entire conversation was so stress-free!

Here are some tips to being successful when flying business class or being somewhere you don't think you belong, for whatever reason[4]:

- Own it#
- Don't feel bad/guilty
- You are a pioneer for other minorities (if you don't do it for you, then do it for other minorities)
- You don't have to be rude, but be firm
- Set the tone: Be friendly and firm from the beginning
- If they don't ask to do things for you that they ask the men, like hanging up your jacket, then ask them to do it for you
- Think of it as practice of how you will stick up for yourself in the real world
- Learn from others around you who don't take any flack but always maintain your own style

Now there is a book with the exact same title: http://salliekrawcheck.com/books/own-it-hc (Check it out if you have time!)

SELF WORK:
Figure out one way you can upgrade yourself to _____BOSS or just BOSS status in your life. Do it. Hint: It's helpful to practice with people who work in the customer service industry, because they kind of have to be nice to you.

The World Is Your Oyster, So Get Out There And Explore!

Back when I was trying to figure out what I wanted to do with my life during my last quarter at UCSD, I remember talking to my sister on the phone. She said this, "Kyla, don't worry too much. You have your whole life ahead of you. The world is your oyster." My mom always encouraged both of us to travel as much as we could before getting married, because she knew that it would be more challenging to travel once we had our own families.

One of my crazier trips was a solo backpacking trip through eastern Europe during the summer of 2003. I planned on meeting up with friends I had made at a Global Communications workshop in Poland, but in between the countries, I was traveling alone. I wanted to prove to myself that I could travel alone, as I was infamous for being terrible with directions, but also I was hoping to "find myself" on this solo trip. On my last stop, Bulgaria, I was dropped off in a town outside of Sofia, the capital, called Bansko. I felt like I was on *The Amazing Race*§§: I didn't speak any Bulgarian, didn't know anybody, and had the daunting task of finding a room for a night and somewhere to eat all by myself.

What an adventure indeed. I totally thought that the town had a lot of "Wanted" people, because there were so many "Wanted" posters posted all over town or so I thought. In addition, I noticed there were seemingly many Mexican restaurants, because I saw *MEXANA* in Cyrillic in front of several restaurants. Later the following night over wine with my Bulgarian friend Dessi (my roommate from the "*laowai* ghetto" apartment in Beijing) and her parents after having hiked the 2nd highest peak in the Balkans (a

§§ *The Amazing Race* is a reality TV show in which teams of two people race around the world and have to perform various tasks in order to win a money prize at the end. Incidentally, Edgar and I applied to be on *The Amazing Race* in the U.S. We never heard back from them.

hike which lasted about 8 hours), they laughed at my observations. The "Wanted" posters were actually obituaries. In the U.S., obituaries are found in the newspaper, but in Bulgaria, they post them around town (!). *Mexana* in Bulgarian means "restaurant" which is why there were so many *Mexana* signs—not that they were actual Mexican restaurants. Sigh. *Wow, I had such an American perspective on things.*

While I realized I didn't have to travel half way around the globe to find myself, there was a certain amount of strength and confidence gained, knowing that I was able to do everything on my own. In a recent FB chat session with Charles (a friend of mine), I asked if it would be ok to include him in the book. He said he would be honored and then followed with this:

Yeah I was out in NYC and DC and San Francisco and all those trips were a lot of good fun, but there's just something special about those first several times that I traveled during a particular time in my youth that hold memories above anything else in my mind for whatever reason.

You were definitely a big part of that. I think I saw how you and your friends were traveling, adventuring and experiencing so much of the world, naturally I wanted to be a part of that too. You inspired me! (February 7, 2016)

There is something to be said about traveling: A time when you are exploring, "adventuring" (as Charles notes), seeing the world, being outside your comfort zone. It is indeed the most invaluable time of all. So what are you waiting for? Go ahead and travel. Remember: it is not the distance that matters, (you can stay in the same country to travel) but what you learn about yourself along the way that matters more.

Look Up!

In my Fall 2015 Communication for Science and Engineer Majors' course, one of my students did her presentation on "The Look Up" Campaign. Based on the simple premise of looking up rather than at your mobile device, the campaign was started by a young guy who created this YouTube video:

A friend of mine posted an article on FB about the benefits of hiking and how it can make you happier, and I do realize the irony, given I was definitely *not* looking up while on FB[5]. However, after reading it, I realized that too often we're missing life around us: the birds, the flowers, and the trees (living in big cities). These are all things that are actually good for our health. Being on your phone actually makes you less happy and healthy. And it's not just about looking up away from your phone, but also looking up beyond your regular field of vision. This is something I learned from Edgar. Since then, I've noticed all kinds of things I would have never noticed before. It has certainly shifted my perspective both literally and figuratively. What are you waiting for? Put your phone away, get hiking, and look up, up, up!

Be A (Positive) Comeback Queen/King

Sometimes family can be challenging or people we see on a regular basis that have almost become like family because we spend so much time with them (think: co-workers/roommates/best friends/etc.). We need a way to let them down easy, without hurting their feelings, especially because we have to see them on a regular basis.

So how do we do it?

Enter the (Positive) Comeback King. To say that Edgar is a (Positive) Comeback King is an understatement. If there were a country that was full of mean people going around throwing shade AT people, Edgar would be that ray of sunshine—the light that warms everything and brings smiles to even the coldest of people. Perhaps it stems from the fact that he has always had to justify where he was in his life or perhaps his family made one too many a joke at his expense, but whatever the case, he is the master of defending himself, but here is the secret weapon: making the other person, the shade thrower, laugh and walk away from the conversation feeling even more positive than they did to begin with. How does he do it?

1. Turn the Tables

> Sometimes, people want to put you down for the sake of making themselves feel better: Their inferiority complex gets fed by how much they put others down. There was one time at work where Edgar's co-workers were fat-shaming him and asking why he doesn't belong to a gym/work out regularly. He started out by saying his wife (that would be me) loves his body the way it is, and then went on to say, "Yeah, let's be gym buddies!" In doing so,

Edgar turned the attention away from Edgar's seeming need to work out to his co-worker's.

2. Confuse + Conquer

Other times, haters try to be seemingly more negative with their put-downs. Distract the hater with something positive, and that is how you will conquer the battle, my friend. One of Edgar's co-workers was making fun of his phone case, because it was dark pink in color. Edgar knew that this co-worker had a daughter, so he asked, "Oh, should I give it to your daughter then as a present?" This is confusing for the hater because he/she expects you to take it negatively.

3. LOL

One of the best ways to end on a positive note, (because let's be frank, usually these things don't end in a positive way at all) is to shut down the hater with a joke. Recently my mom said this to try to guilt trip Edgar and I into coming to Singapore (when she used to live there) for the umpteenth time:

"I have been waiting for 1,000 years for you guys to come!" "Oh, we must be really old then! We must be ancient by now!" Edgar responded jokingly.

4. Seal the Deal

Remember the co-worker that was fat-shaming Edgar? Well, after Edgar asked him to be his gym buddy, he high-fived the co-worker. The co-worker did not know what hit him, because he was trying to throw shade, but was high-fived into conceding defeat. Not to mention, the last thing on that co-worker's mind was becoming gym buddies with Edgar (!). For all of these positive comebacks, you can always seal the deal with a high-five. Yeah!

SELF WORK:
Write Your Own ~~Rules~~ Comebacks

One thing I have found to be helpful is to write down guilt trips my mom gives me, think of a positive/funny come back, and write it down. I actually have a document on my laptop entitled, "Mom Comebacks." It helps to pull it up when I am on the phone with my mom, in case I get nervous or forget what my comeback is. It has actually been super helpful. Try writing your own comebacks for each one of the categories above and then try 'em out!

1. TURN THE TABLES:

2. CONFUSE + CONQUER:

3. LOL:

4. Don't forget to Seal the Deal at the end with a high-five!

Here is a selfie I took with Tarja in the backyard of her house | Finland | May 2015

Here is a selfie Ilkka took of us and his students after we talked about life | Laurea University | Finland | May 2015

Doodles/Takeaways/Reflection Points/

EVERYTHING BEGINS WITH YOU

CHAPTER 3

WITH YOURSELF NOT BY YOURSELF

"Make it a priority to be WITH yourself as much as possible." ~me

Being With Yourself (As Opposed To By Yourself)

I think I am pretty good at being WITH myself: I have managed to comfortably dine alone, travel alone, watch movies alone, and don't really have any hang ups, but I notice a lot of my students and friends do. During cherry blossom season for example, whenever I tell students to go outside and enjoy the beauty of the cherry blossoms, they will immediately moan and exclaim, "Ughhhhhh…we are solo!" Referring to the fact that they are not in a couple, therefore they will not be able to enjoy the cherry blossoms. So in my Career Development course, I always challenged my students to do a task I named "Know Thyself." They have to go out and do something ~~by~~ with themselves, spending time ~~by~~ with themselves, something that is often harder to do for some than taking a test. Some of the results have been awesome though. One male student went as far as taking himself out to Busan!

I thought I had mastered being WITH myself until recently when I came upon a barrage of books on Mindfulness that I started reading. Coincidentally, my friend Fran[*] was working at Mindful Schools, a non-for-profit training organization in the Bay Area. Fran and I will catch up via gchat here and there; she is one of only a handful of friends I keep up with on gchat. I told her about how I had bought a bunch of books on Amazon recently on Mindfulness and how it made me think of her, and she suggested I take one of her organization's online courses. I immediately said, "Yes!" Or rather typed it.

---

[*] Her name is really Amy. We met teaching ESL together in the Bay Area in 2006-2007. Her mom once overheard Amy call me "Friend" and mistook it for "Fran." We have been "frans" ever since (!).

One of the books I decided to read first was written by Tim Ryan. He is an Ohio Congressman and became one at the age of 29. Coincidentally, he also sits on the board of the organization where Fran works. As I began reading the book, I must admit, I was skeptical. *I mean, what is all this hippy dippy meditation stuff anyways and how can it really work and be effective? Can I really incorporate this into my teaching and my workshops?* But the more I read, the more I became hooked and everything just fell into place for me. Ryan describes how he had the perfect outer story of wanting to be the youngest congressman, yet he was constantly struggling to stay present like any one of us in today's omnipresent device world. Then he decided to go on a mindfulness retreat and that is where everything changed for him[1].

The book and the idea of mindfulness reminded me of a movie I watched back when I was living in the Bay Area called *The Peaceful Warrior*. It follows the true story of Dan Millman, a UC Berkeley Olympic gymnast hopeful. He is full of himself, parties, is very popular with the ladies, and doesn't have a care in the world until his dreams of performing in the Olympics are shattered when he gets into a fatal motorcycling accident. One of his legs is completely broken and his doctor tells him he will never be able to do gymnastics again let alone compete in the Olympics. One night, he stops by a gas station in Berkeley and out of the corner of his eye he sees an older gentleman seemingly get from the ground to the roof of the building. A mentorship grows, Dan only knows this man as Socrates; Socrates trains Dan mentally so he can get himself back on his feet physically.

"Take out the trash!" Socrates yells at Dan and subsequently pushes him into a lake on UC Berkeley campus as they are strolling around together. Dan is of course stunned and doesn't understand why Socrates pushed him into the lake and what trash has to do with it. "Take the trash out in here," Socrates continues referring to what was going on in Dan's mind and the fact that he couldn't concentrate, because he was thinking about other things rather than focusing on what Socrates was talking to him about. That was a pivotal moment for me. I think for all of us, it is worth taking a moment of pause here. How many of us think that just answering that next text message, checking our Facebook wall, responding to email is actually helping us become more efficient? Well, ironically it turns out it isn't.

That is what Socrates was talking about, that is what Congressman Ryan is talking about, and other happiness and brain experts alike. Did you know that multi-tasking between devices and other things brings our IQ level down 10 points[2]--an equivalent of pulling an all-nighter? That is how inefficient we are when we multi-task.

But back to Dan, before we get too off track here. After working with Socrates, Dan went on to do gymnastics again, and even compete again.

Looking back, he is not sure whether Socrates really existed or if he was a figment of his imagination. Some time later, he went back to that same gas station, but Socrates was nowhere to be found[3]. I remember practicing what Dan had learned from Socrates and hearing the birds outside my balcony for the first time, feeling the water on my face after showering for the first time, it was a moment of firsts for me. However, as time went by, and especially after having bought my first iPhone, I went back to multi-tasking, thinking I could conquer the world that way.

Last night (June 29th, 2016), on a kick to try to use what we have in our fridge/pantry to make dinner, I decided to make some whole-wheat scallion pancakes. I recalled the simple yet completely profound way we can be mindful in our every day life that both Congressman Ryan and Socrates advocated: take out the trash, follow your breath, and just focus on the task at hand. That is all. I found myself thinking about my mom, worrying about her, and then back to how the whole-wheat flour felt sticky like play dough as I was forming a giant ball. A few more times my mind wandered, I allowed it to, but always brought it back. After dinner, Edgar came home, and I actually focused on what he was saying and made eye contact while doing so. We called my mom, and usually, I will multi-task while on the phone with her, but this time I didn't. I was in the zone. This morning, I refrained from my usual routine: wake up, grab phone, check texts/emails. This morning, I reached for my glasses on my bedside table and started reading Congressman Ryan's book instead.

I won't get into all of the scientific data and research that actually backs this up, but some of which includes: lower stress levels, more productivity, more focus—you get the idea. You can get into more of that on your own, but what I will help you do is get you mentally WITH yourself before you can start being physically WITH yourself and enjoy yourself. Just try for the next five minutes to breathe. That is all. Breathe. When your mind wanders to something else, bring it back gently, and breathe again. When you feel comfortable and confident, start making little changes in your life like turning your phone off, reaching for a book instead of your phone in the mornings, being present in all aspects of your life; you may just find that being WITH yourself can be an extraordinary thing.

Here's a video Fran made on Mindfulness in which she talks about how Mindfulness has had such a profound impact on her life:

SELF WORK:
Write down your thoughts here about breathing and being WITH yourself for 5 minutes.

Some Tips On Being With Yourself:

1. Get to know yourself

This may sound like the strangest advice you will ever receive, but I think there is some truth to it. We often assume that we know ourselves or we truly understand who we are and what we want, but often we don't. There is confusion, because so many people tell us--AT us --what we should be, who we should be, and so on. Also, we are constantly evolving, so there is always going to be something new to work on or self-discover.

2. Create Something that is uniquely YOU

During the spring 2016 semester, I was sitting and chatting over coffee and snacks with a group of freshwomen. One of my all time favorite things to do: hangout with students. We started talking about creating our own brand. Students immediately asked, "But how?" For me, I don't wear make-up that is unique to me, but I do wear big jewelry: necklaces that I found in *Popo's* ("maternal grandma" in Cantonese) jewelry box (so I can feel like she is still with me), big rings (I usually buy from my travels), and a big bracelet on my right wrist. It doesn't have to do with fashion/style, but think about ways in which to create your own brand. This will ultimately help you to be WITH yourself. In this selfie video I talk about the psychological importance of dressing up for yourself and thereby creating your own brand.

3. Take Yourself Out

Who doesn't love getting dressed up and going out on a date or going out with some friends? But what if we applied the same concept, and instead we took *ourselves* out? After all, we deserve it. Practice the art of being WITH yourself. Notice things about yourself that maybe you had taken for granted or that you hadn't noticed before. There is strength in being alone, contrary to what society will have you believe. In this selfie video, I took myself out to a wonderful Thai dinner!

4. Pamper Yourself

This I learned from my college buddy Ping. From a young age, she learned to take care of herself, but not only in the practical kind of way, but in the pampering kind of way. What I love about hanging out with her is that she would go out of her way to pamper herself or pamper both of us. A little donut with coffee here, or a little bracelet there, a massage after shopping, I mean why not?

5. Prioritize YOU

I get that schedules are hectic; there are people to see, places to be, and everything in between. I often hear students say, "Oh, I don't have time to eat." They proceed to show me their schedule, highlighted beautifully in different colors, but beyond the façade of pretty colors, there is neither time to eat nor any down time to relax. This is dangerous for obvious reasons like your brain needs fuel to think/study, but also you are not prioritizing yourself. In another conversation with Edgar, he says, "It is hard for me to do things for myself." To which I replied,

"If you are drowning (i.e. unhealthy, not taking care of yourself, not exercising, etc.), how can you save others?"

6. Be vulnerable

Life is messy, and as humans living life, so are we. Something I have learned along the way is that most people, including my students, don't like to admit weakness, failure, or anything messy for that matter. It is ok. Let go of your perfect image, your perfect selfie, and your perfect job. You just might find yourself in return.

7. Journal

Self-reflection is key to understanding who you are and where you are in your journey. Your journal can also be a "friend" when you need "someone" to spend time WITH, listen to you, and just even something to draw or doodle in. A journal never judges either.

SELF WORK:
Use the 6 tips mentioned here and take yourself out. Write your thoughts about how you feel in your journal (Tip #7).

Doodles/Takeaways/Reflection Points

WITH PEOPLE: DEALING WITH YOUR COMMUNITY

CHAPTER 4

YOUR UNCONDITIONAL COMMUNITY: BEING WITH FAMILY

"You can choose your friends, but you cannot choose your family."
~My mom

Before I begin this chapter, I want to let you know, I love my parents. They brought me into this world, literally and figuratively, and for that I owe them everything…and then some.

My parents are extreme opposites: my mom is an extrovert; she loves people, being social, being the center of attention, and can talk your ear off. My dad is an introvert, loves his quiet time, not being the center of attention, being at home, and would rather communicate over email than over the phone. However, where they come together is they are both *extremely* thoughtful and driven people.

Growing up, my mom would plan and host these elaborate slumber parties in Hong Kong. My dad would drive from the Bay Area to Carpinteria (near Santa Barbara) where my boarding school was located (an almost 8-hour drive in California) to see me on Parents' Weekends and make sure I had all the school supplies I needed. They always made sure my sister and I had everything we needed to succeed and then some. We weren't made to go to after-school programs, but somehow we subconsciously pushed ourselves to be the best versions of ourselves, and still do.

In terms of communication, my mom was an AT communicator. She would scold us, yell AT us, and we had no choice but to obey her. My dad would keep quiet, but when he saw something that really rubbed him the wrong way, he would either have my mom tell us or he would tell us in a less aggressive AT manner than my mom, but still AT nonetheless. Both of them are becoming more WITH-style communicators.

I am still working on my own style of communication WITH my family: I have started communicating more WITH my mom than ever before. I have asked her to be more cognizant of her guilt trips, which she is actively working on. I have started emailing my dad and discussing my life coaching sessions with my own life coach WITH him, and sharing frankly how certain events in my childhood affected me and how what he said or did affected me. Finally, WITH my sister, back and forth over email we have hashed out decades of hurt, miscommunication, and worked on re-building our own relationship too. All of this WITH communicating hasn't been easy, but has it been worthwhile? Hell yes.

My Parents Then and Now:

Out on a date | Singapore | 1970

Celebrating my dad's birthday | Danville, California | March 2018

My mom would often wear a wig out (not in this picture) because Bank employees weren't allowed to date (!).

My parents have never been the "lovey dovey" or playful type of couple, but it has been heartening to see their relationship evolve as my mom's dementia has. My dad now will gently tease my mom and chase her around the house playfully. I love you, mom and dad. Thank you for giving me HOPE that LOVE truly conquers all.

One of the longest running studies out of Harvard on life satisfaction, tracked men in both inner city neighborhoods as well as Harvard grads, and found that regardless of income level/social status level, the men who were the happiest and therefore lived the longest did so because of their social interactions with people. We need to interact WITH people for our happiness and our longevity[1].

Although Edgar and I often spend our winter breaks helping our mothers with their health, trying to communicate better with our respective siblings, sleeping less, worrying more, fighting off dandruff for Edgar/covering up pimples for me (stress-related), we wouldn't want it any other way. After all, it is from our family that our very being was born and created. It is from family that we learned to be. It is from family that we learned to interact WITH humans as they were the first humans we ever interacted WITH. It is from family that we learn, grow, and become better human beings than we once were. And eventually, we will create our very own families.

Getting to a point of WITH communication with your family is the highest level of WITH, I think. From the introduction, you may recall the 10-Day Challenge Project. Some of the most meaningful challenges are the ones where students challenge themselves to communicate WITH their family members more. One semester on the stairs, on my way to class, I ran into one of my former students:

"Hi, how are you?" I asked as I always did when running into students both inside and outside the classroom.

"Good! Thanks to your class."

"What? Why? Oh and thank you."

"Remember you had that 10 day project? Well, mine was to call my mom everyday for 10 minutes. I am still doing it." He was beaming.

"How often did you call her before the project?" I was curious.

"Oh, like once a month…"

"Oh my gosh, that is awesome."

"Thank you so much. My mom also thanks you." And with that he rushed off to class.

Me + "mom" (Edgar's mom) at one of our favorite bakeries 85 degrees C. Incidentally, she is wearing an MIT jumper that Edgar bought for her. She is incredibly proud of him | Irvine, California | January 2017

Dealing With The D Word

Here is a blog post, in fact, my very first blog post that I have ever written. It was written about my mom and dedicated to my friend Nancy's mom (who has since passed away). I realized after writing that post, sharing it on Facebook, that through your own seemingly challenging times, you can still inspire people around you. It was heartening to hear Nancy say after she read my blog post three or four times, "You are an amazing writer, Ky. I have never been able to process my mom's death until now, after having read your blog. So thank you." It was fitting to dedicate the blog post to her mom as well, because Nancy was someone who encouraged me to start blogging in the first place.

Taking Care of Mom + The D Word

5/11/2017

I was recently in Nordstrom's vainly attempting to find some flowy summery dresses. Every other sign read simply "mom" in lowercase letters. As Mother's Day fast approaches, I thought I would celebrate my own mom and my own vulnerability in my very first blog post. For the past few years my mom's short-term memory has been in decline. At first, we made excuses: it's old age, she's not sleeping enough, she's maybe depressed/stressed.

Then it got worse, before it got better.

I'd get text messages from old friends in Singapore saying she had not shown up for appointments. The worst came this past February in the form of a text message saying, "Call me immediately. I am with your mom." It was from a person named Tracy I had never heard of nor met before. It turned out my mom had been hiding her keys, handbag, passport (something she had always done), but this time, she couldn't remember where she had hidden all of her valuables. This resulted in her locking herself in her apartment in Singapore where she lived alone, not able to go out for food, calling a locksmith every day to come change the locks. She called Tracy (who was her real estate agent) at 5am to come help her.

This couldn't be happening, I thought.

My mom ran a successful real estate business in Hong Kong. Back in the day, she was one of the first people I knew to have a cell phone (one of those walkie talkie kinds!). She would rattle off phone numbers of locksmiths, plumbers, repair guys all by heart.

My mom's doctor in Singapore had told my husband that she had early onset dementia. I remember my heart pounding loudly above my chest when he later told me. My mom's only friend Vivian, as of late, would join her at the food court, dine with her and keep her company, echoed the same sentiments. Vivian's own mother also had dementia.

I cried then and have since cried a lot. I cried because I didn't want to lose my mom to dementia. I cried because I didn't want to get dementia. I cried because of the strain it was putting on my family--we have since moved my mom back to California where she is living with my dad. I cried because I felt sorry for myself, because I felt so powerless, and just because.

I realize the irony in all of this: I am the Happy Champion. I give Happiness Workshops all over the world. I have always tried to have a positive outlook on life and in every nook and cranny possible. But this D word creeped up on me unannounced, like a car does in your blind spot.

I stayed away from Facebook not being able to curate the perfect image of my happy self. I stayed away from friends not being able to face them or myself. I stayed away from social gatherings not knowing if I would burst into tears and embarrass myself. I felt guilty when I did have an ounce of fun knowing that my mom wasn't having any. I took solace in the arms of my husband and just cried. I was deep in my own D word: Depression.

Earlier this month, I went home to see my mom for my 39th birthday. I was nervous about what would happen, would she remember me, would my dad be really stressed out from being the main caregiver, would my sister and mom fight, would my niece take attention away from my mom?

And then I realized something. We only ever have moments with our loved ones. Each moment is a precious morsel of time. We may not remember each and every moment, even if we don't have dementia, but when we realize just how precious those moments are, we linger longer, noticing that smile, that hug, that warm hand, that laugh. I found myself wanting to preserve and create as many of those moments for my mom as I could.

For my dad's 75th birthday in March, I wanted to do something unique and special for not just my dad, but my entire family, so I decided to get him a personal chef. Enter Chef Niko: a wonderfully warm Greek-American Girlboss from Oakland. I wasn't able to meet her in person, as I was in Korea, but during our phone call to plan the menu, I immediately connected with her. I opened up about my mom's dementia, shared other idiosyncrasies about other members of my family, and entrusted her to "take care" of them through her nurturing cooking. And boy did she do that.

"Would you like us to get that lady for your birthday?" my mom asked.

I was stunned. The dinner had happened in March, my mom barely remembered when my own birthday was in May, yet she had remembered that dinner. It was a brilliant idea. Thanks mom. My dad and sister ended up getting Chef Niko to come for my own birthday dinner, I got to meet my soul sister in person, and she was a true gem, embracing all of the idiosyncrasies of my family members that I had been initially embarrassed to share with her. Not only is she an incredibly gifted chef, but she is also incredibly thoughtful. She gives back to her community and goes above and beyond what is expected of her in the kitchen. She showed up with a glass vase full of beautiful fresh flowers from her garden for me. Wow.

Chef Niko gave me another unexpected birthday present, just when I needed it. She heard that I was going to travel down to LA to visit my in-laws. "You have to meet my friend Eugene. He is upcycling jeans and T-shirts, and is all about kindness like you."

With that, I reached out to Eugene, and met up with him over Thai lunch at a hole-in-the-wall restaurant near Torrance (not far from my uncle's house). Eugene was that rare human being you meet who had transformed grief into gratitude and then some. He had trekked from Mexico to Canada to raise $80,000 for a complete stranger, so this complete stranger could walk again. Talk about the ultimate random act of kindness. A month ago, he launched a clothing company called KINLOVGRA that upcycles jeans and T-shirts, but in a unique way: all of the fabric is turned inside out to expose the inside, the most vulnerable part of ourselves. As if that isn't cool enough. Each item you buy, will support a family on Skid Row.

He truly lives by his creed posting the most gut-wrenchingly vulnerable posts about his struggles with his new business and his own personal life on Facebook. TOTAL INSPIRATION.

So here I am in all my vulnerability and tears. (Yes, I am crying as I write this too.) I am not perfectly curated for social media, and maybe I never have been. My mom's memory may never improve, but what has improved is my ability to take care of my mom in the emotional moments I do have with her--the way she has taken care of me for the last 3 decades of my own life. And if this Mother's Day, you are completely in the moment WITH your own mom (no cell phones, no texting, no social media), you will see that same smile, laugh, happiness, and joy in your own mom. And maybe, just maybe, it will look something like this:

My mom | Danville, California | May 2017

Happy Mother's Day, mom. I love you.

*This first blog post is dedicated to moms around the globe, but especially to my friend Nancy's mom who is no longer with us. Nancy: Thank you for encouraging me + believing in me like I'm sure your mom encouraged and believed in you. <3

Here's the video of my mom receiving the red gramophone from me and Edgar (the above still shot):

(July 2016)

I had begun taking an online course on Mindfulness during the summer of 2016. *THANK GOODNESS.* What amazing timing. I got back from a trip to Singapore where I found out my mom might have dementia, Edgar had flown to South Africa for work, and I was all alone with my mind. Very alone. All I could do was think: *what is going to happen to my mom? She is all alone. Am I a bad daughter for leaving her alone? Could I have prevented this? What should I do next?* And a million other questions, as well as guilt-trip infested thoughts raced through my mind. I tried mindful breathing for the first time again in a week, as I wasn't really able to do as much as I had liked in Singapore, although I was able to swim every morning.

It was Week 3, and we were learning about mindfulness of emotions in the body. The videos were a bit slow, as were the teachers, although they were super mindful and patient. The more I learned though, the more I was able to understand about how we as humans rarely, if ever, deal with our emotions. We just react to them. I recalled the scene of my mom in the blood clinic, screaming, "What is wrong with you?!" The first couple of times, I let Edgar deal with her, and I just kept quiet, knowing I would explode if I said anything. At one point, I couldn't hold it in anymore, and just yelled. That was me reacting, rather than using mindfulness to respond, and have some equanimity. Edgar was able to patiently talk to my mom and convince her to get her blood work done. He had succeeded. I felt ashamed at how I had reacted and wanted to be better. After all, yelling, does not accomplish anything, and is an AT way of communicating.

This week's task for homework is to feel your emotions, rather than react to them. I began feeling what happens when I get upset inside of my body: my heart starts beating faster, my shoulders begin to get tense, sometimes I can feel my heart pounding up in my head. We were also encouraged to notice how our body feels when it is happy or relaxed: I feel a sense of weightlessness. I recalled a couple's massage session Edgar and I did for our anniversary right before we left for Singapore. We both felt as if we had floated out of the spa. Every single muscle was relaxed, we were good tired not exhausted tired, things were clear in our minds, and this is also how I feel after a good 45-minute swim. *Hmmm. Interesting.*

I know that mindfulness can't solve everything, but it is a start. This week, I begin each morning with 10 minutes of mindful breathing. I have even created a mindful breathing journal, where I record how long I was able to do mindful breathing for, and any other thoughts I had about the experience. One thing that all of this mindful training has taught me is what I least expected it to. Let me go back a little. I had never really been into meditating, even though I knew it was a proven technique to help you become more balanced and the Sergey Brins and Larry Pages of the business world meditated. I guess I never tried it because I was always intimidated, didn't have the patience, felt like it was over-rated. But one of the absolutely mind-blowing (no pun intended) things I have learned is to not judge yourself. So back to all of those thoughts I had about finding out my mom might possibly have early onset dementia. *HEY, I am not allowed to judge myself or blame myself. I am ok. I am going to get through this. One breath at a time.*

SELF WORK:
Remember: Be WITH yourself first before being WITH your family. It will help you tremendously.

Start your own Mindful breathing journal. Write down how many minutes each day you were able to do mindful breathing and how it made you feel. Check out my YouTube video in which I share tips on how to get started:

Popo

Perhaps my love of old people and respect for old people stemmed from the close nature of my relationship with my maternal grandmother, *Popo.* She passed away in September of 2013. Just one short month after my niece was born. Some of my fondest memories were spent with my *Popo.* She came to live with us after my mom started working when I was in elementary school in Hong Kong.

My *Popo* would sneak extra money into my purse for me so I could take a taxi home from elementary school-- a short 5-minute distance up a hill, but a rather excruciating 20-minute hike otherwise. My mom would jokingly scold her for spoiling me too much, but I think she understood where my *Popo* was coming from. My *Popo* and I would spend afternoons together after school. We would either go see a kung-fu movie in Causeway Bay or go to Prince's Building or just walk around Central. She would always ask, "What you want? *Popo* buy." It was the pigeon language we created to communicate and years later as an adult, I think then led me to become an ESL instructor, as I was able to really empathize with my future students, because my first "student" was my *Popo.*

My mom and *Popo* would speak in their dialect called *Say yup*. Soon, I began to understand what they were saying, so they stopped using it to talk about me and my sister. Perhaps growing up listening to Cantonese and *Say yup* made me enjoy languages. Later at boarding school, some of my favorite classes and the classes I performed the best in were my Japanese and Mandarin Chinese classes.

Both my mom and *Popo* were amazing role models. My *Popo* was one of 5 sisters who were only educated up until elementary school, because back in their day, women were supposed to just get married. My *Popo* fought to be educated until high school and when her husband's parents' laundromat became bankrupt she took my mom and moved back home with her own parents. She then went out to work becoming a ticket collector at an amusement park after my mom's father left to go to Shanghai for work never to return. I can only imagine how challenging it must have been for my *Popo* to raise my mother as a single mother herself, back then.

After writing a note on the fridge for my dad, which said, "I am retiring from the kitchen," my mom promptly went to work in the real estate business at a friend's company. She soon outgrew her friend's company and yearned to start her own. I remember answering the phone for her as her secretary first from home, and then in her very own office a little bit outside Central. Even though it must have been hard for my *Popo* to raise my mom as a single mother, I am sure she is extremely proud of my mom for not only starting a business from scratch, but also raising a family, which *Popo* was very much a part of.

July 25th 2016

"Last night, I had a dream that I was picnicking with *Popo* and our future bubba," Edgar casually mentioned during our pillow talk time.

"WHAT?! No way. What did our future bubba look like?" I was so curious. We use the word "bubba" to mean baby.

"Well, I couldn't quite tell, but *Popo* seemed anxious about something. I couldn't quite figure it out. I told her to not be stressed and when she does come 'visit' us in our room, to relax too." He was referring to the doors slamming, as we would leave the windows open to combat the humidity of the summer nights. I believe though that it was *Popo* coming to visit us. Edgar would humor me and say that *Popo* was trying to order Pizza Hut with him. Even though they had never met, they did share a love of junk food.

That night, I attempted to purposefully talk to *Popo* while Edgar was sleeping. I wasn't sure what to expect, nor was I sure if it would work, but I thought I should at least try.

"Also, ask her what we should name our bubba…" Edgar said sleepily before dozing off.

"Well, your mother's name is Daisy and your middle name Hana means flower in Japanese, so I think your baby's name should have something to do with a flower. Yes, I was freaking out in Edgar's dream because it was too hot and the baby had no sun protection," *Popo* explained. She spoke to me in Cantonese, just as clear as day, and that was that. I immediately woke from this trance-like state and researched flower names in Spanish and English. Dalia. It was beautiful. Simple. Elegant. But what if we have a boy?!

SELF WORK:
Go visit and hangout with one of your grandparents. Have a conversation WITH him/her. If your grandparent is no longer with us then set up an invisible counselor's meeting WITH him/her.

Me + Popo in Singapore at the local market by her apartment. Our last selfie together. She was 86. (January 2013)

Grandma Kay

May 7, 2016

It came as it did from my mom, unexpected, except in my dad's quiet way about his mother. My mom had cried and wept, almost yelling that my *Popo* had passed away on the phone. My dad had written one email with the subject heading of "My mom." I knew almost instinctively what the rest of the email was about, not just because of the title, but because my dad had been unusually non-responsive over email during the past few months: Grandma Kay had finally passed peacefully in her sleep. She was 99 years old.

"You can say that we enjoyed our time eating tacos with her, that you were glad that we got to spend time with her, that her memory is living on in the form of you, your sister, your dad, your aunt, and uncle. And most of all, that she accepted me."

Edgar always knew how to be positive in the most seemingly negative black hole. I was struggling with how to respond to my dad's email, wanting to be there and be supportive, but also knowing I needed my own time/space to grieve. I decided to create a YouTube video to honor my Grandma Kay and all of the amazing things she was able to accomplish in her 99 years on this planet for my YouTube channel. It was hard. It was raw, authentic, everything I wanted it to be, but of course, it was not easy at all:

It dawned on me though. As Edgar said, "she is still living on with you in spirit." What if people who have touched our lives deeply, impacted our lives, inspired us to be greater, been incredible role models, mentors, strong independent women (in my case), what if they were still very much WITH us in spirit? What if they weren't really gone? Just their bodies were?

Similar to what happened with my *Popo*, I took a nap today. Emotionally exhausted from dealing with the news and the stress of what to say to my family members, how to break it to my mom, I took an afternoon nap. The window was open, the cool May breeze was going back and forth, which allowed the door to our master bedroom to open and shut, open and shut. I knew, in an instant, just as it had been with my *Popo* in Singapore when the curtain had touched my leg, that it was my Grandma Kay at the door to say "Goodbye." And just as I had said "Goodbye" to my *Popo* in Singapore, I did the same to Grandma Kay. She waved "Goodbye" with a smile, triumphant, head held high as always, not needing help nor wavering in the least. Thus, she left us, today, but spiritually she is as WITH us as she has ever been, as is my *Popo*.

3 generations of strong, independent women: My niece Alexandra, me, and Grandma Kay (97 at the time!) at my Grandma's house | Torrance, California | February 2014

MIU (MY SISTER)

Here is an essay I wrote about my sister after I visited her for the second time in Rwanda. She was working with Partners in Health on community health for her Ph.D. dissertation in Public Health out of Johns Hopkins University.

(February 2012)

To say that my sister is a force to be reckoned with is an understatement. She is at once a tomboy, an athlete, a humanitarian, musically gifted, and cannot stand still. Growing up, when I was still in elementary school enjoying my leisurely afternoons off with my Popo, we would come home to her working out to a calisthenics video (Yes, on VHS!). At a young age, she knew she wanted to play the piano. She asked my mom to buy her one and my mom at first refused, not because she didn't want her to play the piano, but because my parents didn't have enough money at the time to buy her one. Upon my sister's insistence, my mom found a used one and my sister was thrilled. She went on to learn the cello and also sing with an a cappella group at boarding school.*

Whenever I told people what she was doing in Rwanda, people who didn't know either of us very well, would often respond with: "Wow, you must feel like you have big shoes to fill," or something along those lines. In the beginning, I would often put myself down and respond, "Yeah, I am the black sheep of the family." And then one day during a Skype conversation with my sister, I told her of the exchange with yet another person who admired her work and made the usual comment about how she was doing great things compared to what I was doing. To this she remarked, "That is so lame. You know, there are people who are doing even greater things than what I am doing, so I actually don't even consider what I am doing that

* We attended the same boarding school, but she entered as a new junior. We did not overlap, unfortunately.

great. You know, I am always proud of you no matter what." After that conversation, I had an ever greater amount of respect for her-not because of what she was doing, but more so because of her humility.

When we were younger, we would often play together. One of our favorite past times was cutting our Barbie dolls' hair. Things were simpler then. We would play together, eat together, and of course, my sister likes to remind me that I was a brat and would cry to have my own way; I do admit, this was partially true. I think the other part of it is I couldn't stand having her "win" or be better than me. So I would cry. As an adult, of course, things are a little bit more complicated. At times, I do feel frustrated when I can't keep up or she is impatient with me or she is better versed than I am in almost everything; however, I realize now that we are completely different and our differences should be celebrated. For example, I could never live in a remote Rwandan village in a dorm room with cold-water showers. Just as much as she could never teach anything, because she is too impatient.

During my visit last year, she was in a really bad mood after having driven back from Rwinkwavu (the village where my sister worked) to Rwanda's capital, Kigali (an almost 2.5 hour drive). She is not fond of driving either. We were talking about my former headmaster and advisor from boarding school and how he was in Kigali. Before I even asked her, she barked: "I am not about to drive you to the town center. Maybe Chris will take you." She was referring to her husband. It made me so upset that she wouldn't even think about driving me. I would have totally driven her. After that incident, I found myself withdrawing from my sister. It was naturally quite easy given the geographical separation between Korea and Rwanda, but I found myself growing increasingly angry at her selfishness towards not only me, but also my parents.

I decided to write her a letter. We had exchanged letters when I was in boarding school and she was in college. On a recent trip back to California, we sat in my room crying and laughing alternately as we read the letters we had sent each other. It was indeed very nostalgic and characteristic of our personalities, which we agreed haven't changed all that much. My sister's letters were concise, in her signature scribble that very few people in the world can read. My letters were neatly written using a Lamy fountain pen, long-winded, detailing how much work I had or how busy I was. In my recent letter to my sister, I described the incident in Rwanda and how I wish she would be less selfish towards our parents and me. I went on to ask if she could put as much effort into her relationships with us as she has with her work in Rwanda. I cried as I wrote it. I felt it was necessary to be honest and I knew she would be able to handle it.

I think that letter, helped change our relationship. She emailed back saying that she realized she was selfish and that Chris (her husband) was selfish too, so it was hard to change. She ended by saying, as she often did, that at least our parents had one "good daughter." It was not a solution by any means, but it did sort of make me feel better that she had thought about what I had written, and it had affected her as it had deeply been affecting me. This second trip to Rwanda, I was worried that it would be similar to my last trip: wrought with friction and my sister taking out her bad moods on me. But it was markedly different: she planned trips to Lake Kivu† and to track golden monkeys‡, she paid for our accommodation, introduced me to her co-workers in the village proudly, and didn't really complain about all the driving she was doing, as Chris (who usually drove) was away in the U.S. We even spent a lazy afternoon cuddling on the living room couch taking selfies with my iphone and laughing, just as we had done when we were younger (sans iPhone of course). She slowed things down to my pace. She used to bring me "hiking" when I was in my 20s and basically run up the mountain. I was left panting behind. This time, since she knows I am a better swimmer than hiker, we decided to swim to a nearby island together. Even though it was definitely further than it looked, we still had a grand old time getting there and back together, at my pace.

I am forever grateful to have an older sister, a role model, someone to look up to; most importantly though, I know that Miu is someone who will be

† Lake Kivu is considered one of the Great Lakes of Africa. It sits on the border of Rwanda and The Democratic Republic of Congo.

WITH me the longest in our life journeys here on this planet. We often joke that when we are in our 80s, we will be swimming together leisurely enjoying the sun in our retirement. But seriously, just think about it. Fast-forward your life: when your parents are gone, and all your aunts and uncles are gone, those left will be your siblings. If that isn't a reason to spend more time WITH your siblings, I don't know what is.

About to swim to the island in the background at Lake Kivu | Border between Rwanda and The Democratic Republic of Congo | 2012

Eating farm-to-table breakfast the following morning | 2012

Before trekking some golden monkeys | Volcanoes National Park, Rwanda | 2012

Silly Selfies | Kigali, Rwanda | 2012

Know Where You Come From

(August 7, 2016 In Danville, California)

At UCSD in my Japanese class, I remember a discussion on family. Most of the other Asian students rarely saw their fathers growing up and as adults barely knew them. When it came my turn to speak, I told them, "I guess I was fortunate. My dad was always around. In fact he was *so* around, I like to think of him as the rock of our family. In elementary school, he would come home from work and help me with my math homework. In secondary school, we would eat at this Italian restaurant called Grappa's almost every Sunday afternoon—it was our father-daughter date. My dad wasn't absent."

I still relish time alone with my dad. It is uninterrupted time, selfish time, for me to learn more about my dad who is naturally quite introverted and doesn't talk as much when in a large group setting. When I was a child, I loved holding his hand, walking around Hong Kong, and asking him as many questions as I possibly could think of just to get him to talk to me a little bit more.

At dinner tonight, over chicken Chimichurri, homemade flour tortillas, and roasted cauliflower, a meal I often made for Edgar in Korea, I had asked my dad some questions (as I had done as a child) so he began unraveling some of our family history for me:

"Grandpa's father worked at a restaurant to save enough money to open a whole-sale nursery before the war. Grandma's father had a farm in Bakersfield, but he was a sea merchant who worked in Hawaii§. Grandpa would work extremely hard at the nursery, but also after the war, he worked as a gardener and would work 7 days a week. Grandma, in her 40s, after they sold the nursery, decided to get her real estate license. After a few years, she got her brokerage license and started her own brokerage. She also worked really hard with the soul purpose of being able to pass away in her own home, and not in a hospital. And that is exactly what she was able to do in the comfort of her own home." He was referring to my grandma's passing in May a few months ago, and how she had passed in the early morning, peacefully at the age of 99.

"It is too bad that grandpa didn't get to meet Chris or Edgar. Since Christopher is fluent in Japanese, the two of them could have talked a lot in Japanese and eaten sushi together. My dad really liked eating sushi, even after he had eaten dinner, mostly for the social aspect of it, as he would

§ *No wonder people always asked me if I was local whenever I went to Hawaii (!).*

meet his friends at the nearby sushi restaurant. And he spoke Spanish (which was new to me), because he had to talk to other Mexican workers he worked with, so he would have been able to talk to Edgar in Spanish."

I recalled a memory from a photo of me and my grandpa—I had found it in one of the old photo albums tucked away in the cabinets upstairs. We would watch T.V. on the beanbag near the T.V. and cuddle on the carpeted floor; I would go out to the backyard and pick tomatoes and cucumbers from his garden. Grandma Kay would then put them in a salad for us for dinner. Some mornings, he would wake my mom up, who would then wake me and my sister up during the summer and we would go and eat breakfast with him at the local diner. He was up with the sun, and would hit the sack when the sun went down.

I missed him. But I knew he, like my Grandma Kay and *Popo,* is still WITH us.

It may seem insignificant, but understanding where you came from, not only sets the stage after you are WITH yourself, to then be WITH your family. The deeper your understanding of your family, the deeper your understanding of yourself, the more you can be WITH yourself and WITH your family.

Me + Dad in front of our house—about to take a walk together (one of my favorite things to do with my dad). We are wearing matching UC San Diego visors! Except you can't tell, because the top of his visor got cut off in this pic due to my mad selfie skills! | Danville, California | August 2016

(L to R): my dad, grandpa, uncle, Miu, mom, me (!), and grandma. | Torrance, California | 1983

How To Communicate With Your Family: Lessons From My 3.5 Year Old Niece

- BE HELPFUL: As my mom's short-term memory is deteriorating, she often loses things like her glasses, as she doesn't remember where she put them down. Alexandra will immediately help her willingly and once she finds the lost item she'll proudly exclaim, "I found them, Grandma Daisy!"
- BE MATTER OF FACT: Sometimes my mom will guilt-trip us about seeing her more. She will ask Alexandra, "Why don't you come sooner?" To which Alexandra will reply matter-of-factly, "Because we are coming next Friday."
- BE EMPATHETIC: Alexandra knew that my mom would miss us all once we left, so when we didn't make it on our planes due to poor weather and came right back, she immediately went to my mom and said, "Grandma Daisy, you don't have to be sad anymore. We are not leaving yet."
- BE IN THE MOMENT: Alexandra loves playing and enjoys every minute of it. She doesn't dwell on the past or the future. It is helpful that my sister does not allow her to play with smart phones, computers, or watch T.V. for that matter.
- SAY "I LOVE YOU" MORE: Sometimes, when we are coloring together or just playing together, Alexandra will stop, look at me very seriously and say, "I love you." It makes my heart melt.

Me and "Little Gelly" (the nickname Edgar and I created for Alexandra) | Walnut Creek Bart Station, California. Almost matching headbands! | February 2017

SELF WORK:
Think about ways in which you can better communicate WITH your family. Write down some ideas here and start communicating WITH them on a regular basis using your ideas.

Fairy God Mother (FGM)**

As an awkward secondary student who was going through puberty, I loved receiving letters from my Fairy God Mother. She was a very good friend of my dad's from high school, is a reverend, started a non-profit to help empower women in Nepal, used to do colon therapy, and is a world traveler amongst her many accomplishments.

Back when people had pen pals, she was mine. I loved receiving her letters written in fanciful cursive writing on bold colored paper, and the best part? She would include glitter, stars, and confetti that would all come tumbling out of the letters as I unfolded them. I even created a box where I put all of the letters.

I loved visiting her eclectic house. At the time, she lived in a beautiful whimsical house in Laguna Beach with a gorgeous deck from which we could watch breathtaking sunsets. We would make cookies, create cards with glitter and glue sticks, and I would spend the night in one of her fanciful rooms equipped with a waterbed!

As I got older, I would talk to her about boys and sex. She would also encourage me to use protection, have safe sex (she even had a bowl of condoms by her front door!), and make sure that whomever I was dating, knew how awesome I was, and treated me how I deserved to be treated. I always made sure to wink at her and say, "Ok, just don't tell my dad!"

Years later, she married Edgar and me. It was so neat to see her standing up there, waiting for us as we walked down the aisle, all official looking in her robes. She also didn't bat an eyelid when she found out we had (temporarily) lost our wedding rings. She quickly used Edgar's MIT ring and her own ring as substitutes, and went on as if nothing had happened.

Looking back, as an adult, I really appreciate having someone outside of my immediate family be my FGM. She would always encourage me, praise me, create WITH me, never judge me, and all with a sprinkle of Fairy God Mother glitter. And now, Edgar has a Fairy God Mother-in-Law.

After all, everyone needs a littler glitter in his or her life.

** I found out recently from my editor that typically Fairy God Mother is just two words, not three—whoa! My whole life I have been writing it in three. Here though, I think it is important to let you know that this Fairy God Mother differs from the regular/ordinary godmother in the sense that she is magical, uses glitter, and is all kinds of awesome!

Original box I made for my letters from Fairy God Mom when I was in Middle School (!) | Danville, California | 2017.

After Fairy God Mom just married us | Malibu, California | August 8, 2015

SELF WORK:
Think of someone you know in your life who can be your Fairy God Mother/Father or who you would like to be a Fairy God Mother/Father to (!). Reach out to them and ask! One can never have too many mentors in life!

Letter To All Parents

In elementary school and, for me, up until boarding school, I had report cards. My parents knew everything from my grades, to my behavior in class, to how I was doing on my homework. In college, parents don't get report cards, just grades. If I were a parent, I think I would want to know how my son/daughter is doing in college other than just the academics.

Whenever a student decides not to share something (like an eraser) or doesn't take their trash out of the classroom (neither have to do with academic ability, but rather character development), I imagine what it would look like if I wrote a letter to that student's parent. What would I say? How would I say it in a WITH way? Why is it important for parents to nurture and encourage their son/daughter's academic ability but also their character?

So, here is that letter.

Dear Parents,

I know you are well-intentioned. I know you want the best for your children. I know you want your children to succeed and grow into the best possible human beings they can become. I know you must worry at night about whether they had a good dinner, whether they are happy, whether they are getting along with their classmates at school, and a myriad of other concerns. I, too, have some concerns after having worked WITH your children at the university level. I wanted to share them WITH you here.

- COLLABORATION OVER COMPETITION

  When my students (your children) first come to my class, they look at their fellow classmates as competitors. Competitors for grades mainly, but for taking what they think rightly belongs to them. They then compare themselves constantly to their peers feeling that their language skills are not as good as those around them and they feel increasingly insecure. Rather than foster competition at home, foster collaboration: encourage your children to share not just with their siblings, but their friends. So when they start their new lives in university, they don't get upset sharing something as simple as an eraser with a new classmate. Remember: Successful people are those who GIVE rather than TAKE[2].

- IT'S OK IF THEY DON'T GO TO AN IVY LEAGUE/SKY UNIVERSITY

  Sooooooooo much emphasis is placed on where children go to university. This fuels my first point about competition and getting grades, but at what cost? I think many parents (and I have seen this first-hand in my work with younger Korean kids in California) find out that their kids are doing well in school, getting good grades, and lose sight of any kind of character building. Is your child a good person? Is your child kind? Is your child good to others? Is your child compassionate? If your answer is "No" to all of these questions or even some, then you definitely have some more work to do. Even if they get into a name brand school, doesn't mean they are going to be a good person.

- INDEPENDENCE OVER NEEDINESS

I remember going to a talk concert for parents who were interested in sending their kids to one of the SKY universities, as I had been invited to speak there. I saw a video that compared a young elementary school student in the UK with that of one in South Korea. The one in the UK got up by herself, made her own breakfast (cereal, but still), tied her own shoes, and walked out the door with her backpack and lunch box in hand. In severe contrast, the South Korean elementary school student was spoon-fed soup and rice, had her shoe laces tied for her, and was escorted to the bus by her mother. I have even heard horror stories from our admin staff recounting how parents of some of our Yonsei students would call and find out what homework assignments their son/daughter had missed. I have seen first hand how students leave trash behind on their desks. Help them help themselves. I promise you, they will thank you later, as will society as a whole.

- <u>WITH</u> STYLE PARENTING TIPS

When I went back to my boarding school in January 2017 to speak[3], I ran into a faculty member who worked at the admissions office and was an advisor to a Korean freshman. He spoke at length about his frustration working with his advisee's parents and how they put so much pressure on their son to excel. (This freshman was enrolled in Calculus—I was doing pre-calculus as a senior!) This same story was repeated to me time and time again not just at my old boarding school, but in Korea, and even in California. Here is how to break this cycle:

- Listen to your kids: Ask them, "Hey, do you want to go to a *hagwon*? Do you want to study more?" If their answer is "no" don't push them. The suicide rate is the second highest amongst OECD countries for a reason in Korea[4].

- Do something fun with your kids no matter what age they are. Some of my students will write their essays about a fun family trip they took and how they were able to really bond with their family during the trip. Why not take a trip every month? Doesn't have to be far, just as long as everyone is together.
- Talk at the dinner table. I often see entire families out at a restaurant and each person is on his/her cell phone not paying attention, not interacting at all. I once read that the brothers who created the company Life is Good, Bert and John Jacobs, were inspired to create their now million-dollar company because of the one question their mother Joan would ask them every night at dinner, "What is something good that happened to you today?" Bert and John were raised in a lower-middle income family by parents who had escaped a near death car accident. Why not inspire your own children to greatness[5]?
- It's in the little things. At a recent sleepover at Roommate's house in San Jose, I noticed she had written something on the mirror of her children's bathroom: "Challenge is good for your brain. It helps your brain grow." She told me that she changed it from time to time, in order to inspire her kids.
- Play WITH your kids (no matter how old they are and no matter how old YOU are). All too often, kids play by themselves or with other kids. Why not play WITH your kids, bond with them, get to know them on a silly level, get creative. You may just have fun while doing so!

Thank you for reading my letter. I am happy to answer any questions or concerns you may still have lingering. So please do keep me posted on how the WITH parenting style works out for you.

My wish for you and your children is that you help create future global leaders who will change the world.

Wishing you + your children happiness,

Kyla

Doodles/Takeaways/Reflection Points

WITH PEOPLE: DEALING WITH YOUR COMMUNITY

CHAPTER 5

WORKING (WITH YOUR COMMUNITY'S EXPECTATIONS)

"Nobody knows what they want to do with their lives. If they tell you they do, they're lying." ~me

When I was in my last quarter at UCSD, after I handed my thesis in, life was pretty good. I would spend my afternoons at the beach boogie boarding, hanging out with friends over long dinners off campus, and just enjoying my life. Then I realized I had to figure out what I wanted to do. Well, it was a lingering feeling that began almost as soon as I started college my freshman year. I had to pick a major based on what I wanted to do after I graduated, but how could I pick a major when I had no idea what I wanted to do after I graduated?

During this time it is important to listen to your own voice first so you can figure out what YOU want to do, not what your community expects you to do.

When students ask me how I was able to figure it out back then, I usually tell them this: sometimes knowing what you don't want to do is as powerful as knowing what you want to do. So here's what I knew I didn't want for my life:

1. A boring 9-5 job
2. No more studying!
3. An office job

Here's what I knew I wanted:

1. A job that had enough paid vacation I could take time off to travel
2. Explore (the world)

3. Learn more about a culture/language that is part of my heritage (Japanese)

Even though you may not be able to put an exact job title on what you want to be/do, it is still helpful to work WITH yourself to figure out what you may like to do roughly. I mean, how could you know exactly what job you want to do, you've been at university studying for the past 4+ years, right?

The Gun Test

Out on the Newport Pier in Newport Beach, California, Sherlyn (Edgar's sister) and I looked out at the vast ocean. I had always wanted a younger sister. Although we hadn't spent much time together, the time we did spend together was always meaningful and eventful. One time when we went on a museum date to the ICA (Institute of Contemporary Art) in Boston, we ran into Mark Wahlberg (!).

On this particular night, Sherlyn and I were talking about what she should do with her life. She is 24. Incidentally, we share the same birthday. She would always tell me how she enjoyed talking with me because our conversations were always so unique.

"I don't really know what I wanna do with my life," Sherlyn admitted.

"Well, nobody really does. If they tell you they do, then they're lying." I went on to explain everything I went through to figure it out in my 20s. A story I find myself often sharing with my students as well.

"When you are faced with some choices, which one do you choose and how can you know if it is the right choice?" she continued.

"Well, in life, there are no right or wrong choices. There are only choices that are right for *you*. One test I like to do with myself when I am facing a difficult decision is the gun test." I could tell I had piqued her interest.

"What's that?!"

"Well, imagine there is someone who is holding a gun to your head, and you have to make a decision or else this person will shoot you."

"Whoa…"

"Yeah, I know, it's a bit dramatic. But think about it. If somebody was holding a gun to your head right now and told you that you had to get a job tomorrow, what job would you get?"

"It would probably be in customer service. I could get a job in customer service and I kinda like interacting with people."

"Well, there you go. You have your answer."

Me + Sherlyn (Edgar's sister) that night | Newport Pier, Newport, California | January 2017

I bring up the Gun Test not to scare or intimidate you, but to give you the perspective that sometimes all of the answers are really WITHin us, and often we seek validation externally or answers externally to push forward. Really, at the end of the day, we have all of the resources WITHin ourselves to figure it out.

Ok, so if you find the former Gun Test advice a bit daunting and dramatic, perhaps you can wrap your head around this analogy. Here's a drawing I usually give students when they come in and ask for career advice:

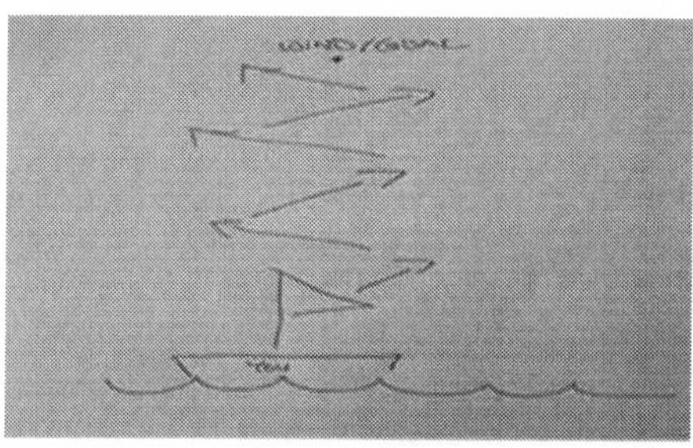

Learning how to sail was one of the best decisions I have ever made. After my then boyfriend had dumped me in grad school, I was determined to get myself back out there WITH myself. I joined a non-profit sailing organization and soon learned how to sail along The Charles River. As you can see from my drawing, what you learn quickly when you sail is that you can't sail directly into the wind. Otherwise, you will be in a situation where the boat doesn't move, or is "in irons." Similarly, with your career path, you will not necessarily get the right job immediately out of college or your first try, so you learn what you like, what you don't like, and you move on closer to your goal. You keep repeating this, until eventually you will get to your goal or your dream job, if one such thing even exists. Keep in mind your goal(s) may change.

SELF WORK:
Work WITH yourself and try to figure out during this time what it is you want and what it is you don't want in a job (maybe choose three things for each category—similar to what I did).

I taught a Career Development course at Yonsei over the course of 4 semesters. I really enjoyed teaching this course, because I could always deeply empathize with what the students were going through, as I remember very vividly how I felt when I was going through my first job search in my 20s—very angsty.

My first semester teaching this course, I realized after having had countless one-on-one sessions with students going over their cover letters and resumes that few students really knew what they wanted to do with their lives. They had spent the past decade or more (depending on how many times they re-took the university entrance exam) poring over books upon books to cram as much information into their heads in order to get that perfect score to then get into one of the SKY universities. Teaching at one of the so-called SKY universities, people in Korea often assume that students are smarter. I don't want to downplay how smart the students are, but I wouldn't say that they are necessarily smarter than any other college student in Korea. It is just that they are better test-takers.

However, they still face the same daunting job search upon graduation that every other college grad faces, and even before that, they still share the same angst:

"I don't know what I want to do with my life..." they often lament.

"What do YOU want to do with your life?" I will ask taking them aback, rather than just giving them advice.

"Well my boyfriend/friend/parents/relatives think I should do this..."

"Yes, but what do YOU want to do?" I often repeat this question until they finally answer it.

Job-Related Myths Or Stuff That'll Help You Get Closer To Working With Yourself (From My Career Development Course)

Myth #1
Everyone Already Knows What He/She Wants To Do With His/Her Life.

I have definitely lived this in my 20s. I would look around at friends who were confidently marching into interviews, jobs, internships where they thought that was what it was they wanted to do with the rest of their lives. Let me tell you, in their 30s, most of those friends are not in those same jobs, especially if they went into corporate law (!). Honestly, nobody knows what they want to do. Heck, if they tell you they know, then they are lying. So stop comparing yourself and figure out what it is you want to do. The only way to do that is to try as many things as possible and get rejected or accepted as you go along.

Myth #2
People Just Have One Job Their Entire Career And That's It.

Back in the day, during my parents' generation, they just did one job their entire life, retired, and that was that. It was an honest living and you had some kind of social security, retirement fund at the end of your many years of work. My dad was one such case. He worked for Bank of America for more than 2 decades and then retired doing consulting work here and there for other smaller banks. Nowadays, the average millennial changes jobs at least 4 times[1]. Also, bearing in mind, often with not too much experience, you may have to put up with a job that doesn't pay you what you would ideally like to make initially. However, all the more reason to pivot, and move to another company or another job within the same company that pays you more once you have gained that invaluable experience.

Myth #3
If I Get A Job At A Big Company Like Samsung, I Will Be Really Happy.

OK, let's not confuse happiness with reputation or prestige. When you hear the names of large conglomerates, people all know that those companies are not going anywhere anytime soon. Therefore, if you are able to secure a job at one of these companies, you will definitely have job security. However, this does not mean you will be happy. Big conglomerates are notorious for making their junior staff members work longer hours, go to work dinners (*huisik*), and generally slave away.

Myth #4
If My Parents Or Relatives Tell Me To Get A Job At A Certain Company, I Should Just Listen To Them.

I feel like I will be walking on thin ice with this question. However, it is important enough to address here and very common amongst comments that come up when I meet with students. So yes, you should listen to your parents and relatives to a certain degree, because they love you and they want the best for you. Unfortunately or fortunately, are *they* the ones who will actually show up to your job and work 14 hours for you every day with a smile on their face? If your answer to that question is "YES" then by all means, listen to them, but if you are shaking your head right now, then you see my point here. Drown out the voices, so you can hear your own more.

Myth #5
Job=Happiness

There is a sense among students that if they just get a job, any job, then everything will be great and they will be happy. In this job climate, the unemployment rate for college grads has been the worst in many years, in fact it's the worst in 15 years since 2000. The number of people in their 20s who are out of a job rose to 410,000 from 330,000 just last year in Korea[2]. But what if getting a job is not really in your control? Beyond the numbers, I can certainly feel the angst and struggle directly when speaking to my students who are applying for jobs, delaying graduation, taking unpaid internships in any hope of actually landing some kind of full-time job.

Myth #6
I Can Only Apply For A Job If There Is An Opening.

Create your own opening, people. Do not wait for an opening to become available to you. A good friend and former colleague from South Africa would tell his students this, "You know when you play tennis, do you wait for the ball to come to you or do you go to the ball and hit it?" The ball, of course, is a metaphor for life and in a more urgent sense, survival. Rather than applying for only job openings, why not email someone at a company where you have always wanted to work? What is the worst thing that can happen? They don't email you back?

Myth #7
If I Work Hard, I Will Get Promoted.

Definitely not true. This all depends on your boss. If your boss does not like you, you will not get promoted. So if this is the case, then leave. Who cares how it looks on your resume. Your mental sanity and professional growth are way more important. Furthermore, it is a good idea to work WITH your experience: if you are not getting promoted at a company you have been with for a while, then one thing you could do is to leave the company, find another job, and get hired at a more senior level based on your previous experience.

Myth #8
I Should Only Apply For Jobs In The Country Where I Live.

One of my former students has the unique advantage of having dual citizenship: she was a citizen of both the U.S. and Korea. In one of our conversations in the hallway after our Career Development course, she pointed this fact out to me and asked if I thought she should apply for jobs in the U.S. Before I even answered the question, she had a list of reasons why she shouldn't, including the fact that they wouldn't want to hire her because her English is not native. Ok, yes, maybe, but you never know unless you try right? Advice a good friend from university gave me was to apply broadly. That way, you can see which opportunities you want to take depending on what the offer is, but you can't know this, unless you try.

Myth #9
I Should Only Apply For Jobs I Really Want.

Sometimes over summer/winter vacations in Boston with Edgar, I would apply for jobs at various ESL institutes in downtown Boston. Even though many of them thought I was over-qualified for the job of institute instructor, I found it incredibly valuable to have an interview, even though I didn't necessarily want the job. First of all, it is not just about the interview. It is about all of the other prep that goes into the interview: dressing the part, doing research on the company, making sure you know how to get to the location, being punctual, and the list goes on. Second, even though you may or may not want the job, you are still being treated like you do, so the questions that the interviewer or interviewers may ask are inevitably going to be challenging. Third, you may find out that it is actually a good fit, not something you were looking for initially, but that may end up working (!). Fourth, there is always room for negotiation. Perhaps you don't like the location, perhaps there is another branch you can work for. You never know unless you ask, right? Finally, there is no better practice than an actual interview.

When You Are Lost

In a conversation with Crystal* in February 2017, she admitted to "being lost" with her job search. She was taking a semester off to figure it all out and landed an internship at a Singaporean bank. I reminded her that this feeling of feeling lost is really normal and comes up time and time again no matter how old you are, so she shouldn't feel bad. Here's some additional advice I gave her, which we both thought I should also share with you:

- ZOOM OUT
  You know on Naver maps or Google maps, you can basically zoom in or zoom out to get a better sense of where you are? Well, when the shit hits the fan sometimes, it is a good idea to zoom out. See the big picture of where you are. Yes, you may not have a job, but do you have

---

* Crystal is a former student of mine from Yonsei University. She first took my Career Development course, later co-headed a leadership seminar we created, and is currently working for a pharmaceutical company in Seoul.

access to food/water, clothes, shelter? Remember: half of the world's population lives on less than USD$1/day.

- VOLUNTEER
  Along the same lines as the first bullet point, you need some perspective on what is going on outside of your crisis bubble. Find a local organization that is doing something you would like to try. You never know, you may end up liking it. Plus, it will take your mind off of the job search, give you something to do to help out those who are in more need than you, and oh yeah, you can put it on your resume in the VOLUNTEER section (!).

- CHANGE THE SUBJECT
  I heard Crystal say, "*They* (companies) won't want to hire someone like me." Similarly, I would hear girlfriends of mine (past and present) say stuff like, "*He* would never be interested in someone like me." To both Crystal and my girlfriends I would say this, "Change the subject from They/He to I. What do *I* want? What kind of company do *I* want to work for? What can *I* offer the company and bring to the job? What kind of person do *I* want to date?

- COMPARE YOURSELF WITH YOURSELF
  This one is hard I know. My students always compare themselves with their peers, in terms of grades, and also in terms of jobs. Crystal was saying, "People who have better grades than I do are going to get better jobs than me." Those people are not Crystal though and vice versa. What someone finds to be a good job, another person may think is a terrible job. The only fair comparison is to compare yourself with the first job you ever had, with the next one, and the following one, and so on and so forth.

- GIVE VS GET
  People often think: I have to get something out of a job. I will *get* skills, connections, something so I can *get* promoted. What people often overlook though is that giving is the way to happiness and eventually success. So rather than asking, "What can I get from this experience/job?" you should be asking, "What can I give?"

And remember, people who GIVE are more successful than people who GET.†

- YOU ARE A ROLE MODEL
I know when your self-esteem has hit rock bottom (thanks in part to the frustrating job search), the last thing you are feeling is *I am a role model.* However, you just need to change your mindset a bit. Think about it for a second: if you are feeling this way, what about people who are younger than you? They must be equally nervous, scared, frustrated, right? Think about how you felt when you were younger. Become a role model for someone younger than you. Guide them. You will feel better. You will have some wisdom to impart.

- CELEBRATE THE SMALL VICTORIES
Did you send your resume out to one company per day? Did you get hired at a place you applied to but don't want to work there? Did you help your friend with his/her resume? Whatever the small victory, Edgar always reminds me to celebrate it. Take yourself out. Heck, you deserve it. Don't wait, until you get that job that you want. Do it now.

Take A Risk

In late January 2016, I met up with two former engineer students of mine Yangjae and Kyuho. They ended up joining the G^2LTS Committee‡. While catching up, they told me they were working on job applications because this upcoming semester would be their last. It was a common story. They were nervous and anxious because the job market is really bad. I encouraged them like I did all of my students to start their own thing.

"Why don't you start your own company or join a start up?"

"Well, you know, it is really risky. And even if the company does well, one of the *chaebol* will either copy the idea or stamp it out," Kyuho lamented.

---

† http://knowledge.wharton.upenn.edu/article/givers-vs-takers-the-surprising-truth-about-who-gets-ahead/

‡ G^2LTS (Global Gender Leadership Training Seminar): a group of 9 hand-picked awesome students I ended up training and working WITH at Yonsei every Sunday evening for about 3 hours during spring 2016.

"Yeah, it is not easy," Yangjae agreed.

"But isn't it the same amount of risk to be unemployed, looking for a job for a year or two years?" I persisted.

Some people are more risk averse than others; some people just take risks like they are drinking their morning coffee. Something I have learned along the way about risk is, if you truly believe in your purpose (the way you see Won-jae and Greg do in the story below), then you won't even think about risk as risk.

Here is a story I wrote about risk:

(December 2011)

RISK

"Kyla, can I be honest with you?" Won-jae looked at me with crazed drunk eyes. The same eyes he had looked at me with, with the same intensity when we won third place as "most mechanical" dancing pair at our boarding school prom. "I don't think you will make a lot of money..." There it was: the phrase that someone who had been wanting to start her own thing for a while now absolutely did not want to hear. "But...I think you will be able to change the world with your own non-profit." I felt somewhat relieved, but not really. The former part of his brutally honest advice, if it could be called such was lingering in my mind latching on and not going anywhere-it was there to stay for good-kind of like the doubt and fear I had within me to start my own thing.

Greg chimed in, "What are you waiting for anyway? If someone like me and someone like Won-jae can do it then you can too." It was true that these guys had built their own "empires" if you will. Greg had recently started his own law firm in San Francisco. Won-jae had started the first lacrosse team in Korea, played on it and is now the coach.

They continued, "Look at us. I mean, we kind of jumped without parachutes. Look at you: it's like you are about to jump with a parachute on your back, carrying another parachute, and you've got 4 or 5 more in hand and you still don't want to jump."

"I am afraid of failure," I admitted rather self-consciously, half-expecting another lecture from the two of them. They backed off sensing that perhaps they had crossed some sort of line, and then we began talking about how the boarding school we had gone to had shaped the adults we have become and our perspectives on life. It certainly had a profound effect on all of us and created an ever-lasting bond between us. They were like family-like the brothers I never had.

After my conversation with Greg and Won-jae, I began thinking about risk and asking others around me what they thought of risk and whether or not they thought they were taking enough risk in their lives.

During my winter vacation in 2011, on the balcony of my hotel room at Sanur Beach in Bali, my friend Frans and I caught up and chatted. She had been teaching English in Bali for the past year. We had met in the Bay Area where we first taught for a Korean company together.

"It's like I think I have courage, but I don't take the initiative like you do," she began.

"But you moved to Bali, not knowing anyone here and not speaking the language," I was trying to play devil's advocate.

"That's different. It's only because I got a job here and there was an opportunity. I just kind of go with the flow," she continued. "Now you, on the other hand, are always creating things and making things happen."

I had told her of this book, the social networking group I had started, and other projects I had lined up for 2012. Her eyes widened as I detailed each project for her. Yet I still had not started my own business.

My first year in the College English Department at Yonsei, I was super ambitious and wanted to create the best Freshman Seminar class ever. Thus, the Innovation, Creation, and Entrepreneurialism (ICE) Freshman Seminar was born; we spent once a week meeting for 50 minutes using hands-on activities to become more innovative, creative, and entrepreneurial. What does that even mean, I bet you're thinking? Well, to tell you the truth, my very own students in that class, had no idea what the "E" part of ICE meant. I put together a series of videos that I found on Youtube which I thought exemplified what it meant to be "entrepreneurial." However, I got the sense that they still did not quite fully comprehend what it meant. So I convinced my friend Aaron to be our guest speaker via Skype.

Aaron had dropped out of USC at the age of 19. He and a buddy from high school decided that they wanted to create an easier way to store large documents online. Thus, www.box.com

was born. Now at the age of 30, he has about 900 employees and has since gone IPO. Incidentally, amongst his many awards and accolades since founding BOX, he was named "Entrepreneur of the Year" by Inc. magazine. It was crazy to pick up a copy of this magazine at SFO knowing our paths had crossed[3]. Whenever we hung out, I would watch him, observe him, soaking him in in the hopes that just by hanging out with him, I could somehow absorb his entrepreneur spirit as if it were some sort of contagious disease or something.

"Weren't you afraid that you were going to fail back at USC?" I asked.

"No, we were more concerned about keeping it going," he answered matter-of-factly.

"You should start your own thing already. You're not getting any younger."

"You're right, but I am afraid of failing."

I recounted this conversation to my Freshman Seminar class after we had heard Aaron speak. One of my students who had been particularly inspired by Aaron's talk, asked me: "So, Kyla, why *don't you start your own thing then?" There it was again: the question that haunted me almost every day since I had the idea to start my own something.*

When I asked Greg the same question about his fear of starting his own law firm, especially in a time of recession, he put it this way: "Kyla, you know, on your deathbed, what are you thinking of? Are you thinking of failed businesses or things like that? No, you are thinking of the people in your life who are important. You are thinking about saying those final 'goodbyes' to the people that really matter to you."

We are told AT from a young age to be "safe." From parents to playing, the rules of society are always to stay away from risk because it is *dangerous.* What if that weren't the case? What if we could actually through practice change our perception of risk? By doing so, we can tackle another AT emotion, FEAR. By taking small risks at first, we can become more comfortable with the idea of risk, change our perception of fear, become more WITH our true selves, and ultimately become better at working WITH ourselves.

SELF-WORK: In my Career Development course, I have students take a risk for their self work assignment. It can be a small, medium, or big-sized risk. The idea is to start out slow. For example, if you are afraid of failure, try something you've always wanted to try that has low risk like learning how to say 1-10 in a foreign language. Then, once you're comfortable, move on to "My name is…" Again, once you're comfortable, learn how to ask a complete stranger how he/she is doing in that foreign language and do it (!). Try your own small, medium, big-sized risks. Write your thoughts below:

Small Risk:
Medium Risk:
Big Risk:

How did you feel? Takeaways?

Won-jae and his wife Jeena, me and Greg enjoying Korean BBQ | Itaewon, South Korea | December 2011

"Frans" | Bali, Indonesia | December 2011: My nickname with Amy. We call each other "Frans" because once her mother had mistakenly thought my name was "Fran" when Amy called me "Friend."

Doodles/Takeaways/Reflections

WITH PEOPLE: DEALING WITH YOUR COMMUNITY

CHAPTER 6

LEADING WITH PEOPLE

"A true leader, leads WITH his/her team." ~*me*

What Kind Of Leader Are You?

We hear the word leader tossed around so much we don't really even know what it means anymore. For the first time, at a women's leadership workshop, I was asked what my leadership philosophy was. I had absolutely no idea. And of course, I had to create a video in which I talked about it. I immediately thought of WITH vs AT and how we can not only communicate WITH intead of AT, but we can lead WITH instead of AT. What does that mean exactly? Well, rather than telling people around you what to do and assuming they will follow your orders, why not ask them what they think first? Imagine marching into battle, looking straight ahead and then nobody is behind you? What would you do? How would you feel? After all, a strength of a leader is not based on the leader. The strength of a leader is based on the leader's team. You can be the best leader in the world, but if you don't have a team that is willing to support you and help you, then there is no point to anything really.

SELF WORK:
Inspired by the Women for Leadership workshop I took with Deidre*, write out your own leadership philosophy. What does leadership mean to you? How do you want to lead? Then create a 1-2 minute selfie video in which you explain all of that! Here is mine where I talk about WITH leadership:

The Leader Within

In an Adaptive Leadership course I took, I learned the very powerful difference between a LEADER and LEADING. The former is a noun and the latter is a verb—seems simple and obvious enough, yet on second thought, wait a minute! Our concept of a LEADER is so fixed. When I was doing research for my GLOBAL LEADERSHIP workshop for the Cross-Cultural Business conference back in May 2014 in Austria, I was struck by how often so-called "leaders" and everything about how to become one of these "leaders" was related to the corporate world. The titles were things like "learn lessons on leadership from CEOs" "How to become a leader in your COMPANY" and so on and so forth. Most of these "leaders" were Caucasian middle-aged men. So this has become what we think about when we think of "leaders."

I did this activity once with all of my students, again in preparation for the above-mentioned global leadership workshop in Austria. I had students draw a picture of what they thought of when they heard the word "global leader." Only one of my almost 140 students, drew a picture of himself. Here he is:

Wongi | Intermediate College English Listening and Speaking Class at Yonsei University, South Korea | Spring 2014

Other students drew pictures of mostly men or globes. When asked to list some global leaders, this was also telling: most students listed American leaders: Barack Obama, Steve Jobs, Bill Gates to name a few. Some students listed Ban Ki Moon, but very few even wrote down former President Park Guen Hye* or any female leaders for that matter. It was disappointing, but proved a point. Before I get to that point, I would like you to take this IAT test and I am not going to tell you too much about it until after you have taken it. Go ahead:

Did you find that you took a longer time on test B? Be honest. Most people do. It is because we have hidden biases. Biases that we would rather not believe that we have, even if we believe ourselves to be the most open, unprejudiced people in the world. I have always thought that I am a pretty

* Perhaps they were foreshadowing things to come? Given her unprecedented impeachment on March 10, 2017.

open and educated person. However, on several occasions since having met and spent time with Edgar, he has pointed out certain biases I have. For example, one day after a run in Boston, we were looking at a construction worker. I noticed that he was Caucasian rather than the stereotypical construction worker who is usually a minority. I made some kind of sweeping generalization about how most minorities are lower in socioeconomic status, and Edgar called me out on it. I was floored, well, usually I am not wrong, but usually I am not THIS out of line. So it happens.

During my global leader workshop in Austria, there were about 30 university undergrad students mostly international business majors—Lusekelo (a former exchange student of mine at Yonsei) had brought his friends from his major. There was a mix of both male and female students, and some other conference participants who were professors from different countries. I had the students take the same test. They argued that it was unfair because you wouldn't necessarily take longer on the second test since you already knew the format of the test. They thought it was lame and did not mean that they were biased.

Ok, fine.

They then had to present their own definitions of what a global leader is in groups. This was very eye-opening: Students would say, "A global leader is someone who is _____. **He** is someone who ______." Time and again, even after I would correct the first students to make this mistake: He *or* she, right? That was actually a better test than the IAT one, even though it is not a bad place to start. I would recommend reading the book *Blind Spot* by Anthony Greenwald (the father of the IAT tests) and Mahzarin Banaji (a professor at Harvard University). Do check out their website for more information:

So here is my point. We need to broaden our definition of a leader to not only include ourselves but also others who don't work in the corporate sector, people who can lead rather than people who are just appointed as leaders. More of us need to take Wongi's lead and seek the leader WITHin. That takes courage, but in the end, I am sure Wongi will agree that it is totally worth it.

SELF WORK:
Write down some non-negotiable characteristics of a leader.

Put an (X) by the characteristics you already have.

Write down how you can work on the characteristics you don't have.

The Casual With Leader: Mrs. Hwang

Interview with Mrs. Hwang

Park Hyatt Hotel Seoul

January 17, 2018

"Thank you so much for coming to join me for breakfast," I said as I tried to subtly slide my credit card into the leather pouch. It was the first time in the 15 years that I had known her that she actually let me treat her.

"I am so happy. I mean, not because you are treating me, but because you are a native of Korea now," she replied with a big grin and a plate full of breakfast deliciousness. She was always happy when she saw people living up to their full potential. She subsequently produced two hand-crocheted coasters from her handbag that she had crocheted the night before, nonchalantly and preceded to scroll through the oil paintings she had painted for her kids--another hobby she had recently started in the past year or so. *Whoa, she is truly living her creed of not wanting to waste a second of her life, but in her casual way, not making it seem like a big deal,* I thought.

After I returned to the Bay Area from being in Japan for three years in 2003, I happened upon a tutoring job at JC Education, Mrs. Hwang's after-school education institute. One of my first students was Brian Bae (who was hearing impaired). I worked with him as a sophomore. He has since graduated from UC Berkeley (undergrad), Johns Hopkins (master's), and is currently working at NASA. Total inspiration. I also speak about him in my TED Talk. I didn't know then, but Mrs. Hwang had moved to the U.S. when she was 15 years old. While she was in Korea, she had been outgoing and had a lot of friends. However, once she got to the U.S., not knowing any English she struggled to make friends, cried for about 6 months, and vowed to save enough money for a plane ticket back to Korea. Incidentally, she did end up saving enough, but didn't know how to go about buying it (!). She turned her months of struggle into JC Education, helping students like her.

It was during my time at JC that I watched Mrs. Hwang and the way in which she treated people: tutors, students, staff, and parents and even her own children. Her oldest son Chris is now 31, Jon is 28, and Katherine is 19. Katherine was running around JC when I was a tutor, Jon was getting tutored, and Chris was helping out as a tutor. Mr. Hwang (whom Mrs. Hwang met in college at SFSU) would come around as the resident fix-it guy. He always had a sense of humor and as a result, would always make us laugh. I can almost hear, Mrs. Hwang saying, "Come on…let's be serious here, Mr. H!" But in all seriousness, they had a rock-solid marriage, supported each other through thick and thin, and raised three amazing kids, not to mention all of their JC "kids." They once told me that they wished Katherine would grow up to be like me and that they were so proud of me after finding out I had gotten into Harvard.

I admired how Mrs. Hwang seamlessly juggled raising three kids, running JC (which started with 1 student back in 2001 to now 60-70 students!), taking care of her mom, making sure the Korean parents were happy, feeding all of us, going to Church, and so much more. She would tell me that at night, her phone would sometimes ring incessantly and she would always patiently talk to people who needed her ear or wise guidance. Then she would check on each one of her kids sleeping in their rooms, and make sure they were ok.

When I returned to the Bay Area again in 2007 after having lived in Boston for three years, she called and asked what I was doing. That was Mrs. Hwang speak for "I have a job for you." The next week we met for lunch, which also ended up being the start of my job working for a Korean education company that brought Korean kids to the Bay Area, and handled all of the logistics from A to Z of helping them get settled in a private school in Dublin, California. I ended up working there first as their head tutor, and then replacing Mrs. Hwang as Academic Director, not to mention, I was also their first non-Korean hire. It was an awesome job: I got to experience Korean culture, food, students, and people first-hand. Eventually the students I met there planted the seed for what would become my long love affair WITH Korea.

Mrs. Hwang would often treat me to lunches at a Korean restaurant in Concord, California. Over lunch, she always had wise, insightful, deep golden nuggets to share, but she always shared in such a casual way, it was never intimidating, but rather stuck with you that much more. Like the time she told me not to worry about the things I cannot control. "Kyla, you know, life is like this: Imagine a giant boulder has been dropped down from a mountain. If you try to control that boulder, you will get crushed. Just go with it. It will be easier that way and less stressful for you." She would often begin her sentences with "you know."

At a shabu shabu restaurant in Kangnam the night before, we had dinner with another JC tutor, Krystal and a former JC mom, Heewon. Both agreed what an incredible woman Mrs. Hwang was. That night, she admitted to me while giggling, (which was disarming and adorable at the same time) that she loved hanging out with different aged people. She felt as if they helped her see different perspectives and kept her young. At 58, she was as youthful as ever. My attention turned to Heewon, as Mrs. Hwang began a conversation with Krystal.

"How do you know Mrs. Hwang?" I asked Heewon.

"She took care of me and my husband when we moved to the Bay Area. We didn't really know anybody or speak English that well, but we met Mrs. Hwang at the Korean church and she was so kind to us," Heewon responded. You could tell how grateful she was to Mrs. Hwang by her facial expression and the fact she had commuted over an hour to see her for a few hours—in fact we all had.

"Yeah, the director of the *hagwon* ("academic institute" in Korean) where I teach now is so different from Mrs. Hwang. We don't get to go to nice restaurants or get treated to good food like what Mrs. Hwang would do for us at JC," Krystal lamented. She was half-Korean and half-American and had come to Korea for a year to teach English and learn more about her own heritage.

I thought about all the times that Mrs. Hwang would invite us tutors to her home for *karaoke*, *kalbi* (short ribs), and mountains of *chapchae* (stir-fried glass noodles). Mr. Hwang would be outside on the balcony grilling the *kalbi* and Mrs. Hwang's mom would be in the kitchen helping her prepare the *chapchae* and other *panchan* (side dishes). I thought of the time when I found out I got into Harvard, and then got a position working at Yonsei, and how each time, Mrs. Hwang had shrieked with complete and utter joy for me, and just glowed from the inside and out. She knew, but would never admit, that her support and encouragement (how she is with everyone who crosses her path) played a crucial role in getting me--and all of us-- to reach our fullest potential.

1. What makes a good leader?
   A good leader is someone who can distinguish right from wrong. Not just in terms of morality/ethics, but every facet of life. Nowadays, people cannot distinguish between what is right or wrong, so they tend to stay in the middle--

grey areas. That is where things go wrong and they can make wrong choices.

Earlier you talked about processed sugar and how our bodies are not meant to eat processed sugar, because our bodies haven't evolved to process it. Similarly, humans are humans. Our minds need to distinguish between what is right and what is wrong. From there, you can have an impact. You can have a positive impact on others and voice your opinion clearly. People will follow you from there.

2. What is your message to young people?
   When people think of leaders, they think there is only one person or a "One Man Show." Think about it: if there is only a show with one person, that "show" can only go along so far. It won't last. There are other characters around that support the main character: YOU! You are the main character of your life. Make every second count. Live in harmony with others. I keep in touch with around 100 people around me. I make sure to make them happy, give them joy. That is what I tell my kids. You only need a certain amount to be happy yourself: food, shelter, the necessities. After that, you can help others. Just look around you. There are a lot of people who need help.

3. What is your life motto?
   I want to live happily and positively. I had arthritis before. Some mornings, about 4 months ago, it was so painful to even write anything with my writing hand. But then I would think to myself and say to myself: I still have 9 other fingers. You will not get the best of me today, arthritis. I am stronger than this. I believe that if your mentality is strong, and you have a positive attitude, you can really overcome anything both physically and mentally.

Thank you, Mrs. Hwang. You are a great example of a <u>WITH</u> leader.

SELF WORK:
We would start our G^2LTS meetings by sharing what we had learned about ourselves the previous week. Why not join us? Get a journal, and start writing one thing or as many things as you like that you learned that day. For example, *today I learned that it is not so scary to eat lunch by myself.* My students commented on how it made them reflect back on the day or days, actually recall what they did, they felt more aware of themselves and more grateful. Why don't you try it? What have you learned about yourself so far in this book?

Being A With Communicator: The First Step In Becoming A With Leader

Whether you are a teacher, manager, leader, student, office worker, the best way to communicate with someone is to communicate WITH them rather than AT them. How you ask? Here are some tips:

- Be a good listener. Make eye contact—don't look at your phone/watch. After you listen, and listen without interrupting, you can then ask questions to clarify or try to better understand what the other person is saying.
- Empathize. Even if you haven't been through the exact same situation/experience that the other person has, try to put yourself in his/her shoes as much as possible. In that way, you will not only be able to see things from that person's perspective, but you will be in a better place to help him/her out. Bring up a time when you went through something similar and how you dealt with it.
- Relate. This is kind of like empathizing, but taken to another level. After you empathize, use a story or an experience that has

happened to that person. For example, if that person has lost his/her pet, refer to another time when that person lost something. You will be helping that person recall past feelings or experiences such that he/she can help him/herself without even knowing it!

- Don't judge right away. Again, continue to listen, listen, listen, and hold back your judgment. One of the quickest ways to be an AT person is to judge someone or judge what he/she is saying before he/she has even finished.

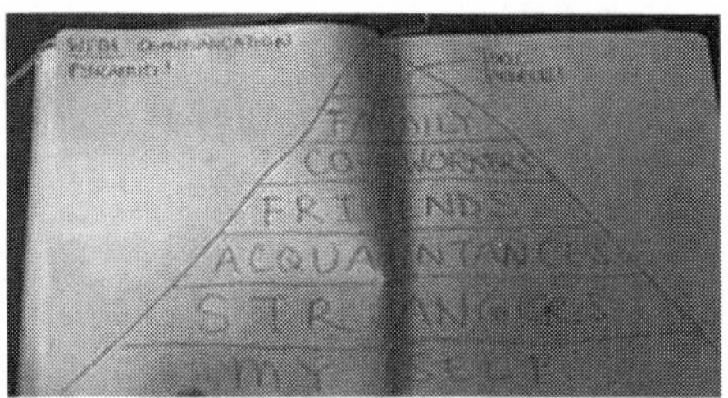

The WITH Communication Pyramid: Build your communication WITH yourself first to set up an incredibly strong foundation so you can work up the pyramid. My finger made a cameo in this photo!

*

DIFFERENT TYPES OF AT "LEADERS" YOU MAY ENCOUNTER:

Negative Nellie: Everything you say is wrong; life is negative; bleak outlook; why are you even working? Everything is doomed! Cue Darth Vadar music in the background.

Commander Cole: Do as I say or else. Barks orders. You should listen and obey. Old- school authoritative.

Stressed Out Sidney: No time to meet; always stressed out; no time to sit down or eat.

I like the sound of my own voice Val: They just want to hear their own voice; they don't care what you say or what anyone else says for that matter; AT style. Very exhausting.

Incompetent Iggy: Because they are incompetent, they have other people do their work for them either overtly or covertly.

WITH vs AT

10 TIPS ON HOW TO BE A WITH LEADER:

1. Have an open door policy: Never be too busy to listen and learn WITH your team members
2. Don't be an asshole/negative/yell AT people
3. Lose the hierarchy/attitude/ego
4. Create an environment where people will want to come to work
5. You don't know everything
6. Be a lifelong learner
7. Don't discriminate against anyone you work with based on age/gender/race/ethnicity
8. Help your team succeed, such that they get promoted
9. Encourage Collaboration over competition
10. Encourage everyone to be open and share everything

Quote People You Know (Who Are Still Alive)

My first semester teaching my World Issues class at Yonsei, I was so inspired by what my students had to say on their midterm exams about what makes a leader a global leader, I sat down and wrote down the best of what each student had to say. The following day, I handed it out to my students and posted a copy on my "wall of hope" (where I put letters from students and inspirational student work) above where I sit to inspire me to be a better person and educator. Here is that sheet:

World Issues

Fall Semester 2011

Famous Quotes From Future Global Leaders

"As we all know, sometimes dreams are always just dreams. Dreams are also just "what ifs" and will never come true without humans' abilities." ~Hades

"Diversity is always the key to development. Unless there is diversity, on the surface things will look calm and peaceful, but soon groups or countries will disappear because they cannot adapt to change." ~Min A

"I have learned three precious things: knowing myself better, passion, and effort and courage. These are the keys to having an inspiring life. If I practice what I have learned, I could reach my dreams with happiness. Also, it could expand to making the world full of inspiring things and happiness." ~Miso

"The whole journey of searching for my dream and finally fulfilling it will never be a straight line. One might make many mistakes and confront obstacles. However, it is okay to make errors. It is okay to fall away from your perfect plan." ~Minjeong§

"I felt that being concerned about other people's opinions should not be the reason or standard when people make decisions about their own lives. It is so easy to accept socially accepted guidelines for life especially in Korea." ~Jiyun

"One should not settle down and keep up with reading people's wants and needs. Once well-founded faith is prone to collapse in a second when one doesn't cope well with unpredictability and changeable thoughts of others. What one needs is change everyday." ~Yeon Jin

"If I could change one thing about the world to make it a better place, I would want to imagine the people of the world not being able to find any fossil fuels, because I think fossil fuels have created more problems than benefits." ~Jong Keun

"Being a global leader means that the leader is not tied to just one ethnic group, nationality or affinity to a region. Having an open mind in any situation and having channels open to everyone are the steps to being an 'open' leader." ~DaAeh

"Most world issues and problems involve vulnerable people. They are killed and exploited because they have no power to keep their safety and belongings. The awful part of the problem is that we don't give enough attention to these people. So if someone wants to be a global leader, he/she has to listen to what they are saying and pay attention to them." ~Dajung

"Listening skills do not mean just listening to someone's words. These skills mean listening to someone's words carefully and also responding pertinently with a sincere mind. Therefore, these skills are a fundamental pathway to communicating with each other." ~Goeun

---

§ The same Minjeong who wrote the Foreword (!).

"Changing is not a passive word meaning 'not doing,' but rather an active word meaning 'do better.'" ~Ji Hyun

"People usually confuse communication skills of global leaders with English skills. However, communication skills are not only about language ability. Communicating is more about being a good listener and knowing how to deliver one's thoughts effectively." ~JooYeon

"I thought humans were an independent unit ultimately even if people have friends, family, and colleagues. However, after entering university, I learned that making people feel happy can also make me feel happy." ~Min Kyeong

"Being a global leader is different from just being a leader of a class, company or a country. A global leader should be prepared to be what others cannot be." ~Hye Geun

"I think that happiness comes when people do what they truly want to do. If they have passion and the will in whatever they do, the money will follow." ~Woo Jung[**]

"Embracing others is one of the most important and difficult qualities of a global leader. I can be sure that the global leaders who have to embrace their enemies have more difficulties. However, if we are ready to embrace all the hard times, we can all be global leaders." ~Gakyung

"To be a good global leader, the most important thing is to take care of yourself and think carefully about other people not just yourself. By respecting individual voices, we can be one and not separated." ~Song Yae

"Experience is something that cannot be bought with money, but is critical in adapting to the different views of the world. Naturally having more knowledge than others is also crucial, but this knowledge does not necessarily mean how many As one got in his or her college years or how many books one has read. It is more about the ability to think further than others and the ability to put these thoughts into action." ~Jennifer

"We are living in a world with incredible convenience and abundance. People can go everywhere by cars, trains, and ships or even by spaceships. However, there is a place where we cannot access with any form of transportation, a paradise: a world without poverty." ~Yeo Seol

---

SELF WORK:
Quote yourself. Think of something that is important to you and come up with your very own quote:

The Last Word: Career Advice From My Dad

My dad has had a pretty stellar career by any standards. He started out bagging groceries as a university student, and then upon graduation he took a job with Bank of America (BofA), so he could travel and see the world. After more than two decades with BofA, he went on to work for a smaller bank called Bank of the Orient in San Francisco. I actually asked my dad to be in a selfie video, but since he's a bit introverted, he decided he would write his advice down instead. So here it is (it's actually pretty darn good!):

- Have a clear idea of your career goals and work towards them in some logical manner. However, don't be afraid to make changes if you are unhappy with what you are doing, including returning back to school. The job you're likely to do in ten years probably does not currently exist. Be prepared to improve and broaden your skills so you are in a position to perform newly created jobs and then grow with that job and become an expert at it.
- Travel to other countries and get to understand how others live and think. Do not be afraid to work in other countries. Most careers will require international experience and will greatly enhance your long term potential.
- It is very important that you work compatibly with co-workers, particularly your supervisor. All highly successful executives have the ability to get along well with others. A charming personality will win you many discussions. Socializing with co-workers will provide you with the ability to meet new co-workers in a convivial environment and allow you to get to be known by others who may help you in the future.
- Establish and maintain a network of friends and co-workers in other companies in your industry. Collect business cards, email addresses, etc. These individuals can often help you if you are in need of important information. Additionally, they may

provide assistance if you decide to shift jobs. Industry conferences, seminars, workshops, etc. are great places to meet others. Don't forget your former schoolmates.

- Don't be afraid to volunteer to be on a committee. It will help you to meet others in the company whom you may not know. Pay close attention to the manner the committee chair runs the meeting. This is a skill that you need to learn as you may be called to chair a committee yourself at some point.
- Do not assume that your work will speak for itself. You must let the right people know your capabilities and successes. Don't be afraid to bring new ideas or ways to improve things to your supervisor. But make certain you properly research and evaluate those ideas so you don't embarrass yourself.
- When you join a company there will be those co-workers whom you need to communicate with in order to do your job effectively. Be nice to these people. There are other co-workers who may need information from you but are below your level. You need to maintain good relationships with these people as well because at some point they may be above your level and in a position to give you grief.
- Join a professional club relative to your job. You will meet others in your industry and perhaps learn what other companies in your industry are doing, which may be of benefit to your job/career. The more you learn about your job or industry the better for you and your company.
- Consider joining community volunteer groups that perform important services to those less fortunate. You will be a better person for doing it.
- Try to find a co-worker who can act as a mentor. Generally, these are older individuals who have been with the company for many years and are very well informed about the way the company really runs. He/she can help you with your career or if you encounter a problem. Be careful whom you select. Selecting the wrong person may harm your career.
- Identify a young co-worker that looks like he/she may have a rapid upward move to his/her career. Become friends with this person. Note how that person does his/her job and try to learn why he/she is so successful. This person can help your career, even if he/she leaves and goes to another company.
- As you progress in your career note the good and bad traits of those individuals who were your supervisors and make a mental note to avoid all the bad traits they have displayed and

promise yourself not to do them when you become a supervisor/manager. Try to model yourself after the very best managers you have worked with or been involved with.

- Stay away from Facebook and other social media sites. You never know what someone might say about you that is untrue and negative. Employers often review these sites and it may impact your career or job potential.

Thanks Dad. I love you. Oh and thanks for nurturing the inner WITH leader WITHin me.

Doodles/Takeaways/Reflection Points

WITH PEOPLE: DEALING WITH YOUR COMMUNITY

CHAPTER 7

BEING WITH PEOPLE

"I generally trust people I first encounter until they prove I should do otherwise." ~me

Close Encounters With Terrorists

The closest I came to a terrorist incident was just another visit to Boston to see Edgar when we were doing long-distance. What awaited me upon my arrival was something I could have never predicted nor even expected. I wrote a story about it. Here it is:

(April 14, 2013)

Last Chances or Everyday Chances?

"Kyla;

I hope you are being practical about your safety during the next few days given Kim Jung Un's crazy threats. I don't think he will be dumb enough to fire any rockets or bombs into South Korea but there's a very real probability that he might kidnap some U.S. citizens and demand some type of payment from the U.S. for their return. I know you are not particularly concerned but it would be wise to practice a little common sense safety steps.

Love;

Dad"

This is the email that I put up as a warm-up for students in my World Issues class on Wednesday, April 10th in place of the usual background music I played. The same Wednesday, April 10th that crazed leader Kim Jung Un said he would send out his missiles and kill all of us "capitalist pigs" or whatever he calls those of us living in South Korea in his propaganda. This propaganda used, on the one hand, to manipulate those same "capitalist pigs" into thinking he would be crazy enough to push the button and launch nukes when really at the end of the day, I think his people just need aid. And on the other hand, the same propaganda used to unite a starving (both in terms of hunger but also freedom) nation into thinking that they are better than the rest of the world, led by their "beloved leader."

Wednesday has since gone and past, but the rhetoric is still around. Friends in the U.S. have been reaching out to see whether I am in some bunker asking if I have been evacuated. Ping's mother recently told me that I should know the location of the nearest bomb shelter. A co-worker from Canada has been carrying her passport around with her in the event she needs to flee the country. A student from Paraguay has actually fled to Taiwan, abandoning Korea and his upcoming midterm. It seems everyone has been cast under Kim Jung Un's spell of pandemonium.

"I think that we should treat North Korea as if it were a baby and we its mother," a student suggested, back in my World Issues class. My dad's email had sparked more of a discussion in a class where discussion was hard to come by given the culture surrounding learning in Korea. The students were trying though to get their opinion out there. "They just want aid. They are not going to start a war." Another student chimed in. I was thinking, perhaps there should be more imminent threats of war, so that my students can be this active about discussing global issues all the time

(.!).

"Are you guys worried? I mean, is there a real threat of war?" I looked out at the sea of young faces. They were not panicking at all. In fact, they were more worried about their impending midterm the following week than any kind of threat from their neighbors in the north. It made sense: they were the generation that grew up coddled by the hard work of their grandparents' generation. The same generation that had worked to build a "miracle economy" out of the ruins of the aftermath of the Korean War. This generation could indulge in luxuries a mere 5 decades ago, that did not exist-often overly so. They were the Smartphone generation. It was not uncommon to see students coming to class and texting on their phones on Kakaotalk rather than talking to each other face to face before the class began.

On Glee* this past week, rather than the usual mash-up songs, gunshots rang out through McKinley High's halls. The next scene is one of high dramatics for sure, pushing each actor

* An American musical comedy drama TV series that follows a high school glee club that aired from 2009-2015 for 6 seasons.

literally into a corner of the choir room, but also into perhaps the most dramatic acting of the season. They start recording their last words on their smart phones, crying and hugging alternately, and basically saying their "goodbyes" to each other. There is a sense of regret, things unsaid, and making up for any wrongdoing. At least I am sure that is the message that the producers wanted to send out to its viewers.

I thought about the past week and all of the rhetoric that had been blasted out all over the world through various news channels, Social Networking Sites, and everything in between to make people think that North and South Korea would be engulfed in the next World War. Even Richard Engel (NBC War Correspondent who was notorious for showing up right before war broke out, and had thus become known as a War Omen) had arrived in Seoul. A friend of mine who worked at the Westin Chosun Hotel, where he had checked in, further confirmed this. What would it be like if the world did end on April 10th? It certainly was a point of reflection.

"Going to a Concert Alone." This was the title of a narrative essay by a student in my reading and writing class. She had done what I had never had the courage to do: gone to a concert alone. It wasn't just any concert either. It was a Taylor Swift concert. As I read through her narrative outline, I couldn't help but feel a tinge of jealousy topped with a huge scoop of admiration. Later in the week during a one-on-one feedback session, she had encouraged me to try going to a concert solo. She had detailed how liberating it had been to overcome those fears of being alone when she had sung with fellow Taylor Swift fans from around the globe at the actual concert. She admitted not knowing all of the words, but that wasn't the point. She had put herself out there knowing if she hadn't, she would have regretted it.

So, perhaps it is about living our lives without regrets. The mountain behind my dormitory building has served as my running grounds ever since I arrived in Seoul; upset that I couldn't find a decent 25m swimming pool, I took to running. Over the three years I have been here, I have never run past a certain point. In the beginning, it was sheer physical endurance. As the years past, it turned into a series of excuses: if I ran further, my knees would start hurting, I'd have to wake up earlier, and so on and so on. "Have you seen the new wooden walkway they built up around An San?" A co-worker asked knowing I run up there in the mornings before classes. A little embarrassed to admit that I hadn't, I shook my head.

The next morning, I ran past the usual point and low and behold, as if a metaphor for life, there was a whole new world that had been in existence this entire time that I had never known–or never felt confident in knowing. The views were breath-taking: amongst the back drop of forsythia bushes, cherry blossoms slowly blooming dotting the mountain side, the buildings below seemed far away and insignificant. The more I ran, the more I wanted to see: it was like a drug.

Perhaps that was the lesson. I mean, we live in an unpredictable age. The Kim Jung Uns of the world could press a button to end our lives forever, in less than a minute we could get hit by a bus, so many things could happen to us. Why don't we live our lives as if we were dying everyday–not just on the April 10ths/impending war threats? Beyond this, why don't we take these chances to push ourselves to be better humans both physically and mentally? Go to a Taylor Swift concert alone, run further than you've ever run before. You may just be pleasantly surprised by what you find on the other side. Just put your goddamn smart phone away and start living your life.

I remember when that hash tag YOLO came out. I remember thinking, another acronym? What does this one stand for? I didn't clue in until years later, when people had forgotten about it in the abyss that is the Internet. Now I think about today, each day being my last one on this planet. What are the things that I would want to say to those around me whom I deeply care about? What are the things I am deeply grateful for? What are the moments I am so deeply involved in that everything else fades away? This is how to live WITH your life.

(April 18, 2013)

A week later, excited to see Edgar (by then we had been dating for almost 8 months), I left Incheon airport for Boston. Bracing myself for a long flight, and even worse service from the United flight attendants, I stuffed my hand carry full of my usual goodies: magazines, M&Ms, and my last Coffee Bean & Tea Leaf ice-blended before boarding. Little did I know what was awaiting me...

Instead of the usual excited boyfriend waiting with anticipation, and some sort of big romantical gesture†, I was greeted by the same message in three different apps:

"Hi honey-I'm going to be late to pick you up. There's been a shooting on the MIT campus. An officer has been shot. I'm safe and so are our friends. I'm currently on lock down by the MIT police and we're waiting until the situation gets resolved. It's on the news. I love you very much. I'll be there as soon as I can. I can't wait to see you."

Skype, imessage, Kakaotalk, and finally a CNN message all popped up to greet me. The latter, of course, was not

† The first time I went out to see him in Boston, he showed up at the airport with a hand-made painted signs in my two favorite colors (pink and orange).

from Edgar, but corroborated everything he had texted. Fortunately or unfortunately, I was in such a daze after having traveled for close to 24 hours, I wasn't fully with it. I assessed my situation: 8% battery life, battery charger dead, Edgar on lock down, no key to his apartment, almost 1 am. As I texted back and forth with Edgar, I recalled the conversation I had had just before leaving with a co-worker of mine:

"Well, you're probably a whole lot safer in Boston than in Seoul. I mean, what with all the threats from Kim Jung Un," my co-worker chuckled from behind his cubicle.

"Yeah, I was just trying to convince my mom that nothing ever happens in Cambridge, and it is super safe," I agreed, trying to convince myself perhaps more than my co-worker or my mom. "After 9/11, New York was pretty safe, because there was so much security," I continued.

"Ma'am, you do know what just happened at MIT, right? You still want me to drive you there?" My cab driver looked confused, but surprisingly willing at the same time.

"Yes, my boyfriend is there with his sister and some friends. I have to go pick him up and the others..."

Edgar and I had decided that it would be better if I came to pick him up, so we would both get to his apartment and I wouldn't be left outside waiting for him.

"You know, I have never once felt fearful living in Ethiopia," my cab driver chatted away with me. We were talking about the events of the Boston Marathon in light of the recent shooting at MIT, not realizing at the time, that the two events were actually linked. He went on to explain that he had been some sort of financial advisor back in Ethiopia, often traveling to remote towns and villages to help people with their accounting. He had never once though, feared for his life, the way he admitted feeling merely going out with his buddies on a Friday night in Boston.

Recent events across the U.S. painted a picture fraught with gun massacres, including one that had actually pushed a gun control debate so far, it had gone to the forefront of Obama's policies. Ironically, many of the marathoners in

Boston were running for those who passed in this same massacre in Newtown, Connecticut‡; 16 had even lost limbs running for this very cause because of the bombs the Tsarnaev brothers had detonated.

As we neared MIT campus, most of the streets that led to campus were blocked off by police cars and roadblocks. Not realizing the driver was lost, I panicked thinking there was no way I could get closer to where Edgar, his sister and his friends were. Then, the unspeakable happened: my cell phone finally died. With no way to get his cell phone number, I must have looked like a child who dropped her ice-cream cone when the driver asked me if I wanted to use his cell phone to call Edgar. It may sound weird and cliché, but in times of crisis, when you are pushed to try and recall something, somehow your brain goes into adrenaline/overdrive mode and you are able to come up with it. Somehow the 9 digits I needed to get to Edgar came to me in an instant; then the next thing I saw looking out the taxi window was Edgar, his sister, and two

‡ The deadliest mass shooting in U.S. history at a grade school. Adam Lanza who was 20 years old, shot and killed 20 Sandy Hook Elementary School students in Newtown, Connecticut and then shot himself.

friends running out of the off campus bar like fugitives just minutes after I was able to call him. I was relieved his sister was with him.

It was my first time seeing Edgar in more than 2 months. I wanted to embrace him, like we usually did when we saw each other for the first time after months of missing and longing. However, there was no time for that. His sister and friends jumped into the cab, as if it were the last taxi they would ever see. I held on to Edgar's hand in the cab, as we drove off into the night to safety. In that moment, we were indeed all fugitives. Not knowing if the gunman would reappear and promptly conduct another massive shooting spree not unlike what had happened in Newtown, Connecticut.

The following day, amid the endless drones of sirens, helicopters, and media, I lay next to Edgar. I wanted to leave the house, but everyone was on lockdown until they found the younger brother. As the news unfolded in front of our eyes, at times, almost a stone's throw too close, I felt so fortunate to be alive. I thought about all of the things I had done in my life and consoled myself thinking if the gunman came knocking, I would be with Edgar. But then I thought, wait a second! There is so much more that I want to do. I am not even 35 yet. I wanted to make it back to Korea, so I could go paragliding for my birthday in May. I wanted to dive the Great Barrier before all the coral reefs eroded away, I wanted to go to Santorini, and I wanted to start my own company-something I had been talking about for years.

Why is it that we put off things until we are near death? My thoughts were interrupted by Edgar's return home.

"How was the memorial service, honey?" I asked Edgar when he got home.

"I cried for 2 hours. I feel better now."

They had held a memorial service at MIT for Sean, the police officer who had been shot at MIT. The same police officer who had frequented the bars where Edgar had worked part-time on campus. The same police officer who had loved listening to country music. The same police officer who was just 26 years old-two years younger than Edgar. I felt like a terrible girlfriend. I should have been there for him while he was crying, I should have known that they were closer than I thought they were, I should have something. Then I thought: well, how could I have known? How could anyone have known, some kind of disaster would show up in the form of two brothers from Chechnya setting up bombs, hijacking a car, ending in a police chase and later in Watertown in someone's boat?

Who would have thought that just 3 short years later, they would have made a movie called Patriot's Day starring Mark Wahlberg and I would be sitting in a movie theater in California watching it with Edgar, and seeing him cry again.

The thing is, no one ever knows. You trust people-the way in Korea you trust that if you leave your laptop, cell phone, and any other personal item on your table to go to the restroom in a cafe-it will all be there when you get back. You trust that people aren't crazy. Turns out, the brothers ended up living four short blocks away from Edgar and his sister. A house we passed a million times on our morning runs. A house that could have housed a family of intellectuals, students from nearby MIT or Harvard, or even three kidnapped women -like those who resurfaced a decade later in probably a similar looking house in Ohio[§]. You just never knew.

So how do we go on?

"In Ethiopia, you knew who your neighbors were. If you needed butter or salt, you could go knocking on their door and get it. They were more than your neighbors-they were your family."

The cab driver had a point. In our increasingly disconnected, supposedly technologically sophisticated society, we have so many ways of connecting with one another: just as Edgar had desperately tried to get a hold of me using Skype, Kakaotalk, and every other messaging app he could get his hands on; we have so many ways of getting in touch with each other, we aren't actually touching each other anymore. Literally. We aren't touching each other's hearts; we aren't touching or influencing each other's lives the way we used to. We would never go

---

§ Ariel Castro kidnapped three women and held them captive between 2002-2013 in his house in Cleveland, Ohio. One of the women managed to escape in May 2013, which led to the rescue of the other two women and the eventual arrest of Ariel Castro.

knocking on our neighbor's door for fear that they may be some kind of terrorist or because we simply did not know who they are. Would it make that much of a difference if we started touching each other more? Would that prevent those of the likes of the Tsarnaev brothers from committing such acts of terror?

Honestly, I can't tell you either way, but what I can tell you is I think they would perhaps think twice before hurting those that they thought actually cared about them enough to touch them. As the Bible says, "You shall love your neighbor as yourself. There is no other commandment greater than these" (Mark 12:31). I know, I am by no means religious, nor have I gone to church since I was a kid, but perhaps there is some truth here. I mean, at least, love those around you in the hopes that they will not turn against you? Reach out to those around you for they may need you more than you think. This goes for not just North and South Korea on a macro level, but the likes of the Tsarnaev brothers on a micro level.

Take some time to get to know your neighbors. And not through text either.

You may just get some salt or butter out of it.

Building a community, you have to do it WITH others. Whether it is an online community or an offline community, we humans need connection. Just think back to our ancestors who lived in villages, together, helping each other. In parts of the world, our lives have become uber modernized and more convenient with technology, but at the same time, technology also helps to isolate us more and more.

SELF WORK:
Create your own community. Think of something you enjoy doing, a hobby, something you would like to share with others and connect WITH them.

Staycations + Reverse Discrimination: Severe At Behavior And How To Deal With It

To be discriminated against is to be judged AT quickly, purposefully and without much thought and consideration or kindness for that matter. In June 2017, I decided to take a life coaching certification course. Boy, did I learn a lot about myself. One of the things that stayed with me though was an explanation of why we shouldn't judge others or ourselves. You see, when we put others up on a pedestal, we put ourselves down. On the other hand, when we put others down (judging them/discriminating against them/stereotyping them/etc.), we then falsely put ourselves up. Thus, the only real way to see other people is equally. Neither judging, thinking they are greater nor you are greater.

I love doing staycations. The whole notion of staying somewhere close by was coined in 2009 shortly after the global economic recession. Marketers of tourism needed a way to still get tourists and other vacationers to pay to stay, so rather than marketing vacations, they began marketing staycations.

In August 2015, Edgar and I moved to Songdo. It was something we had thought about doing, but became a reality because he was fortunate to score a job at a bio pharmaceutical company in this new smart city in Korea. We are about 1.5-2 hours outside of Seoul by public transportation. This distance, was at first, a bit of a challenge. My commute to work used to be a 15-minute walk, but had now become an hour bus ride campus to campus. Yonsei had built a satellite campus in Songdo in 2010 equipped with dorms for all freshman and provides a free shuttle bus between the two campuses.

I decided rather than commuting back and forth on some weekends, where I had engagements, it would be great to have a staycation. It was the perfect plot: I could combine my love affair with staying at hotels with my aversion for commuting long distances, and I would drag Edgar along with me (!).

In October 2015, I gave my Happiness Workshop at COEX at the International KOTESOL conference. Of course, I was excited that my proposal had been accepted, especially given it hadn't been the previous year, but I was also secretly more excited at the prospect of staying at a hotel with a pool, club lounge, and being pampered. While I was gone, on one of the conference days, Edgar was working at the club lounge. It was during the afternoon, when they had some snacks out, and he noticed (he has a knack for observing people) how the young female staff were fawning over an older Caucasian gentleman.

What then ensued, sad to say, I have seen time and time again. Not just at 5-star hotels across Korea, but on business class flights, counters at airports, but more generally all over Asia. The older gentleman became increasingly irritated that he had to share the attention of the female staff with Edgar, so he began giving Edgar dirty looks. He would stare Edgar down. I mean, Edgar wasn't doing anything other than working on his laptop and getting up from time to time to get some snacks. Finally, Edgar had to say something, "Oh, you're reading that book? Have you gotten to page 200 yet? That's when it gets really good." The gentleman had nothing to retort back, so he left in a huff. If anyone should have left in a huff, it should have been Edgar, since he was not getting any attention from the staff as they were ignoring him.

Edgar and I are no strangers to this kind of discriminatory treatment. We are an Asian/Mexican couple. At first glance, no one would know that we went to MIT and Harvard respectively, but it would also be elitist and not like us to broadcast this just to receive the same kind of treatment we feel we deserve, because we are essentially paying the same amount of money as the white gentleman who threw a tantrum.

Edgar and I have fond memories of the Hyatt Hotel in Cambridge. It was where I stayed when I first met Edgar back in the summer of 2012, and we subsequently make it a point to stay at Hyatt hotels around the world. I even signed up for a Hyatt credit card shortly thereafter.

In June 2015, to celebrate our 3rd anniversary and Edgar's graduation from MIT, we stayed at the Hyatt in Cambridge once again. During one of the buffet breakfasts, we were sandwiched between two tables of older Caucasian people. Servers should have come around to ask if we wanted orange juice, something to drink, give us ketchup. However, no one came. The servers served around us. They served the older Caucasian people on either side of us. After about 10 minutes of this, I got up and asked a server to help us. He said he would come, but again, he never came. Finally, a server came by saying he was busy, and that he hadn't even known that we were seated there. I decided to not let it go, because in these types of situations, you have to call people out. Believe you me, I am not a fan of confrontations. My preferred method is avoidance, but if I do actually confront someone, I cry. Calling people out, especially in these hotels, has been a great personal challenge for me. The result was chocolate covered strawberries and champagne, a box of chocolates, fruit, a hand-written note from managers, a free lunch with the manager and F+B manager, but no one ever *actually* admitted that there had been any kind of discrimination.

At a hotel in Seoul, the Sheraton D Cube, MK and I were doing a girlfriend staycation in February 2015. We went to breakfast about 10 minutes prior to its closing down. The F+B manager (we didn't know of his role at the time) came to us and told us quite curtly that the buffet would be closing and we would not have enough time; he was basically trying to persuade us to not eat there or at least that is how it came across. We did not heed his warning, believing that we were paying guests, and that we were welcome to the 10 minutes of eating time. As we should be. A few minutes later, a Caucasian gentleman arrived. He was greeted not with time constraint warnings, but with a plate, and a female server who kindly explained what everything was; it made us both sick to our stomachs.

Over breakfast, MK and I talked about bringing it up. We had to bring it up. Even MK, who is a generally shy and introverted person, believed that the way we were treated was not right. It was just not the right way to treat us. We wondered why Koreans (and this is true of most other developed countries in Asia I have been: Singapore, Hong Kong, Japan, China) treated their fellow Asians with less respect than their Caucasian counterparts. Beyond the argument that all hotel guests should be treated equally, if there should be any preferential treatment, it should be given to those who most closely resemble them? No?

So we brought it up after we checked out. We sat uncomfortably in the lobby waiting for them to refund us for the discriminatory breakfast we had to suffer through. We did not feel that we should pay for that kind of treatment or service. We talked to the manager and the F+B Manager again.

He was sorry, but honestly, I don't think he knew what he was sorry for. He did not feel that he had treated us any differently. Then I do what I normally do when I talk to managers of hotels on pointers to improve, I say: "I could write about this behind your back on TripAdvisor, but instead, I choose to tell you to your face, so that you can improve." Then with a smile, I hand them my business card, and tell them I am available for training should they see that their staff need to start working WITH their customers rather than discriminating AT them. I never hear from them, but when you feel as if someone has put you down, or you have been treated unequally, call them out and speak WITH them about how you felt. That is how change is created.

With Service

The number 1 hotel on TripAdvisor** in Seoul is none other than a JW Marriott boutique hotel in Dondgaemun that was built 2 years ago. Upon first glance, one would overlook this hotel. It is not ostentatious, nor grandiose on the outside, but it is thus so on the inside, where it counts. Walking past the various shopping areas, you would also walk past this hotel if you didn't know about it. What a pity that would be! From the bell boys to the reception desk staff, everyone is friendly and nobody judges you based on your appearance (in my case, young-looking, no make-up, no brand-named clothes or accessories, etc.). The staff at the executive lounge actually had a meeting about when Edgar would arrive (!).

They also went out of their way to make sure we got to dress up in traditional Korean clothing *hanbok,* had staff send up the *hanbok* to our hotel room, and take pictures for us and WITH us.

Now *that* is WITH service--the first level of it. We'll get to the second and harder level next.

** At the time of writing it was #1. It has since moved to #7, but will always be #1 to us!

Hanbok couple | JW Marriott Dongdaemun Square, Seoul, South Korea | Fall 2016

It dawned on me, almost a year after I wrote this section on WITH service that I was coming AT it from a not very WITH perspective. Namely, I was looking AT it from the perspective of the customer. Makes sense, as I usually am the customer. Something clicked though on a recent trip to Bali in December 2017: I was staying at a women's retreat and the staff were over the top with their customer service. Each staff member remembered each one of our names, our favorite drinks, would greet us every time they saw us, they would say "you're welcome" and make eye contact, and the list goes on.

Then one lazy afternoon, I decided to hang back and stay at the retreat while the other women were off surfing or yoga-ing. I wanted to give back to the staff, because they had treated me so well throughout my stay, so I shared the steamed palm sugar dumplings coated with grated coconut (*Kue Lupis* in Indonesian) I had made in my cooking class. The staff was delighted. I heard them say, "Suksma!" ("Thank you" in Balinese, the first Balinese word I learned WITH them!). It was so gratifying and satisfying. Then I heard them say, "Kyla, you are our favorite guest! We will miss you."

It got me thinking. If I expected a certain level of customer service, in a WITH fashion, I had to also display a certain level of guest service in return: Not being entitled, asking rather than demanding, saying "Suksma" every time I received something while making eye contact, asking how *they* were doing, remembering *their* names. Now that is truly <u>WITH</u> service—the second level and optimal level for both guest and staff.

Noncomplementary Behavior: The Ultimate With Behavior

I think fear begets fear. Fear creates more AT feelings such as violence, hatred, bullying and so on. However, kindness begets other WITH feelings such as positivity, inclusivity, acceptance, and so on. Whenever students around me are dealing with negative people around them, I always tell them the story of noncomplementary behavior. As humans we often mirror other human behavior. So if someone is angry around us, then we become angry. If someone is sad, then we become sad. Rarely do we respond to someone's behavior WITH noncomplementary behavior. If someone is aggressive, we could show that person kindness. One summer night in Washington D.C., a gunman walked into a dinner party demanding cash, and was instead shown kindness. The dinner partygoers invited him to join them while they drank wine and ate cheese. So he did. He left not harming a single person at the dinner party and even got a group hug out of it, even though he had wanted their cash not a single person at the dinner party had cash on them[1] (!).

In 2007, something called the Aarhus Model (based on the name of the town where it originated) was introduced to address the issue of reintegration of potential ISIS fighters in Denmark. With the exception of Belgium, Denmark produced the highest number of citizens per capita joining ISIS in the EU. The mayor of Aarhus, Jacob Bundsgaard responded by saying that it was because the Danish community had failed in making them feel welcome. So they came up with a program in which they used noncomplementary behavior. Rather than ostracizing those who returned from Syria more radicalized, they instead embraced them: the police would ask them out for coffee, they would then pick out a trained mentor and follow up if there was anything suspicious. They are happy to report that as of 2015, only 1 Danish citizen made it to Syria. In 2013, the number was 30[2]. How cool is that?

Masterchef Junior

I started watching *MasterCheff*[††] a few years ago. I found Gordon Ramsay to be somewhat abrasive, and the adult contenders extremely unkind to each

---

†† An American cooking competition TV show starring Gordon Ramsay as one of its three judges--it began in 2010 and is now in its 8th season.

other (AT behavior), so I started watching *MasterChef Junior* (kids 8-13 years old) instead. I have been absolutely fascinated about what we can all learn from them in terms of having good WITH behavior:

1. Be encouraging
   Before and after each kid goes up and showcases what they made for that particular competition, the kids will yell stuff like, "Go ______!" "Good job, ______!" Even when the judges decide on the bottom three junior home cooks, the bottom three are usually surrounded by their friends who hug them and say, "Don't worry. You did a great job!"

2. Make it a good sendoff
   When a kid has to leave the show because he/she was at the bottom that week, the other kids will create a group hug around that kid and tell him/her that he/she will be missed and many of them will be crying.

3. Celebrate small/big victories
   When the kids did something well, or they were excited about something, it was very noticeable and palpable. They would jump up and down: literally and figuratively jumping for joy!

4. Don't talk shit
   When interviewed separately about other talented kids or kids that were doing really well on the show, they wouldn't say anything negative, they would just say how impressed they were.

5. Be a good loser
   Even if some of the kids lost a particular competition, or they didn't do well, they would cry and not put others down in the process. Meanwhile, other kids would yell in support.

6. Get excited
   Every show, the kids would run into the *MasterChef* kitchen as excited as ever. They had the same amount of enthusiasm before every task, not just at the beginning of the show.

SELF WORK:
List some of your own AT behavior below. Think about how you can change it into WITH behavior. For example, sometimes I am quick to judge people with dark skin. I can smile at them instead to make them feel welcome. Incidentally, smiling makes you feel good too.*

AT BEHAVIOR → WITH BEHAVIOR

Doodles/Takeaways/Reflection Points

WITH RESPECT FOR WOMEN: THE MOST IMPORTANT PART OF ANY COMMUNITY

CHAPTER 8

(AT) WOMEN

"It should *always* be the woman's decision to get married, have a baby, and any other major decision that affects their bodies." ~my husband

In many ways, this is the most important chapter of this book. Of life. Of everything and anything. Life starts with women. Women no longer need men to create life. But we do need men and women to work together, WITH each other to get women to where they need to be. So if you are multi-tasking, not fully paying attention, texting, picking your nose, eating/drinking, STOP what you are doing and pay full attention.

I grew up in a household that from the outside may have seemed traditional: my father worked and my mother stayed at home and took care of me and my older sister. Then shortly after I started elementary school, everything changed. Namely, my mom "resigned" from the kitchen. Yes, she literally left a note for my dad that said just that on the fridge. Armed with her high school diploma, she went to work for a real estate company owned by her then friend Beverly. My *Popo* came from Singapore to look after us, and you will be happy to hear, I stopped throwing my lunches away, because my *Popo* would make lasagna and other yummy hot lunches in a hot flask (no more soggy ham and cheese sandwiches on untoasted white bread); my mom was out of the house and would later go on to start her own successful real estate company.

So you see, I grew up thinking that I could do anything that boys could do. Sure, I had body image issues (doesn't everyone?!)—if you look through my journal entries from middle school up until high school, almost every other entry has to do with how fat I felt or how I was insecure (we will get to that later), but I knew what gender equality was all about so much so that I never even really talked about it out loud until grad school.

Actually, it was shortly before grad school. After teaching English in rural Japan for 2 years (my first job out of undergrad), in the classic quarter-life-crisis fashion, I had no idea what I wanted to do with my life, so I decided like any rational-minded 20-something that the next logical thing to do would be to study Japanese in Yokohama for 8 hours a day. *I mean, I loved languages, I loved learning languages, what better way to while my days away then to learn one?* And it was just that. I got to spend my days with 5-6 other students around a table learning about the ins and outs of the subtlety of the Japanese language, conjugating verbs mathematically, and learning how to deflect a compliment like a pro. It was a dream. Oh and at nights, my fellow language lovers and I would spend hours perfecting our Japanese at karaoke places singing our hearts out to Britney Spears (her old stuff like "Baby One More Time") and The Backstreet Boys, as well as other classic hits from the 90s. It was wonderful to enjoy the perks of city life in Yokohama after having lived in a small town for two years previously.

For our final project, after 10 months of intensive study, we had to give a final presentation in Japanese for 10 minutes. *Scary.* In order to do that presentation, we had to have researched something. I remember thinking: *Shit, what am I going to research about? I don't even know what I want to do with my life? How am I going to find a topic for a presentation?*

Little did I know, that was going to lay the foundation for my eventual research for grad school. Don't you love when this happens: Past you sets yourself up for future you. I began researching domestic violence shelters, because my older sister had volunteered at one and I thought it sounded interesting. I soon found a shelter, (the only one that helped foreign women) and started volunteering. To this day, it remains one of the most important things I have ever done, and am proud to say I have done.

At Women

The most extreme form of behavior AT women, to me, is violence or abuse of some kind. At the domestic violence shelter where I volunteered in Japan, I heard stories of foreign women who had been trafficked into Japan, forced into some kind of sex work to pay off an insane debt (to the trafficker who "helped" them get into Japan), all to never really pay it off ever. With no language skills, no passport, and no rights, the women were left to fend for themselves. Whenever anyone asked me if working WITH these women was depressing, or there was that uncomfortable silence when I told them what my presentation topic was, I would remark quite frankly, "Actually, they empower me. Their strength empowers me and gives me perspective on my own life."

I think at one point or another, we have all been victims of some form of abuse. While working on my presentation, I learned that abuse is not only physical; it can be invisible, in the form of financial, emotional, mental, verbal abuse. One of the toughest things I have ever had to do (while volunteering at the shelter) was escort a woman back to her abuser. We were on the subway. I looked at her, her bags. I remember the sinking feeling in the pit of my stomach, feeling as if I had failed, as if the shelter had failed her, society had failed her, and all around us, Japanese commuters had no idea. They were safe in their ignorance.

People often assume, why don't victims of abuse just leave? Why would they stay and suffer? Why would they go back? Why wouldn't you do something about it? I too was one of those people asking those questions, and it wasn't until I experienced verbal abuse first-hand at work that I realized how judgey I had been before. Even those around me, closest to me, those I respected the most told me that I should just "stand up for myself" or "stick it out and not quit, because it will look bad on your resume."

But it wasn't until I found out that my own mother-in-law was a survivor of abuse--not once but twice (first from Edgar's biological father and then his stepfather) --and I asked the same questions of Edgar's mom that had been used against me, that I realized I was victim-blaming. I am grateful to Edgar for pointing that out to me.

Most recently, through my Finnish collaborator Ilkka I met an overcomer of abuse named Emilia. After she overcame a 6-year physically and emotionally abusive relationship where she was almost killed, she looked around and realized that everywhere she turned in society, she was the one to be blamed. People called her a "victim," which led her to believe that her very own story of abuse was not her own. She set out to change the way we look at those who can come out of abusive relationships/situations calling these amazing individuals "overcomers" rather than "victims." She ran across the span of New Zealand-1500 miles in—the equivalent of 50 marathons to raise awareness around this issue (!). Check out her inspiring video + story here:

I got to meet her in person in February 2017 in Palo Alto, California. Emilia had not only survived, but also *overcome* her very own physically and emotionally abusive marriage, but she had come out of it stronger, more determined, and with an entire movement to prove it. She was about to take off for her very first Iron Man in New Zealand, but she created the time and space to speak WITH me about issues surrounding IPV (Interpersonal Violence), her work, and how she believes she can create change one run at a time. Something she said still plays in my head, "This movement is not about me. It is greater than me. My body is just the vessel." *What a badass.*

My SHEro Emilia + me at Peet's Coffee | Palo Alto, California | February 2017

Her-Ass-Ment

Here is a story I wrote about my boss at China Travel Service (CTS) in Beijing who sexually harassed me, but I made sure I had the last word.

(December 2005)

#MeToo: Sexual Her-ass-ment

Charlize Theron once again, had another stellar performance in North Country as a female worker in a mine in Minnesota who led the very first sexual harassment class lawsuit in the United States. Like many sexual harassment lawsuits today, it really just boils down to one person's word against another person's. I went to see it with a girlfriend from grad school. We were both left feeling very helpless and at the same time in awe of Charlize Theron's character's courage. My girlfriend said this: "I feel like there is something that I should or could be doing to prevent this kind of thing." I replied, "There are lots of ways you can go about preventing this thing without having to go to Law School. You can sit on a board, you can volunteer, there are other ways to help." Although I wanted to convince her and I perhaps sounded convincing, I still wasn't convinced.

The movie reminded me of something that happened to me while studying abroad in Beijing-a story I rarely shared with anyone. During my internship at CTS, I got to learn a lot about the way people conducted business back in the 1990s, but also a lot about what happened outside office walls.

Guanxi is one of the most important words to know in Chinese. It means "connection," as in how you know someone. Everything is about who you know in China, rather than who you are. Through our own guanxi, my friend Dessi helped me land an internship at China Travel Service's head office, the largest government-owned travel agency in China at the time. My boss' name was Sun Ni Jia. He was 44, single, had a terrible temper, and drove one of the few BMWs in Beijing at the time. He was also very kind to me and treated me like a daughter, or so I thought. Later, I found out that he had become the laoban, ("boss" in Chinese) through his own guanxi.

During my time at CTS (China Travel Service), I saw a lot: pre-WTO days, Chinese people were not allowed to leave China. However, if they could provide the following that ensured their return, they were allowed to leave:

Proof of job

Proof of spouse and/or other family members

Proof of bank account with enough money in it

Proof of residency

One day, a man came into the office with a suitcase full of money. It was just like the movies-the suitcase was filled to the brim with wads and wads of Ren Min Bi. It looked like he was bribing someone. Upon asking a colleague, she said that he had to prove he had enough money in his bank account. If he did not come back, all of that money would go to CTS. Whoa.

On the weekends to beat the sweltering humidity, I would seek solace in a swimming pool. I was thrilled to find a pool in the same building as CTS. One Saturday afternoon after a nice swim, I ran into my laoban in the lobby. He wanted to take me to see the new office. I naively agreed. One minute we are looking at the new windows, the next minute he is hugging me and telling me to stay in Beijing longer. Within the blink of an eye, he lifted up my shirt and tried to feel my breasts. My heart leapt and must have skipped several beats. I wanted to scream and run, but I felt paralyzed. I knew I had to do something. I pulled his hand and told him that we should go back up to our old office and head to lunch. Five minutes later my laoban was chatting away in the elevator with my other colleagues as if nothing had ever happened. Yikes.

I went home and told Dessi. I wanted to cry, but I didn't even know what to cry about. Dessi comforted me and said, "Imagine you are like a precious pearl, running from one person's hand to another. If the hand closes around the pearl, the pearl will stop running. But you won't let it. You will keep running." If it weren't for Dessi, I think I would have been more devastated. It took me months before I could even come to terms with it myself, before I could tell friends, and even talk about what had happened.

On the night before I left, my laoban invited me out for a farewell dinner. I wondered whether or not I should accept the invitation. If I did, he might molest me again, if I didn't, I would offend him. I decided to accept and I gave Dessi his cell phone number in case I didn't make it home. Dinner went pretty smoothly without any molestation. On our drive home, I gathered up as much courage as I could and in my broken Chinese I confronted my laoban.

"Don't you find me attractive?" he asked coyly.

"You are old enough to be my father! I am 21 and you are 44. You should learn to control your temper, you should find a girlfriend your own age, and you should stop chasing girls half your age!!"

"OK, I guess you are right."

"Of course I am right. Thank you for dinner."

That night I felt lucky. I got away with giving him a lecture (or piece of my mind) and getting a kiss on the cheek in return. It could have been far worse. That incident made me think about blind trust. Every time I meet someone, I always give him/her the benefit of the doubt. This time, I felt completely and utterly vulnerable, even though I had the last word. Why is it that more frequently than not, women are the victims? Why are women more vulnerable?

It brought me back to my gender theory class I took at MIT while at Harvard (we were able to cross-register). A class I struggled with and my final B- grade only reemphasized my struggle. In class, we talked about gender binaries: not all men are masculine, and not all women are feminine. Globalization tends to focus on men and forgets the millions of third world women in factories exploited by globalization. Ok, so what are we left with? A feminization of poverty, jobs in the informal sector, and exploitation of women. Women are increasingly marginalized around the world.

Questions still plagued me: Why is it ok for men to exploit women? Why doesn't gender studies focus on getting more men involved instead of only women? Even though men are generally physically stronger than women, does that give them the right to physically assault women? Why aren't men as vulnerable? Is all this theory really helping women after all? And is it some cruel joke that harassment sounds like her-ass-ment?

SELF WORK:
#MeToo. I shared this story on Facebook after this hashtag went viral and I was both shocked and inspired WITH all of my other female friends who had also posted #MeToo. Share your own #MeToo story here. What did you learn about yourself?

Here is another essay I wrote on feeling unsafe in Cambridge, Massachusetts in the U.S.

0.31 mile (0.5km)

(July 19, 2014)

0.31 of a mile: the distance between Edgar's apartment and the nearest available Zipcar*. 0.31 of a mile: the distance I needed to walk alone, at night, alone. 0.31 of a mile: in the time that it took me to walk this distance- about 10 minutes-I pondered the #YesAllWomen Elliot Rodger killing spree in Isla Vista, California in May of this year, just 2 short months ago, and how it had sparked a fear in me.

Ann Hornaday of the Washington Post had written a thoughtful response to all of the backlash she had been getting after criticizing the latest Judd Apatow movie Neighbors as yet another means to justify and condone the objectification of women. The same objectification Elliot Rodgers used to condone his killings because women had "rejected" him in the past[1].

What worried me was not the

* Zipcar is the world's largest car rental/car-sharing company. It was actually founded in 2000 in Cambridge, Massachusetts where this particular story takes place.

Hornaday article. I rather liked it, actually. I liked the video, and how she had stood up for herself and all women for that matter, for what she had written, how she had taken the time to explain her case. What worried me was the response that followed by a man: Phil Plait of Slate.com. It was not that it was misogynistic nor was it poorly written. It was on the contrary, on point. Plait basically breaks the Elliot Rodger killings down to a simple hashtag: #YesAllWomen[2]. How many men do you know who fear they will get raped, sexually harassed, and have other atrocious things done to them without their consent? I am sure not a whole lot, if any.

It was then that my heart began pounding, walking along the neighborhood streets of Cambridge, back to Edgar's apartment, not too far from where the Boston Marathon bomber brothers had fled from police after visiting a 7-11 in the area. Cambridge was ironically one of the safest cities in the U.S. Yet there I was scurrying along, looking over my shoulder, and nervously walking faster whenever I sensed someone was walking behind me. I did not want to become yet another statistic, but more than that, I didn't feel safe.

I had gone out on a whim to buy stuff to make chorizo sausage from scratch. I had wanted to surprise Edgar and his sister. She had once been followed home, and some guy tried to wrestle with her to get into the door. That story lingered in my head like a repeat song that wouldn't stop. Was I overreacting? Surely, I wasn't this paranoid when I was in my 20s.

1.5 hours earlier, I had rented a X1 BMW. They retail at about $30K. Zipcar is that guilty pleasure: you can get it for $15/hour. I could hear Edgar's rational and logical voice in my head: "Why do you need to drive a BMW for an hour when you can just rent a hybrid for $8?" I didn't have a logical explanation for him, other than the fact that I have always wanted to drive a BMW. I know.

After buying all of the ingredients that go into making chorizo, including Sherry at Trader Joe's (one of my favorite grocery stores in Cambridge), I decided on a whim to extend the car for an extra 30 minutes and treat myself to some JP Licks (my all-time favorite ice-cream place) in Harvard Square. I told myself: Only if I find a parking spot close by. If not, that would be a sign that I didn't need it. I found a spot.

I walked taking in the summer night breeze. Looking at the young people around, walking leisurely, not worried about being attacked or raped. Well, seemingly. People were in groups. Were you safer in groups? There have certainly been several gang rapes recently, most notoriously in India, where a young female medical student who was gang raped was actually escorted by a male friend/boyfriend.

My thoughts are interrupted. I see an older South Asian Indian gentleman persuading a young Caucasian female beggar to stay at a homeless shelter. On my way over to JP Licks, I eavesdrop and hear her say, "I don't do shelters." She had a nice necklace and backpack: she looked as if she had had a shower within the past few days. Not that you can't have those things if you are homeless, but there is a new face of homeless people since the global recession of 2008.

I looked back at her, but soon forgot her as my eyes perused the dizzying amounts of flavors on the JP Licks chalkboard. I don't know why I always look to see, but my go to Coffee Cookies 'N' Cream (formerly Coffee Oreo) is always up there. I ordered my cup of ice cream, thinking about Edgar, as it was our first ice-cream date place. He usually got a large coffee, since he doesn't have a sweet tooth. On a more recent trip with Ping†*, we were sitting outside, and an African-American man came out of nowhere, stumbling, mumbling, and apologizing for scaring me. I was indeed scared.*

That woman was still there begging. I walked passed her thinking that I could be in her shoes, and she could be in mine. She could be the one walking carefree back to her X1 BMW Zipcar rental. She could be the one eating her Coffee Oreo ice cream. I stopped in my tracks, turned around, went back to the ATM machine and withdrew $40. I never carried cash. I

---

† Ping had flown out from Taipei to visit with us for 5 days, because she had wanted to meet Edgar before we got married. Incidentally, she is the only friend I have who has visited me in every single apartment I have lived in since I graduated from UCSD (!). She is due for a visit at our current abode in Songdo!

never gave money out to people on the street: homeless, environmentalists, NGO workers, and so on. But for some reason, I couldn't not give her money.

I was struck at the huge inequality of the entire situation. There we were, across the street from the most prestigious university in the world. A university I graduated from 8 years ago--A university with a whopping $30 Billion endowment and the largest non-profit on the planet. Harvard alums go on to head Fortune 500 companies, change the world, heck, Zuckerberg and Gates didn't even graduate.

Research suggests money makes us meaner. In a rigged Monopoly game, Paul Piff shows players who were rigged to win, became more aggressive, ruder to the other player (who was losing), more likely to showcase how awesome they were doing, and the list goes on[3]. It makes you want to gag, except I think this is true of my own behavior. As I mentioned, I never gave out money before. It had been a long time since I volunteered. As an educator, I always knew that the trade off for changing and shaping the lives of bright young minds would always be money.

Walking back to the apartment, I got home, put all of my groceries down and heaved a huge sigh of relief. I could have been her.

When I bent over, leaned in, and shoved the two $20 bills into her hand, she didn't even realize how much I had given her. She was too absorbed in what seemed to be her new situation. She didn't have that forlorn, I am used to this F&*%$-ing situation face, and seemed to be sobbing. Her eyeliner had created the dreaded badger eye look.

As I walked off, proud of what I had done, worried about what she might do with the money, and in a bit of a rush to make the deadline to return my BMW Zipcar rental, so I wouldn't be charged extra...she realized what I had given her, and called out to me meekly, "Thank you...thank you...I love your dress." It was a compliment that I felt guilty responding to, so I didn't.

I cannot think of any fast remedies, save forking your change over to the new face of homeless people or the old face, or even to the middle class that is becoming no longer in the U.S.

However, what was encouraging to see in the same Monopoly study was that it wasn't all bad news. Those who did have, who were exposed to others who were giving, were more likely to give as well. Research shows that we are happier when we give, we are happier when we help others, it is a natural thing for us to do, and people are doing just that, even those Harvard drop outs Gates and Zuck have done just that: forked over significant change to create change. I too hope to follow in their footsteps in the not-too-distant future.

And perhaps, just perhaps, those two $20 bills have helped that woman in Harvard Square make her own 0.31 mile journey safely to her next destination, wherever that may be, so she -unlike me- doesn't have to look over her shoulder.

From Beijing to Cambridge, that sinking feeling that something could happen to you isn't a good one. I was fortunate that nothing more happened with my laoban that fateful afternoon in Beijing, and again while walking that 0.31 mile to the nearest Zipcar in Cambridge.

Globally, 1 in 3 women have experienced some sort of violence AT them[4]. This is not about feeling sorry for them or wishing that this wasn't the case. This is an issue of AT.

During my time volunteering with overcomers of abuse, I learned the beauty of true strength and felt completely empowered by their stories of survival. Cooking meals together in the kitchen I still remember feeling so completely in awe of how they walked away from these utterly seemingly impossibly violent situations and were better for it. I admired and respected their strength. Not to mention the food was absolutely delicious.

Everywhere else I looked though, I realized how women are treated as objects: from magazine ads to T.V. to movies. Nobody talks about this treatment of women and how it deeply affects all of us. A student of mine survived and overcame an abusive relationship. Her boyfriend tried to force her to have sex with him in the library. She tried to go to the Gender Equality Center on campus, but they blamed her. She tried to go to the police, they told her to "keep the peace and harmony" on campus and to "not cause trouble." It was devastating. Fortunately, she was able to turn her experience into a presentation to educate the rest of the students in my then World Issues class about sexual assault on campus.

Whether abuse is happening behind closed doors or in broad daylight, we have to keep in mind, the majority of those that it happens AT are women and girls. Rather than blaming women and girls for dressing a certain way, not keeping the peace, speaking out, we should work WITH them to ensure that these kinds of incidences never happen in the first place.

SELF WORK:
What are some creative solutions you can think of to make your own neighborhood and/or places you frequent safer?

Doodles/Takeaways/Self-Reflection Points

WITH RESPECT FOR WOMEN: THE MOST IMPORTANT PART OF ANY COMMUNITY

CHAPTER 9

CREATING CHANGE WITH YOUNG MEN + WOMEN

"Two heads are better than one." ~Korean Proverb

The Beginnings Of A Global Gender Leadership Training Seminar (G^2LTS For Short)

In the fall of 2015, I ran into Crystal on campus. Crystal was a rare breed amongst female students at Yonsei: she was a leader. She would lead whichever group she was in throughout the semester during our Career Development course in the spring of 2015, and at the time she was a sophomore. When we met for coffee for the first time at Coffee Bean in Sinchon, she went on to tell me how she missed our class. She missed specifically how there was no hierarchy between not just the students and me but between the students themselves. Everyone was free to interact WITH each other however they pleased without being restricted by formal language. She went on to say how it was challenging to find classes like mine elsewhere on campus. *Wow, that's great*, I remember thinking.

I went home feeling really re-inspired and re-energized from my coffee date with Crystal. My head was spinning in a good way: Perhaps I was doing something right? Perhaps there was something to my WITH teaching style? Perhaps it was hitting all of the right spots? But what could I do to help students like Crystal? Surely there were more students out there who were seeking similar experiences in a course? How could I give female students more leadership experiences and empower them?

Then I thought back to my cupboard back in the studio I lived in on Yonsei campus. After my very first World Issues class in 2011, where I had met Minjeong (my former student who wrote the Foreword) and some other very stellar female students, I had been inspired to create a leadership club. I had posted all of my ideas on post-it notes for this club, along with the original list of student members on my cupboard. Things never really got off the ground save for a leadership seminar we had on campus, where we invited my friend Katherine to speak on finding happiness. She spoke about her solo back-packing trip around the world for 10 months and how she found happiness within rather than externally, even though she had had all of these jobs with high-profile companies like Samsung.

It struck me. Perhaps I could have a group where I could empower young women and men. I could be sort of like a mentor/older sister (sans hierarchy). They could come to the meetings and freely talk about what they wanted to talk about: The stuff that they couldn't talk to their relatives/parents/even friends about. It would be a free space to think out loud and not be judged. I did not want to lead this, because that would be missing the whole point of empowerment. I wanted to lead from behind and just help, should the girls need my help, but I wanted them to steer it. I knew the perfect person to lead this: Crystal.

I shared my idea over dinner at the Cancer Center at Severance Hospital. One of my favorite places to go, because the food was healthy, Korean, the staff knew me there, and it was relatively close to the South Gate of campus where the shuttle bus departed for Songdo campus (so I could get home to my apartment in Songdo quicker). She said she was interested and that she would talk it over with her mom and some other friends to get some more ideas. Her father had passed away a few years prior with a heart attack, but her father had treated her and her brother equally. They were always given the same opportunities growing up. *No wonder she's a natural born leader.*

During one particular meeting, we got on the subject of room salons, and how most important business decisions happen in these room salons, even though female employees aren't really invited nor feel comfortable going. Crystal told us how she had actually gone to a room salon because her father had taken her to one when she was 11 years old. At first we were all stunned. How could a father take an innocent child to one of these establishments? She quickly calmed our judgments and explained that he wanted his business partner to see that if an 11-year old girl did not feel comfortable at a place like that, they should not be having a meeting there at all. His business partner soon got the hint, and never invited him to have a meeting there again[1]. *Genius.*

After a few one-on-one meetings with Crystal, she invited one of her good friends Chaeryoung. They were in the same major, same year, but

Chaeryoung had taken the semester off; so she was free, but studying history to prepare for part of the exam to be a government official. She was the opposite of Crystal. While Crystal was bubbly and talkative, Chaeryoung was quiet and introspective. It was a perfect balance. The two had both spent the majority of their lives abroad, so they also had a very open-minded perspective. Crystal had lived in the Philippines and Chaeryoung had lived in Uzbekistan. Then I invited a former student of mind, Kyuhee to join us. She had just gotten into medical school at Kyunghee University. She was interested in making sure we include women's health issues in our discussions, and was always the first person to comment in all of our Facebook group discussions.

During winter vacation, I invited them over to my apartment in Songdo. I must admit I was a bit nervous. *What would we talk about? What would we do? Would they be nervous?* Since I have been super into baking (now that I have an oven in this apartment in Songdo), I decided to give them a team-building task of making healthy chocolate chip cookies (with coconut oil instead of butter and just 1 tablespoon of brown sugar) together. They immediately washed their hands and got excited about their hands-on task. In no time, we were talking over the baked cookies and tea. *Ok, I get how this could be misconstrued as an activity to reinforce gender stereotypes, but we all know plenty of world-renowned bakers and chefs for that matter who are male.*

We ended up talking about possible topics for us to discuss during the spring semester (over our freshly baked delights and tea), if we were to actually create a seminar that met weekly for about 1-2 hours.

A few weeks later, at a Starbucks in Itaewon, I had come from my OBGYN and wanted to tell Crystal and Chaeryoung everything about what had happened during my visit. I was a little bit hesitant, because I had never talked about sex WITH them and I knew that students tended to be shy when talking about this topic. The closest I had come was having students watch a TED Talk about HIV/AIDS in the DRC and then have them design condom packets[2].

"So, I just came from my OBGYN, and I thought that it was really timely, since we haven't really talked about health issues. Would it be ok if I shared what has been happening to me?" Crystal and Chaeryoung nodded looking curious. Kyuhee had since dropped out of the group, letting us know that she would support us from a distance, because she was worried she wouldn't be able to fully commit given her new status as a medical student.

"Well, a few weeks ago, I went in for my annual pap smear and I had an abnormal pap. Do you guys know what pap smears are?" We went on a tangent for a bit to clarify what pap smears were and whether or not it was common for students to get them.

"So I had a biopsy and I got the results today, and it was not cervical cancer (thank goodness!), but a very low-risk, mild form of HPV." We went on to discuss what HPV was and how I had just gotten the first in a series of three vaccinations because the vaccinations would further prevent the high-risk HPV series.

The meeting went well. I felt so exhilarated that beyond any class I have taught and the great evaluations I have been awarded with, beyond the three teaching awards I had received while at Yonsei, this reward was priceless. I was able to get these girls to talk about sex-related topics, I shared something that was quite private, as did they, and we mutually listened, respected each other, and felt empowered WITH each other by doing so.

Sex Ed

I have been told from students here that there is a lot of room for improvement in terms of sex education in Korea. In informal discussions WITH students, many admit having limited knowledge of contraception, using contraception, abortion, and other issues surrounding sex. It is no wonder. A brief look into the sex ed curriculum reveals that beginning in elementary school up until high school, students learn about issues surrounding sex, but not really about the act itself. For example, part of the material they use states, one way to avoid sexual violence is to "Make sure you are not alone with your boyfriend." To further fan the flames of controversy, the Ministry of Education decided to opt out of any discussion surrounding those who associate themselves as Lesbian, Gay, Bisexual, Transgendered, Queer and Asexual in their 2017 sex ed curriculum[3]. If students were given accurate information early on, they could then make informed decisions, be open to different kinds of people with different kinds of sexual orientation.

Recently, in an NPR article, it came out that the sex ed guidelines which basically haven't changed since 2015, even though they have been blasted and criticized considerably for victim-blaming and sexism, warned women to pay for dates. If not, they warned, this could be a cause for date rape. What?! When asked to comment, one of the officers from the Ministry of Education responded that they had no idea that the material could be construed as sexist, and that they should carefully check each detail and be more thorough. This is the starting point, and the fact that the people who wrote it have no idea that it is steeped in sexism, in and of itself is extremely problematic.

Given all of this, it is no surprise that the Kangnam Murder case was also steeped in the same kind of sexism. In May 2016, a woman was murdered in a public bathroom in Kangnam. At first, it seemed like just another murder. Later it came out that the murderer was mentally unstable, and fatally stabbed and killed the woman in his own words "because women have always ignored me."

What disturbed me was not just the murder itself, but how it was perceived in Korean society. People were mistaking misogyny for feminism saying that feminism is bad, rather than misogyny. Once our G^2LTS classes were up and running, we met on Sunday evenings once a week for 3 hours. I was eager to hear what the female and male students alike had to say about this Kangnam incident. I was met with a long silence, avoidance of eye contact, and then Crystal finally said something, "Well, I think people are worried to say something that may be offensive."

So what sex ed should be about is not just educating students on the physical act of sex itself and all of its repercussions, including how to use a condom, but also the differences between misogyny and feminism, as well as the fact that it is OK to speak up and talk about this kind of stuff. This is how you teach sex ed WITH students as opposed to AT.

Jealousy: An At Emotion

At our farewell party at my apartment, I asked my G^2LTS seminar students whether "좋겠다!" (*joketa*) was considered negative, or if someone said that to them, would they feel bad or negative about themselves. For the most part they answered "No." I was still not convinced though, because after talking to several American girlfriends of mine, and telling them about something great that had happened or something great that was going on in my life, they would remark, "I am so happy for you."

"좋겠다!" and the equivalent in Japanese "いいな〜" (*ii na~*) translate into English as, "I envy you!" Whenever I hear either from my students, I definitely don't feel positive. Furthermore, I feel as if the person who says this is comparing him/herself with me. Perhaps the envy-sayers are well intentioned, perhaps they honestly do envy me or others, but doesn't that also mean that in some small way, there is some small bit or large bit of dissatisfaction in their own lives?

Facebook and other social media are breeding grounds for jealousy. People love posting their best travel photos, captioning their best selves, Instagraming another sunset, perfect smiles, yet rarely do we see people who take a sad selfie, a depressed caption, a photo sharing when they first wake up. I certainly feel inadequate when I compare my life with the life of social media pros. I begin comparing myself, asking questions like: *Why haven't I done that? Why haven't I gone there? Why can't I do that?*

Unfortunately, jealousy is our ugliest selves. When I say "ugly" I don't mean superficially, but internally. It is our mind wreaking havoc on us saying, "You are not good enough, you should be more like person X, and I don't like you." I have a lot of students who will often compare their grade with another student's, more likely than not, their friend. I will inevitably get an email, "My friend got this grade, why didn't I get that grade too?" Sometimes it is more subtle. When students receive graded exam papers or tests, they will look at what their friends got and secretly compare it to their own score. I have certainly done this in college, high school, and middle school.

In order to preempt any jealousy or comparing, I usually nip it in the bud on the first day of class. Along with writing a shared list of core values for the class with the students, I ask students a rhetorical question: "Are all students the same?" They all shake their heads vigorously. I then pick up a pencil case from one student and a pencil case from another student. I ask again, "Are these two pencil cases the same?" Again, they all shake their heads. I continue, "So if I were to compare these two pencil cases would it be fair? I mean, one is green, the other one is blue with stripes, one is big, the other one is small…" Then I start seeing that light bulb go off in their heads. The blank stares are gone, and they understand how unfair it is. "The only fair comparison is to compare yourself WITH yourself. Today on the first day of the semester, what is your English comprehension level? What about your first test? And your second? Always try to be better than you were before. That is the only true and fair comparison."

During my 6 years in the College English Department at Yonsei, I have won 3 "Teacher of the year" awards. These awards are supposedly based on student evaluations, our portfolios, and whether or not we upload our syllabi online. The second time I won the award, like an excited child who brings back a trophy to his/her parents, the first person I saw after I found out was my then office-mate and someone I considered to be a good friend. Rather than congratulating me, which I naturally thought she would, she just retorted one word, "Again?!" I find other women often the ones who sling envy AT me and when I least expect it too.

During that semester, I grew to resent her and that word haunted me. I played that word in my head over and over again. At our end of year dinner party, I finally gathered the courage to let her know how it had really hurt my feelings and I began to cry, of course, which is my natural go-to response for anything hard and confrontational. She replied, "I had no idea it affected you that much. I just thought you seemed really arrogant when you said that you had won the award." A year later, thinking things had smoothed over between us, I asked her to write a letter of recommendation for me. I remember showing it to Edgar at a restaurant where we happened to be in Singapore; he shook his head, "This is awful." In *my* head I thought, jealousy is definitely an AT emotion.

SELF WORK:
You see, jealousy is an AT emotion that makes you compare yourself AT someone else. The reason it is one-directional is there is NO ONE on this planet quite like you. So, look deeply WITHin yourself and compare yourself WITH yourself. What is something you did in 2017 that you improved on in 2018? Write it below.

2017:

2018:

Doodles/Takeaways/Reflection Points

WITH RESPECT FOR WOMEN: THE MOST IMPORTANT PART OF ANY COMMUNITY

CHAPTER 10

OTHER ISSUES THROWN AT WOMEN

"Women are the most important part of any community and should be respected as such. Period." ~me

At The Movies: The Bechdel Test

Another extreme form of AT can be found in Hollywood. Images projected on a screen AT you. In mainstream movies, there are a select few main characters, usually male and white. Women are pigeon holed into supporting roles, and are also usually white. I came across this test at a TESOL conference workshop I attended. It was given by two female professors who taught in Japan. The Bechdel Test[1] was quite simple and straightforward:

1. Are there two or more women in the movie and do they have names?
2. Do the women talk to each other?
3. Do the women talk to each other about something other than a man or a boy?

I assigned this to the G^2LTS students and they went and watched *Joy* together. At a cozy hot chocolate café in Sinchon, we discussed how even though Joy passed the three requirements, because Jennifer Lawrence's character talks to her mother and grandmother about topics other than men or boys, she was still defined by her role as a housewife. Amy, one of the students, worried that Joy was going to sleep with one of the male characters to get her mop approved.

If we look at movies that win academy awards, marvel comic movies (my favorite personally), and big Hollywood blockbusters, they almost never pass the Bechdel Test. Beyond not passing the test, what this AT behavior shows us, is we don't see women represented in the movies, women who look like us, dress like us, work like us, and we can't do anything about it because it is one directional.

SELF WORK:
Go watch any movie playing in a theater near you. Do the Bechdel Test. Write down whether or not it passes below and anything else you might have noticed about the female leads.

Body Image

In class during the fall of 2016, in a handout on "50 Reasons to Exercise" (Can you tell, I was trying to motivate my students to exercise?!), two words came up that I had to explain: BODY IMAGE. In my usual go-to move, I borrowed the student's pencil, and sketched a mirror, and a stick figure in front of it: "Imagine, this is you, and you are looking in the mirror. Someone with a positive body image would say back to the mirror, 'I am so beautiful.' On the other hand, someone with a negative body image would say back to the mirror, 'I don't like the way I look' or avoid the mirror entirely."

While explaining this concept to my student, I couldn't help but feel I was not doing it any justice. I knew it was more complex than that. I wanted to share that I too, had up until quite recently (in my late 30s) come to terms WITH my own body, after years of not really liking my own image staring back at me in the mirror. Ok, to be fair though, when I was chub (my sister's word, my mom's word is "pleasantly plump," and my dad just stays out of it altogether—smart man), I actually didn't have a complex about it. It wasn't until I started losing weight, I felt trapped in my chubby body, no matter how much weight I lost, or no matter how many people told me I lost weight and looked good.

One summer, in my early 20s, my sister, mom and I were driving around the South Bay. I think we had just finished eating lunch at one of the only Cantonese restaurants in the South Bay that my mom trusts to go and eat at. We would usually go eat dim sum/fried noodles and vegetables for lunch, go to 99 Ranch (Asian Supermarket) next door, and then squeeze a movie in, if we could. Usually, my sister wouldn't join us, so this was a rare occasion. Anyways, back to the driving around part. My mom was in the front seat (where she sat depended on where the sun was, as she did not like the sun shining on her face; she thought the sun was giving her sunspots), she glanced down, and saw my belly protruding from whatever I was wearing and proceeded to comment. I heard fat, time to lose weight, and then the last thing I recall, as if blacking out in a drunken stupor was my sister coming to my defense: "Mom, why don't you try using words like *beautiful* instead of *fat* to describe Kyla?" I always loved the way my sister said my name, because she rarely used it, since we went by our nicknames* we had created for each other most times. I remember wiping my tears, driving silently, and getting lost around where the Google Campus was.

Even though my sister and I have disagreements, I have to say, I always really felt that she had my back and for that, I am eternally grateful. Thank you, Miu. (But don't worry, we have since worked out all of our issues and are back to being best sissies!)

I don't think I ever really felt self-conscious about being chub until I graduated from UCSD. Most of my high school and university life, I wasn't obsessing over my weight, even though I had probably gained the "Freshman 15" at boarding school. Don't judge me, I was introduced to sweet cereals for the first time, as well as a whole host of other junk food not available to me in Hong Kong. That combined with not-so-great-cafeteria-food all accumulated in ordering Domino's Pizza during double block lunches with my pizza posse, eating entire boxes of Triscuits† and wheat thins in one sitting, and a whole host of binge eating I will not go into detail here.

What I realize now is that often to feel better, we stress eat/binge eat our feelings away in an AT way. We eat fast food, snacks, sweets, that are bad for us and attack our bodies in an AT way. Rather than treating my body in an AT way, I've recently come to realize that I can actually be more WITH my body: try to eat healthily, stay away from processed foods, processed sugars, and anything else that would attack my body in an AT fashion and therefore make me feel yucky and gross.

---

* My sister's was Miu (short for Miu Miu. Nothing to do with the fancy brand name store, but everything to do with the first syllable of her name her Cantonese teacher gave her in secondary school in Hong Kong: Miu Tit Sa). Mine was Momo. I have no idea why. Ask my sister.

† Triscuits are square whole-wheat wafer crackers. You can eat them plain or with a dip, cheese, any anything else your heart desires. I preferred them plain.

When You Feel Chub: Do Stuff WITH Your Body (!)

- Do not compare yourself to others (everyone has his/her own unique and beautiful figure)
- Do not read any magazines, watch T.V., go to the movies (only a small percentage of people actually look like models/actors/actresses)
- Do exercise (not to lose weight, but to give you confidence, keep you mentally strong)
- Do say something nice WITH yourself in your head (rather than putting yourself down) while looking at yourself in the mirror
- Do get dressed up and take yourself out (dressing up helps with self-confidence)
- Do nourish your body WITH good fuel like whole grains, vegetables, fruit, and cut down on your processed sugar intake

SELF WORK:
1. Write down ONE thing (or more than one) that you LOVE about your body + why.

2. Complete the sentence: I am beautiful because ____________________.

How To Deal With The Toxic Co-Worker/Boss

According to the Harvard Business Review, a toxic worker can cost a company USD$12,500 annually, at least (!). Toxic workers are defined as people who are generally bad for a company and although talented often are perpetrators of sexual harassment, workplace violence and fraud[2].

So I work with a lot of men. I use the term "work" broadly. I don't just mean my colleagues at Yonsei (2/3 of my colleagues were white men), but generally other speakers I may encounter when speaking abroad, or collaborators I may have. Most of them are awesome, but occasionally you bump into that *one* toxic person. During a Google Boot camp at Chadwick International School in December 2016, I was the only woman amongst 6 white men (one of whom was the trainer). We were sat around a seminar table, and *all* of the men sat on one side of the table. Not one wanted to sit on the side I was sitting on. 2 of the 6 did not look at me when I spoke, nor acknowledged my existence. Fortunately, the trainer was really cool, and took an interest in my Happiness Workshop (which I made sure to drop during my intro). Here is how I dealt WITH this situation and other past seemingly toxic situations:

STEP 1: KEEP CALM

If you need to buy yourself some time, because the toxic person has just said something mean, degrading, condescending or all of the above, you do that. Ask him/her to clarify a point, ask him/her to repeat his/her question. While this is happening, you should be gathering your ammo (ammunition) in your head.

STEP 2: FEEL YOUR EMOTIONS RATHER THAN REACT TO THEM

Have you ever regretted saying something or doing something after a heated debate/argument? I certainly have. During my mindfulness training, I learned that we often do this: we react to our emotions rather than feel them. So when you are upset or feeling any other kind of negative emotion, notice and become aware of what is going on. For example, for me, my heart starts beating, and my stomach sinks.

STEP 3: KILL THEM WITH KINDNESS

Once you have FELT your emotions, rather than reacted to them, you can be kind in how you respond. Do not fight anger with anger. Do not mirror. Instead use non-complementary behavior[3]. It will work. Go back to Step 1, keep calm and be kind.

STEP 4: USE HUMOR

If you can make a joke at your own expense, this is key. For example, if someone is asking you to do something that you can't do or you don't have the expertise to do (this actually happened to a friend of mine), rather than telling them you can't do it, you can make a joke at your own expense: "Oh, I *wish* I could read contracts...we may have to get a lawyer in here. Things are getting serious!"

STEP 5: GIVE + FORGIVE

If you haven't already read *Give and Take* by Adam Grant, I suggest you pick it up. Basically, givers are more successful than takers. So, even if a co-worker pissed you off or a boss said something you didn't like, pick up some chocolate/candy and leave it on his/her desk for Valentine's Day or another special occasion. You will be surprised by how far a small gift will take you. Oh, and you will feel happier making others happy, as well as be more successful. I brought some chocolate to a male co-worker who had put me down in the past. During our meeting, he was blissfully chomping away on the chocolate as if nothing had happened. Remember: Forgiveness is about you, not the other person. Holding a grudge is not good for your mental sanity.

STEP 6: BE VULNERABLE

I didn't want to admit that I was afraid or intimidated, but somehow admitting that in front of all of the men in my Google Bootcamp set me at ease. I told them, "I am humbled to be here and think I can learn a lot from all of you, and am pushing through my own fears surrounding technology." I think being appropriately vulnerable can give you the right amount of respect if used correctly.

STEP 7: CALL IT LIKE IT IS

Nobody likes to bring up the elephant in the room. What if you are that elephant? In the Google Bootcamp when asked how we deal with participants who don't want to be in our workshops I said, "Well, I am usually younger, Asian, and female among all white male speakers, so I have to work extra hard to gain their respect. But it is totally worth it in the end when they come away having loved my workshops."

STEP 8: SOLUTION TIME

Think of a solution that includes a "we" or an "us" in it. That way, the toxic person will not walk away feeling as if there is no concrete path forward. Continuing on from STEP 4, say something like, "Should *we* call a lawyer? What do you think?" Using this strategy, the toxic person thinks he/she is involved, even though of course, you will have to call the lawyer, but at least, the heat is off of you and there is a solution looming. Done.

STEP 9: FIND A DAD/BROTHER/ALLY

At that same Google Boot Camp, I ended up talking WITH one of the men who had a daughter. I realized that he could empathize WITH me because of this connection. Find a connection WITH those that seem toxic-there is usually a connection out there. They can then start naturally empathizing WITH you more.

Confidence

I think I had a ton of confidence after I graduated from my boarding school. When I got to UCSD, I was brimming with confidence. I could walk into any situation, academic or otherwise, fearless. I would go and visit professors during office hours, also unafraid. When I got out into the real world, things were a little different. I wanted to be confident, but at times, I just felt as if I had gotten slammed in the face time and time again.

At the Global WINConference in Rome, in September 2015, I sat by the pool with a Danish guy who had just come out of my Happiness Workshop.

"You know, one of the things that keeps coming up is confidence," he responded when I asked what he thought of the conference thus far. For every 1 guy there were about 10 women.

"Yeah? How so?" I asked curious to hear more.

"Well, women keep saying that they don't have confidence and they need more. We men don't have confidence either. We just don't talk about it."

"Hmmm…so what do you do about it then?"

"Well, for example, I started teaching a business course at the University of Copenhagen and I had no idea what I was doing, but you just keep practicing. Slowly, you will get better."

"For me, I do things that I know I am somewhat good at, like swimming." I nodded in the direction of the pool and subsequently went in for a 45-minute swim. After I got out he gave me some pointers, which I am sure he would be happy to know I have since incorporated into my swim practice.

So there it was. Men also don't feel confident. It is not just a women's issue. Students often ask me, "How do you gain confidence?" So, I thought I would leave some tips.

1. Do something you are somewhat good at
   For me, this is swimming. Swimming is my zen time: I am able to think about anything and everything that is on my mind, uninterrupted by devices, people, technology. It's just me and the water. Sometimes I am able to think so clearly, I come up with more epiphanies. Edgar has nicknamed these poolpiphanies (!).

2. Observe Your Inner voice
   My friend Jules (whom I also met at Global WINConference in Rome) is a confidence coach. In one of her videos, she talks about watching what we say to ourselves. We can be quite negative and harsh AT ourselves without even noticing it. Once you become aware of it, you can change that inner voice. For example, I will often say, "I am so bad at technology." However, I've since starting saying instead, "I can improve on technology."

3. Do something that scares you a little bit (that has nothing to do with work/school)
   I took a selfie vacay to Honolulu in early 2017, and decided to learn how to surf. It was a bit scary, because I had never done it before and I thought I would definitely fall into the water, or badly injure myself (~~I have absolutely no upper body strength whatsoever~~ → I can build up my body strength), but that feeling of standing on a surf board for the first time and riding my first wave into the shore--it was actually quite simply one of the best feelings I have had in a long time. Pure awesomeness.

4. Power Pose
   Amy Cuddy's TED Talk[4] is great for this. We all know how our body language affects others, but did you know that your body language also affects YOU? In her talk she

describes her research and how after just 2 minutes of power posing, subjects were more confident and performed better on their tests. In her book *Presence*, she goes on to talk about how the smaller your device, the less assertive you are, because you are continually hunched over in a less powerful pose[5].

5. Look at something you're proud of (it can be a small thing) I know this may sound really nerdy, but whenever I go home to my parents' house in California, I will inevitably go into my closet and dig out something I wrote, drew, journal-ed about when I was in boarding school or some time in the past, and I smile, smugly, deeply, knowing I was a badass and still am.

Here's a video testimonial by that same Danish guy in which he talks about how The Happiness Workshop was so different from any other workshop he has been to:

Doodles/Takeaways/Reflection Points

WITH RESPECT FOR WOMEN: THE MOST IMPORTANT PART OF ANY COMMUNITY

CHAPTER 11

TALKING WITH REAL WOMEN

"Have a conversation WITH a real Woman. It may just change your life." ~me

Interviews

Often we are blinded and awed by famous women who are doing amazing things. Here I wanted to show that ordinary women (my friends and former students!) are also pretty darn extraordinary and inspiring. I know some pretty fabulous women. I decided to interview them to get some much-needed inspiration and I wanted to share that WITH you here. Rather than being jealous (AT feeling), why not feel inspired by or realize you are not alone in your struggles?

August 8, 2016

Ozumo, San Francisco, California

Joanne

At one of my favorite Japanese sushi places in the city, there I sat with Joanne. She has had an amazing career run: she worked her way up the corporate ladder at Credit Suisse, after their exit last year from the U.S., she joined UBS where she is currently the Senior Vice President. We had both studied Chinese History at UCSD together some 20 years ago, which seemed a lifetime ago, sitting at the sushi bar that night.

Amidst the chomping down of *edamame* (soy beans), *karaage* (Japanese fried chicken), sushi and sashimi, I looked at her and felt so grateful to her for our years of friendship. She gave me the pivotal advice to take the GRE and apply for grad schools when I was fearful. She gave me a spare set of keys to her apartment in North Beach (the Little Italy of San Francisco), where I would crash on the weekends when I was living in Walnut Creek (a suburb in the east bay area outside of San Francisco).

In that same time frame, she had had an explosive argument with her dad at her parents' home in the south bay, and I had driven to pick her up at her parents' in the south bay, then dropped her off at her apartment in the North Beach ("Little Italy" of San Francisco), and then drove myself back home to the east bay.

With true friends, there are defining moments in your friendship that you will never forget. For me, it was Joanne supporting and encouraging me to go to grad school and generously giving me a space to party/crash on the weekends. For Joanne, it was my dropping everything, and coming to "rescue" her that fateful night she had an argument with her father.

As we reminisced, she nodded, but didn't even take any credit for that particularly pivotal moment in my life she had swayed. That is a true friend. I am incredibly proud of her. Not just for what she has been able to accomplish in her career, but for the person she has remained.

"I mean, I never imagined I would be advising Chinese CEOs," she remarked, surprised at her own success. "I never really even liked my job during the first few years. It is only recently that I have begun to actually enjoy it."

"What made you persevere through the challenging first few years?" I was curious.

"Well, my work partner always supported and encouraged me. He told me that he had seen other people who were not as talented as me quit, but he saw something in me. That encouraged me to stay."

"Why do you think you are different from other people in your industry?" I probed further.

"I think I have conviction. I don't talk down to people, I tell them like it is. A lot of these CEOs have never been told what to do or given solid advice, because others are afraid of them. I feel as if I am an advocate for them. I am an advocate for my clients."

"You work in a particularly male-dominated industry, how do you think you were able to survive?" I was getting into more difficult questions.

"I never really thought about it, but my partners at work always treated me as their equal. Right now, my partner is male, and most people go to him and assume that he is the lead on things. It gives me the time and space to keep my head down at work. I also work with a younger more progressive generation who aren't really sexist. I am lucky. There are a few occasions where I will answer my phone for my partner, and the person on the other end will just assume I am his secretary. I don't take that personally."

That's cool. What made Joanne so successful on her own terms was the fact that she talked WITH her CEO clients not AT them.

Me + Joanne | Ozumo, San Francisco, California | August 2016

February 4, 2017

Café in Seoul

JJ

My friend JJ, an art aficionado in both work and life, asked me out for another museum date. This time we went to see Olafur Eliasson's exhibit at Leeum.

"He is half Danish and half Icelandic…" JJ went on to explain about the artist. I was watching the fan that was seemingly precariously hanging from the ceiling. Later I would learn that it was part of the exhibit.

Even though I knew nothing about art, and always wanted to consider myself an art aficionado (it sounds cool, doesn't it?), truth be told, I learned everything about contemporary art from JJ. She was a force to be reckoned with. Once when we met at the Westin Chosun Hotel, she could name every piece of artwork in the lobby, and tell you some interesting facts about the artist. She never allowed me to pay for anything, always treating me to meals, saying that it was her way to "treat" me. She was humble, thoughtful, gentle, and a veritable walking encyclopedia of contemporary art.

"I loved art because I loved looking at beautiful things," she remarked when I asked why she had gotten into art.

"Why do you think you are so different from other people?"

"I think I was just born this way. I was always like this. My dad was a positive man, but he was a business man. My mom wanted me to become a competitive person, but that just wasn't in my nature. My dream is to improve humanity."

Over her Americano and my peppermint tea, after our museum date, we talked about women. Our conversations inevitably flowed towards women one way or another. JJ had gotten promoted the year before, and had to deal with an older male colleague who ignored her, and more recently 3 female colleagues who quit because they wanted to focus on their marriages.

"You know, when I was in New York, meeting major art directors and CEOs, one of them told me that he thought I was a nanny!"

"WHAAAT?!" I was shocked. Then again, as an Asian female who is often surrounded by older white males, I understood. Once at a meeting with a new white male co-worker, and another co-worker, the new co-worker mistook me for my other co-worker's TA. When I told him I had been teaching at Yonsei for 5 years, he was shocked.

"I guess it is because we look younger. I mean, you have to dress up. And you have to be a bit more aggressive," JJ suggested thoughtfully.

I knew what she meant. Thinking back to the times when I had to assert myself more knowing that people wouldn't take me seriously because I looked younger and I was an Asian female. It upset me that when women were more confident, they were seen as aggressive, but when men were more confident, they came across as more competent and therefore more hirable.

"We have to keep on working so that other younger women see more of us in the upper ranks, and not just men," JJ went on to say, referring to the fact that most upper management positions in the art field were filled by men. I knew that she also worked particularly hard to nurture the young female talent in her office.

"Yes, agreed." With that, we clung our paper cups together in a tea toast.

It was JJ's unique view of not looking AT art, but approaching art from a WITH perspective that made her successful; and her willingness and openness to work WITH younger women to make sure they had positive female role models so they too could be successful like her.

April 1, 2017

On the phone

Ping

Ping and I were catching up over yet another 3-hour phone conversation. We reminisced at how I would always call her falling apart after yet another breakup, no matter what the time difference. She was always there with a non-judgmental ear and insightful, thoughtful advice. She and her mom were two of the most thoughtful and successful corporate women I knew. During the summer of 2005, they generously let me stay in their apartment in Tokyo when I was interning for an anti-trafficking non-profit while doing research for my master's thesis.

Ping was not only a great friend, but also a phenomenal daughter. She had spent a decade working for her parents' font company and shared her time between their family home in Taipei and Tokyo (where I had stayed that summer of 2005). I always looked up to her and sought her advice for anything work related, and she would do the same for advice on dating and social relationships. One incident stood out to me so I wanted to interview her more about it.

"Can you tell me more about what happened to you a few years ago at one of your work drinking parties?"

"Well, it was me, that guy, and another more docile guy. As the night went on, the creepy guy got more touchy feely with me. He insisted on putting my jacket on for me. I refused a couple of times, but since he was so insistent, I just let him. On our way to the subway station, he kept trying to touch me. I told him a few times to leave me alone and get his hands off me, but he persisted. I finally, just left abruptly, and went home on my own."

"So, was the creepy guy married?"

"Yes, he was married and had two sons."

"Oh gosh…"

We talked about how women working in Asia face sexual harassment landmines just waiting to be set off at drinking parties and at the workplace. Women had to tread carefully, because at any moment, a landmine could be detonated.

"So what advice would you give to working women who are facing similar harassment issues?"

"Well, young women and all women need to *fight*. They need to not roll over and play dead. I 'fought' my way out of that sexual harassment issue that night, but as you have mentioned before, we can find allies. For example, at another drinking party recently, the creepy guy started saying inappropriate things again, and two older men in the company told him off. They both have daughters."

"What would you say needs to happen in order for things to change?"

"We need to start embracing *all* kinds of women. Whether you decide to stay at home and take care of your children, or you decide to be a career woman or both, whether you wear leotards like Beyoncé or you don't cover your mouth when you laugh, you don't look like a K-pop idol star, it's ok. Let's embrace different women. Let's embrace the women of our future."

Well said, as always Ping.

It was Ping's ability to not just work WITH all kinds of women and men but also embrace them and their differences that made her successful.

Ping and I | Her company's booth at Tokyo Big Sight in Tokyo, Japan | May 2016

September 8, 2017

Over email

Crystal (former student)

1. Talk about 3 struggles you have overcome since graduating from Yonsei. Be as specific as possible.

> Struggle 1. Finding what I want to do
>
> When I first entered Yonsei, I thought I would definitely become a diplomat, and getting there would be super easy. However, during my first year of uni I realized that it was an unrealistic dream with the amount of effort I was

willing to put into it. I wasn't that enthusiastic about my major Poli Sci (Political Science). Also, wanting to be a diplomat was something I decided on in a day or so when I went to an MUN (Model United Nations) conference in Qatar so I wasn't that desperate to become one.

I thought that in the 4 years, there would be something else I'd find that I would really love to do, and by the time I'd graduate, I would be ready to start my work there. However, even after 4 years of uni, I still don't know what I really want to do. There seems to be no balance between realities and dreams, something I really want doesn't seem to be realistic at all, and something so realistic, I don't feel like doing at all.

So, I started out with random internships, from the Legal & Compliance Department at DBS (a Singaporean Bank) to the Respiratory Marketing Department at GSK (a pharma company), I've tried out jobs that are not even close to Poli sci. What I realized from these two jobs and observing the people around is that I don't think it is "what job I do" that matters to me but "who I do it with" that matters more. I was more than content with both jobs because the people I worked with were excellent. So, in searching for what I wanted to do, I figured out that I want to get a job where the people who I will be working with everyday are good people, enthusiastic, cooperative, and value teamwork. If working WITH a team could be happy everyday, whatever the work is, I think that would be what I would want to do everyday.

Struggle 2. Getting a job

I think the biggest struggle for any college grad is getting a job after graduation. I don't know if it's the same all over the world but Korean students don't usually get a job they dream of or really want. They usually just get a job that is high-paying, stable, and has good benefits. We are usually taught from a young age that if we graduate from Yonsei, we have to and SHOULD get a job working for a *chaebol* or "conglomerate" company. But because everyone aims to get a job at a *chaebol*, getting in is very difficult:

there are several stages before you can even get a full-time offer.

I have gone through these processes as well, and most recently, I ended my 2-month summer internship. I don't know the results yet so I don't actually know if I successfully have overcome this struggle, but one thing I can say is that the 2 months were priceless and worthwhile. I learned a lot about marketing and how a company runs, so even if I don't get a full-time offer, I think I now have a glimpse of how marketing works, so it will be easier for me to apply elsewhere.

Struggle 3. Learning to rest

This is my biggest struggle. I've studied non-stop since my elementary school years, and taking a semester off at uni was meant only for my internships. Going through 16 years of education without a proper break, I feel like I've not learned to take a rest and have some time to myself, which is why now, even if I am given that time for a proper break, I don't know how to use it. It feels like I should be at an academy learning something to get a certificate, or be at school to take extra credits, or be at a company for another internship. It doesn't seem right that I have nothing to do, which is why this is a struggle for me.

However, I've started with baby steps. Today, I booked a flight to Fukuoka to completely opt-out of the stress my own reality has been giving me and to try to stop worrying about my internship results, or my school grades, or more job applications. I think the fact that I've decided to take this break is a start to overcoming this struggle!

2. What role (if any) did I (Kyla) play in helping you in a WITH-style?

Kyla has been a great part of my time overcoming struggles. When I didn't know what I wanted to do, she was always there to reassure me that there's nothing wrong with not knowing. From the first day I met her in our career development class, she has been the biggest support. Through her guidance in writing cover letters and resumes, I took my first step in applying for jobs, through the courage she gave me during our mock interviews in class to overcoming my greatest fear of job interviews, I was able to go to actual job interviews and get the internships I wanted. My whole journey of finding a job started with her guidance, and if I do get a job, it would all be thanks to Kyla.

The reason her guidance was of a greater help than the guidance of others is because she was never a demanding leader, nor was she one-way in all her lessons. She would always emphasize doing things together, finding solutions together, making decisions together. Her way of empowering students has made me gain the courage to stand in front of greater people and not be afraid to show my talents. I learned not to conform to the hierarchies of Korea by having a great professor like Kyla who would approach students as a friend, not a professor.

Also, whenever I had any problems, and would go to her with questions, she would not give me an answer straight away, but would rather question me again, in a way that I could think of my own solution. Her questions that guided me were really helpful, especially when I had to make important decisions. (It worked most with my relationship problems).

Thank you so much Kyla.

3. Tell us more about your dad's WITH-style of parenting (ie. how he treated you and your brother equally).

My dad was different from typical Korean dads. He, like Kyla, never thought he was above of us. He always respected our decisions, and never underestimated our decision-making even when we would make wrong decisions because we were young. When I said I wanted to quit ballet in my 2nd year of elementary school, after doing it for 4 years, because I wanted to go to Korean school on the weekends instead, he respected my decision and enrolled me in a Korean language school right away. When I said I wanted to quit learning piano, which I had been playing for 6 years, to play the flute instead, he took me to the music shop and bought me the best flute they had. When I said I didn't want to take hip-hop classes after trying it out for a month only, he never got mad at me and was always ready to support my next interest. Thanks to such a supportive dad and mom, I have tried so many things during my early years, from playing the piano, the trumpet, the saxophone, the flute, the violin, to dancing ballet, hip-hop dancing, belly dancing, and taking art classes, cooking classes, baking classes, traditional brush painting classes, also doing all kinds of sports such as taekwondo, swimming, golf, table tennis, and basketball! Through it all, my dad always thought that my decisions were the most important because it was *my* life. He never claimed ownership as a father, but he was rather a companion in my decision-making processes.

Also, my dad brought me to a room salon for a business meeting with one of his business associates to prove a point: they should not have meetings there if it was inappropriate for a middle school aged girl to be there. My dad always encouraged me to experience many things even at a young age. I was allowed to go to Hong Kong alone as a 4th grade elementary student because my dad trusted that I could find my way around a new neighborhood. Also, since middle school I registered for school by myself, because he trusted me with money. Moreover, I always decided what school I wanted to go to, what subjects I wanted to take, and what I would like to become in the future because he always believed that I would work harder if I chose my own path. My father, treating me as an equal, was the reason I was able to make my own decisions from such a young age, and eventually grow up to become such a strong independent woman.

4. What advice would you give your younger self?

Although I have no regrets with my life at the moment, there is one thing I am curious about. Growing up so independently, I have never actually lived a steady and slow life. I was always busy studying, exploring places, fulfilling credits, and looking for jobs. So some advice I would like to give to my younger self is to try living a steady and slow life. I am curious how my life would have turned out if I didn't rush to graduate high school, and if I didn't rush to finish all my credits at uni.

5. What advice would you give to the readers of this book?

> **Never struggle to solve things by yourself. Seek help.** Like I had Kyla to guide me through my lost years of uni, there is always someone around willing to help you. I hope that if you're ever in trouble, or if you ever feel lost, don't try to solve things by yourself! Try asking a friend, a teacher, your parents, or even your professor from some advice! They will provide you with a perspective you might not have even thought of before, and it might even be the solution to your problem! I believe that things will get better for you if you're willing to really open up and share your difficulties/challenges **WITH** someone.

Thank you, Crystal.

Me and Crystal | My apartment in Songdo, South Korea | September 2017

August 26, 2017

In my apartment

Gabi (former student)

Gabi had come to celebrate her engagement to her now fiancé Tim. He was a British guy who was teaching English, but wanted to eventually start his own thing in Korea. Gabi was in her last semester at Yonsei, and had spent a semester as a TA teaching English to middle school students.

> Me: Gabi, do you remember the day that you came to my office and you told me you wanted to get plastic surgery?

How everyone around you told you that you should get it? I think that out of all my days teaching at Yonsei, I felt like I had failed. Failed you, mostly, because I wasn't able to convince you to not get plastic surgery.

Gabi: I'm so touched that you remember that conversation. First of all, you didn't fail me. I had people in my life at that time telling me that I should get plastic surgery to have a better life. I was fragile. You were actually the first person to tell me not to. I went to you for advice because you seemed confident and I knew you wouldn't judge me. So, no, you didn't fail me.

Me: Oh phew. Thank goodness. What would you say now to those people who told you to get plastic surgery?

Gabi: You know, I am fine now. I have met a lot of good people who don't care about looks. I think it was good to find people who don't care about how I look on the outside. Like Tim and I went to Mount Fuji recently. We didn't shower for two days, my face was super greasy, but he didn't care.

Me: That's awesome! So cool you went to Japan and hiked Mount Fuji! What is your advice for young people?

Gabi: I am totally fine now with myself even though I don't have a job and I haven't graduated yet from Yonsei. It takes time and people who care about you to get to this point though. Maybe ask people like Kyla who are not judgmental for advice, and try to hear that advice over and over again until it sticks WITH you.

Thank you, Gabi.

Me and Gabi | My apartment in Songdo, South Korea | August 2017

2750

Imagine a world without a single Korean person. The year is 2750. No Korean people, no Korean language, no Korean culture. It sounds like the title of Murakami Haruki's next novel. When I first started hearing and reading news that due to the shrinking birth rate and the aging elderly population, Koreans would become extinct[1], I thought to myself: *Come on, that is ridiculous.*

When I was living in Japan and teaching English back in the early 2000s, the same issue was discussed in the news, and I remember thinking: nobody was talking about how a lack of governmental policies and corporate infrastructure were not supporting working mothers. It made total and utter sense to me: women were dropping out of the workforce to give birth, if that was what they decided to do, and then coming back again once they were older in their 40s or above—the so-called M curve.

In 2015[2], South Korea was the worst place for working women amongst OECD countries. And in 2014[3], and in 2013[4], you get the picture. From a statistics point of view, I once thought, *how can ranking-obsessed Korea stand this? Isn't this embarrassing for you and everyone else in the country?*

Over tea, about a year ago, one of my former star students who had taken almost every single one of my classes, told me about her struggles to get a job.

"I always get to the final round. Then it is between me and many other male candidates. And I am never chosen," she lamented.

She told me a story of how she had to go stay in this dorm room outside of Seoul with other potential candidates, put together group presentations, sweat through group interviews, and at the end of it all, there was not one single job offer.

"One of my other students told me that even though you are a SKY graduate, since you are female, companies will look for non-SKY male graduates over you. Is that true?" I asked her fearing her response.

She nodded. I knew it was true, but I almost didn't want it to be true. So on the ground, this is what my students and other female graduates around the country are facing once they graduate from university. *This sucks*, I thought.

Companies were judging female candidates AT: companies assume women who drop out of the labor force to give birth would make companies lose money, but is this really true? Or is this just their perception?

A study led by Kathy Matsui, Vice-Chair of Goldman Sachs Japan and Chief Japan Equity Strategist for Global Investment Research at Goldman Sachs revealed that closing the gap on gender in female employment would actually increase Japan's GDP by 13%. She recommends that the government, private sector and society take a three-pronged approach to combating this dire issue[5]. Another case for hiring more women is diversity: diverse teams at work are not only smarter, focus on facts, process these facts more carefully, more innovative, but perform better. In a study done by McKinsey in 2015, companies with the highest quartile for gender diverse teams, were 15% more likely to have returns above their industry average[6]. If these aren't reasons enough to work WITH women, I don't know what else would be.

Doodles/Takeaways/Reflections Points

WITH RESPECT FOR WOMEN: THE MOST IMPORTANT PART OF ANY COMMUNITY

CHAPTER 12

CREATIVE SOLUTIONS ON WORKING WITH WOMEN

"The women's movement cannot move forward WITHout men." ~me

Let's Ask Some Men!

A Talk With Ilkka

In Finland, dads can have a whopping 9 weeks of paternity leave paid out at roughly 62.9% of their salary[1]. In addition, the government also doles out 172 Euros per child/month for private daycare expenses[2]. Ilkka told me that when his daughter Hilma was first born (she is now 4 years old), he took 6 months of paternity leave. The first 9 weeks were subsidized at about 70%, but thereafter, he still received partial subsidy. During one of our Skype calls in early 2018, I decided to ask him more about paternity leave and what men can do to work WITH women.

Skype

January 18th, 2018

Kyla: Why do you respect women?

Ilkka: Ohhh, that is a big question. You know, I think it is about attitude. Understanding that in order to succeed in business and in life, diversity is a plus and adds an extra perspective.

Kyla: That is so cool. You once told me that you stayed home with Hilma when she was first born for 6 months. How was that?

Ilkka: Yes, it remains today, as one of my most important periods bonding WITH her. In that way, Hilma got to know both my wife and I--not just my wife.

Kyla: That is unbelievable. Finland is such a great leader in that respect for gender equality. What do you think is a way for us to work WITH women moving forward based on your experiences working and living in Finland?

Ilkka: We need to create new experiences, open up dialogues; we need to talk about this online and offline. If we can share our experiences, it is really up to our imagination what we can do together WITH each other.

Kyla: Yes for sure! What message would you give to your daughter when she is like in her 20s and to our readers?

Ilkka: Wow! That is a great question. You always come up with the best questions! First I would say, learn to believe in yourself. You know, life has ups and downs, but understanding that the downs happen for a reason, and there is a seed lying in the down parts. I know it is easier said than done, but if you can believe in yourself, you can build your self-esteem. Second, carefully choose whom you surround yourself WITH. You can easily become like the people you hangout WITH, so make sure to choose wisely, and show gratitude to them as much as you can. Third, life is really valuable. As a father, I understand now how valuable it is to spend time WITH my daughter Hilma. In a short time, children will grow up…make sure to spend time WITH your loved ones. Finally, give back to the world. It has given you so much, make sure that you give back to it.

Kiitos ("Thank You" in Finnish), Ilkka.

Me and Ilkka | Finland | April 2016

An Email Exchange With My Dad

My dad has always stood by my mom and supported her as a husband. When she wanted to "retire from the kitchen," when she wanted to start working, when she wanted to start her own business, he always supported her. As a father, he has always supported me and my sister. When we wanted to work in non-profit, when we wanted to live at home, when we wanted to go to grad school, and the list goes on. I never really questioned how supportive he actually is or really thought too deeply about it until my editor brought it up. So I decided to ask my dad some more questions about why he so deeply respects women.

Email

January 11th, 2018

> Kyla: Why do you think you respect women?
>
> Dad: I believe respecting women came about because of my early experiences with my aunt and mother; then much later on what I came to realize about my mom and then finally, what I saw at the workplace.
>
> Kyla: What happened when you were younger?
>
> Dad: As you may know, after the War, the Mitsunaga and Miwa family moved into a three-bedroom house in Hawthorne, California. Because we were so close physically my aunt and mom often shared certain household duties like preparing meals. I would always

watch them make dinner and in particular the baking of apple pies. It seemed to me they were always working and basically took care of everything involved in keeping a household in order. Each New Year's Day both families would make *mochi* ("rice cake" in Japanese), which was a lot of work. Everything I know about the Buddhist religion came from my aunt explaining it to us kids (Mas, Brian, Gerald, me) on the drive back home from church each Sunday. My aunt and mom pretty much managed the nursery; ordering inventory, pricing merchandise, waiting on customers, doing the books, etc. Most of my growing up lessons and advice came from my mother, and to some extent my aunt.

When I took a history course in college I finally discovered what happened to the Japanese-Americans during the War because this was never discussed at home. The hardships my mother must have experienced were beyond difficult. I was less than a year old and my brother was born a year and a half later in camp. She told me how the FBI showed up one night and took away their Japanese books and some family photos. She also said she remembers how smelly the horse stables were. I don't know how she got through it all. Even after the War life could not have been easy assimilating back into a white society.

Kyla: That is crazy and must have been so tough for both grandma and grandpa but it just speaks to the kind of strong people they were! I remember finding out when I was at grandma's house in high school and being totally shocked that you and the whole family were put in internment camps during the War. Did grandma always want to work?

Dad: My mom told me that she always wanted to get a college education but her father thought women should get married and have children, which was a common thought amongst most fathers in the 1930s-40s. She was raised on a farm with three brothers so life wasn't easy. Anyway, she was able to do two years of junior college. Once the nursery was sold, she decided to get a real estate license and then later a real estate brokerage license. She started her own real estate company and was very successful and kept working until she was into her seventies. I think she wanted to prove to her father and others that a woman could be just as effective as any man.

Kyla: That is amazing. What happened when you started working?

Dad: When I started working at Bank of America I had a couple of women managers who were very competent whom I enjoyed working for. One of them told me that they didn't earn as much as their male counterparts and that their promotion to higher levels was very limited. I felt very odd when I heard this because as my career progressed I received regular salary increases and promotions while my female counterparts were left behind. It was something I always remembered.

Being a member of a minority race, I know what it is like to be overlooked when other less qualified individuals are given the opportunity to move ahead, so it's not difficult to empathize with women who are also at a disadvantage for unfair reasons.

Kyla: Thank you so much for sharing, dad. You have overcome so much but at the same time are always so deeply empathetic. And thank you for raising me and Tisha in such a way that we never felt like we couldn't do anything other than succeed as women.

Dad: I saw inequalities throughout my life and did not like it. I did not want my children to be similarly disadvantaged so I made certain they had the best advantage: a quality education. More importantly, they are using their learned skills and have put everything to good use.

P.S. I lived with your mother, my mother-in-law, and you and your sister—4 women! So I had no choice but to remember to put the toilet seat down!

Thanks, Dad. Thanks for working hard to become more of a WITH husband, WITH grandpa, and WITH dad.

SELF WORK:
Find a male friend in your life you trust and respect. Ask him why he respects women. Brainstorm ways that you can create a community of people who respect women!

Can Women Still Have It All?

In the fall of 2016, I met up with a good friend from grad school. She was in Seoul for work. I took her to my favorite Buddhist vegetarian restaurant place for dinner. In that zen space we talked about the possibility of having kids.

"Do you want to have kids?" I asked.

"Well, you know, I wish I could just be the father…"

With that one word, father, I knew exactly what she meant before she even began to explain how if she were the father, her body wouldn't change, she could go to work the very next day as if it were just another day after *her* partner gave birth.

In 2012, Anne-Marie Slaughter wrote an article for *The Atlantic* magazine entitled, "Why Women Still Can't Have it All."[3] It was one of the most widely read articles in the magazine's history. It was so widely read, she decided to write a book that came out three years later in 2015 entitled *Unfinished Business.* If you haven't read either, I suggest you get your hands on both.

In her book, Slaughter outlines a number of concrete solutions for businesses, governments, and ordinary people alike. People say that her article was written in response to Sheryl Sandberg's *Lean In* book, but regardless, she has some worthy and astute advice.

Here's mine:

WITH vs AT

HOW TO WORK WITH WOMEN (ON A MACRO-LEVEL)

- Create day care centers at the company
- Allow women to work from home
- Allow flex time
- Get rid of *nunchi* ("judgment" in Korean) such that women can actually take maternity leave and not feel guilty or bad
- Allow paid paternity leave (men can help too)
- Test yourself and do gender blind interviews[4]
- Read this book: *Blindspot: Hidden Biases of Good People* by Banaji and Greenwald and take the Implicit Association Tests
- Do the research: adding women to the labor force also adds TONS of money[5]
- Be open (!)

HOW TO WORK WITH YOUR PARTNER (ON A MICRO-LEVEL)

- Make sure to have the conversation with your partner before you decide to have a baby: who is going to do what household chore? Who is a better cook?
- According to statistics, working mothers still do the lion's share of the housework, so creating a schedule/chart to divide out the chores is helpful
- Take turns
- If your partner can hold down a full-time job, your partner can also do the laundry, cook, clean. It might not be *exactly* the way you want it, but you have to also let go of your own expectations or communicate them
- Make sure to continue to prioritize (as much as possible) time with just the two of you: date nights, movie nights, and anything else that will help strengthen your bond

Military Service=Maternity Leave?

Every semester, my male students moan and groan about having to complete their 21-month military service. Those who survive the experience are rather tight-lipped about it, but usually describe their experience in two words: "Cold and hungry." Although no Korean male really wants to do it, each and every able-bodied male has to do it. Many of my students apply for the highly coveted position of KATUSA (Korean Augmentation To the US Army) so they can serve as a translator for the U.S. soldiers, and enjoy other privileges of being stationed on the U.S. military base.

On one of my swims recently, I had a pool-piphany: no one gives men a hard time for joining the labor force 21 months later, and nobody expects anything of them during this time, why can't women expect the same when *they* take their maternity leave? Aren't they serving a critical national service too? Isn't the birth rate shrinking in Korea?

Ilkka once told me one of the most important things he has done is take 6 months off for paternity leave when his daughter Hilma was born. In Finland, fathers are entitled to a whopping 9 weeks; they receive 70% of their earnings up to EUR 36,686, 40% up to EUR 56,443, and 25% of their earnings if they exceed this level. The minimum daily benefit they can receive is EUR 23.936. In Korea, paternity leave is 5 days. 3 days are paid 100% and the other 2 days are unpaid. What a contrast! Wouldn't it benefit not just daughters and sons to spend more time WITH their fathers, but society overall?

War -> Day Care Centers

On the deck of her parents' 1920s Laguna Beach cottage in California, we sat as we had sat many nights in college, chatting about life and what matters to us in our lives—this time almost 20 years later. 'Trina and I had met in the laundry room at UCSD our freshman year. We went on to volunteer for CORE (Community OutReach Effort), a community service oriented student group that put together soup kitchen trips amongst its many other volunteer efforts. Sophomore year, when we lived in different apartments on campus, I would go over and visit her for baked Brie—that was her thing.

'Trina had taken the train to meet up with me in Laguna Beach from her own house which was more inland, leaving behind her husband Baber, and two children Sara and Nathaniel. The weekend was glorious: we laid in her parents' bed chatting, 'Trina attempting to read the first draft of this book, chatting more over 2-hour brunches on the deck, taking walks on the beach, gulping down milkshakes at a local diner, and just good ol' catching up. I relished the time with her, and how generous she was at sharing it with me, as well as how generous her parents had been lending us their awesome retirement home. (They were away in Thailand visiting 'Trina's middle sister with her youngest sister.)

"You know, back in World War II, there were government sponsored day care centers for kids," 'Trina bemoaned. It had taken her more than a decade to regain her sick days after having two kids, whereas her husband had stockpiled his. They worked at the same elementary school.

"No way!" I was shocked. I mean back in the day, one would assume that things were more conservative, people were more conservative, but wait, this is war we are talking about.

"Yes, what's more, it was full-service. You could pick up medicine there, your kids could get fed there. You basically could go there and just pick your kids up, and be on your merry way home."

"Whoa…"

'Trina was talking about the Lanham Act programs that were established in 1942. These day care centers were set up in every single state in the U.S. with the exception of New Mexico (poor working moms in New Mexico!), and between 1943 and 1946, every year, 3,000 centers took care of about 130,000 kids. By the war's end, it was estimated that 550,000-600,000 kids had benefited from this program[7].

Why was it so difficult for people to accept that this is what actually needs to happen? I understand we are currently not living in wartime, but do we have to go through a war in order to help working parents make end's meet? Why can't governments step up to the plate and fund day care centers?

For more, check out 'Trina's video she created on that very deck in which she talks about things she wished she had known when she first became a working mom:

Girl Squad

I am unabashedly a Taylor Swift fan: I absolutely love her and what she stands for. She writes her own music, she actually cares about her close group of girlfriends, but also her fans and says that they ground her, she is a fashion/style icon, she is constantly reinventing herself/those around her/inspiring her fans, and I know this may sound as if I am completely full of myself, but I see some parallels. OK, bear WITH me here.

Taylor respects her fans. Before she released her 1989 album, she invited her fans to each one of her homes, baked cookies for them, and played the entire album for them from start to finish. She is also known to send fans Christmas presents, show up at a fan's bridal shower unannounced, help out those in need. In the same way, I respect my students. Every semester, I memorize every single one of my 100+ students' names in my 6 or 7 courses, rather than tell them what they did wrong during feedback sessions, I ask them what *they* think they could have improved on. I have them call me "Kyla," rather than "Professor," so they feel less intimidated.

We all know that Taylor is extremely loyal to her girl squad made up of mostly models and other hot women like herself. Something MK said when she came to be a guest speaker in the G^2LTS seminar during the spring 2016 semester struck a chord, "Surround yourself with good and positive people--the kind of people who will be there for you through the good, of course, but also the bad. When they stick around for the bad, you know that they are good people." Life is going to throw all kinds of stuff AT you, but it is those friendships that will keep you sane, keep you from stress eating that bowl of ice-cream, or be there to eat it WITH you.

At our wedding in California, I looked out at all of the people who came to celebrate our love. We couldn't afford a big wedding, so we chose carefully who we wanted to share our special day WITH. On Edgar's side it came down to mostly family, as he comes from a large Mexican family, and a few of his close friends from MIT (who were mostly his groomsmen), and on my side, a few family members and mostly good friends who were as close to family as ever. I remember looking up peeking as I walked down the aisle flanked on one side by my dad and on the other side holding tightly to my mom's hand. Everyone stood up as I got closer to them, the mariachi band was playing the traditional wedding song in the background; and then it dawned on me, these awesome women I knew, were absolute reflections of me and how I would like to live my life and exactly how I live my life now. They were *my* girl squad (with the exception of some male friends), even though we didn't all live in the same country nor did we ALL hangout together at the same time all the time.

Many of these women (and men) are some of the most accomplished humans I have ever met. I am eternally grateful for the profound impact my friends have had on the course of my life and continue to have. These incredible human-beings have never judged me, always supported me, been there through my ugly cries (and there have been a lot), and shown up for me, WITH me, just as much as they did that special day. As cheesy as this may sound, I am also so grateful to have them WITH me on this journey called life—through the ups, downs, and when life/society throws those AT balls AT you, having a girl squad in place to shield/take a hit for or WITH you is absolutely what it is all about.

Spirit Guides

During the spring semester of 2016, in one of our weekly Skype calls, Ilkka brought up the idea of invisible counselors. He began talking excitedly, abashedly, and again excitedly as he always did when he wanted to share a new crazy idea. The idea comes from a book *Think and Grow Rich* by Napoleon Hill. The idea is to have a chat WITH someone who is not necessarily alive or you may not have direct access to and seek their advice on something that's troubling you. Here is a YouTube video on the invisible counselors idea:

While I couldn't relate to actually having talked to invisible counselors such as Napoleon, Socrates, Aristotle and the like, I did recount the story of reconnecting with my *Popo* after she had passed away. After my *Popo's* wake in Singapore in 2013, I said "Goodbye" to her before I went to bed telling her that I would be leaving the following day to go back to Korea and that I loved her very much. In my sleep, the curtain by my bed touched my leg (even though there was no reason for the curtain to move, as the window was not open, nor was the AC on). It was as if my *Popo* was acknowledging everything I had said and she also blessed my journey home. Ilkka recounted a similar story and admitted being close to his grandma as well before she passed away.

Several days later, I decided to have my very own invisible counselor meeting inviting: Michelle Obama, Hillary Clinton, Taylor Swift, Ellen DeGeneres, and Sheryl Sandberg. I later recounted my "meeting" with Ilkka during another Skype chat, but this is roughly how it went down:

> MICHELLE: You know, when Barack was a senator, it was really difficult for me to raise two daughters without him around. I asked my mom to come help me. It wasn't easy, but I survived, we survived.
>
> HILLARY: When the whole Monica Lewinsky scandal broke out, I was shocked and mortified. I didn't want to believe that it was true, but it was and very publicly for me.

> SHERYL: After my husband passed, I didn't think I could go on. I wanted to throw in the towel, but I just knew that I had to keep going. For my kids, but for all those women out there.
>
> TAYLOR: When *Red* didn't win album of the year, I was upset, but I knew I had to do something different--something completely different. And that's how *1989* was born.
>
> ELLEN: You know, when I came out, and nobody would hire me as an actor I didn't know what I would do. I would have never imagined I would be able to serve people in the way I do now with my show –16 seasons later! Be kind to yourself!

Each incredible woman told me, and took turns sharing an event in their lives that was so horrible, so insurmountable, yet somehow they were able to overcome it. Hearing each one of their stories was so moving, because I adored and idolized these women. They had accomplished so much already in their lifetimes, yet were still completely down-to-earth and humble about everything. They ended the meeting by saying, "You can do it Kyla." And that was that.

One night I decided to take myself out to see *Spirits' Homecoming*, a movie based on the life of Kang Il-Chul who is currently 88 years old and living in the House of Sharing in Gyeonggi Province. The movie was an incredible feat on multiple levels. First, it reveals the remarkable life story of a teenager who persevered against all odds: she was taken at the age of 16 to serve the Japanese military during the war at various "comfort stations." Second, the movie features not just one story but two. The second story takes place in modern day Korea. It follows Kang Il-Chul as an elderly woman. She happens to cross paths with and take in a teenager who can connect with spirits. Finally, the movie itself struggled with funding, because everyone was afraid that it was too political, but it eventually came to fruition due to the generosity of over 75,000 people[8].

Of course the brutality and abuse of the young comfort women brought me back to my own grad school research on human trafficking and domestic violence. Watching scenes of the women being forced to have sex night after night was almost unbearable, but something I learned was that there were large pits where the women were first shot and then burned to get rid of any evidence that comfort stations and comfort women for that matter ever existed. Even though many people don't like to talk about this issue because it is too political or people blame war and the natural tendency of brutality of wars, this is no different from modern day slavery in the form of human trafficking that is going on all over the world. The only difference is it is 2016 (when I wrote this) and it was the 1940s back then. Not much has changed over the past 80 years.

My *Popo* once told me when the Japanese soldiers were occupying Singapore and she was also a teenager, she and her friends would smear black tar on their faces to look unattractive, so they wouldn't get raped. The movie made me immediately think of my *Popo* not only because it was a movie about her generation, but also because of our spiritual connection. That night, my mind in a fog after coming home from the movie, I talked to my mom:

"Do you know if grandma was ever raped during the Japanese occupation of Singapore, mom?

"Well, no, I don't think so…I mean, I think she would have told me. We had a pretty open and honest relationship. Why do you ask? Is it for one of your classes?"

I had to admire my mom's openness. She didn't even skip a beat when I asked her that question out of the blue. She even went on to say that she could perhaps find out for me, ask a cousin or another relative. That night, I decided to connect with my *Popo* spiritually again, inspired by the teenager who had been able to do just that in the movie. I could sense that my *Popo* knew as well. The week before I had been hearing sounds in the apartment and even noticed that things were not in their proper place. I know, it sounds crazy. I woke in the middle of the night, knowing I had spoken to her. I couldn't recall everything, but I knew she had been there. I moved a photo of us closer to me, on my bedside table, so she could be physically closer to me.

I won't know if she was ever raped, but I do have faith that creating change for this next generation of women leaders will help create stronger, more confident women. If they have someone who believes in them like my *Popo* and my mom and my sister believed in me, then the sky is the limit for them.

SELF WORK: Sometimes it's helpful to know that there are people you don't know out there who support you—an invisible girl squad, if you will. Create your very own invisible counselor's meeting. Ask them some questions you are dying to know.

Kyla Mitsunaga

Women For Leadership Workshop*

Over a weekend in March 2016, I attended yet another workshop at Chadwick International School. I was beginning to feel like a bit of a groupie. Chadwick had everything: resources, open-mindedness, creativity, collaborative spaces for actual collaboration, professional development, awesome facilities, super duper nice teachers, and administrators who were all very diverse not to mention actual paper towels in their bathrooms!

Over the course of two days, I met women who were at different stages of their careers, all in the education sector, mostly from Chadwick, but we were all heading towards the same goal of upping our leadership skills. During the introductions, one of the few Asian women talked about how she doesn't see anyone else who looks like her around when she goes to conferences. Another woman said she is always surrounded by men in her leadership position, so she wanted to spend time with women instead. We talked about role models, traits of good leaders, had to create our very own leadership philosophy and elevator pitch.

I went in thinking I would breeze through this. Ok, some of the stuff I actually did in my classes, but some of the stuff was definitely challenging being on the receiving end. I have students do an elevator pitch, so I am very familiar with the concept, but doing it as a role play in front of everyone with the workshop facilitator, I got my ass kicked. She actually walked away from me, because I was boring her (!). It was hard! I shared that story with my students too.

I did ask a question that I was dying to ask other women in leadership positions, which was this:

"How do you deal with people who discriminate against you just because you are a woman or you look young even though you're a badass?"

Yes, I actually wrote badass, which initiated a chuckle out of the facilitator. She said that she herself has never faced that, so she threw it out to the rest of the participants. The same Asian woman spoke and said, "If you talk to the person long enough, they will find out in time who you really are and what you really have to offer." Another woman a few years younger than me shared her story of how she lost her confidence and regained it through spirituality/meditation. Before ending the workshop, we talked about action plans for ourselves individually but also for us as a group. The facilitator wanted to know what was happening in Asia for female leaders? Throughout the workshop, she would mention how she found it odd that in Asia, there were very few heads of schools who were actually Asian and

---

* A workshop put on by Deidre Fischer who has headed several international schools all over the globe: http://deidrefischer.com.au/.

female. I didn't find it odd at all. I knew exactly why. Women were not seen as "leaders."

Edgar happened to be in New York with two younger female colleagues. He recalled how his business trip was going and how it had been particularly challenging because the two colleagues were younger Korean women in their 20s who were not confident enough to approach CEOs/VPs at this pharma conference they were attending in New York. Recently, a Korean female student came to my office crying about how she was afraid to ask questions/for help in my English Communication for Science and Engineering class, because she was afraid people would judge her. She had lost *her* confidence.

These stories are not one off stories, unfortunately. These are the stories that need to be heard, but also the stories that need to be changed. These women (including myself) need to be empowered. When Edgar was coaching his two female colleagues and giving them a pep talk asking them what would be helpful to them to be more confident they responded by saying, "Well, a leadership workshop for women would be helpful, but even if we do attend that workshop, because of the culture in Korea, we have no way of implementing change."

WIN (Women's International Network) Conference Tokyo | May 18-20, 2016

Please no one come, please no one come, please no one come. I was pacing around my studio apartment that I found 4 times cheaper than The Shangri-La Hotel in Tokyo where the actual conference was taking place. I had actually applied to challenge myself, get myself out on the women's conference scene, try to be a different kind of speaker younger women could see and hopefully be inspired WITH, and yeah, I didn't want to pay the conference fee that was about 57,000 Yen, so I thought if I get accepted as a speaker, I would only have to pay for my accommodation and plane ticket. I had heard about the conference from Ping who was thinking about attending herself.

Here is a Youtube clip of me before the workshop where you can see just how beautiful the space is:

The room where my workshop was held was beautiful: it was called the Pavilion. I imagine weddings took place there as a long aisle led from the double doors to the end of the room. It was circular in shape with floor-to-ceiling windows, and was perhaps the most majestic place I have ever given a workshop. After a while, my wishful thinking of having no one come, actually came to fruition. 7 participants ended up coming total. At first, I wanted to cry, but then I remembered why I was there and what I had come there to do: change people's lives. And that is what I did. I channeled my inner-Kyla and got to work.

Before I knew it, older Japanese women were working alongside younger African-American women, and the one Japanese male who came, who barely spoke any English was actually having fun, engaged and looked as if he was enjoying himself. How awesome is that?

At the end of it all, I received a bouquet of flowers, but the best reward of all was the conversation I had with the *one* male participant:

"Oh, can I take pictures of everything for my work?" he asked innocently.

"Sure, go ahead. How was the workshop for you?"

"Oh, it was good. I think there are many toxic workers here in Japan and most of them are men. Women are actually very smart and capable." I hesitated before saying this, but I knew I had to get it out there, "Yes, most of those toxic employees are middle-aged men who are super conservative…"

"Yes, you are right. They are just waiting for retirement!" he remarked.

It was perhaps the best outcome of any women's conference possible: making sure you hear from the other half: men. We cannot have any women's movement or any movement on any front unless we include men in the conversation. There are some awesome men out there, like this Japanese one who attended my workshop and Edgar who was willing to coach his female colleagues. They may be hard to find, but once you do find them, it makes it all worth it in the end. Moreover, going back to why there are so few Asian female "leaders" or perceived as such, I think it is because there are so few Asian female role models out there. If young Asian women actually see other women in positions of power who look like them, they will increasingly think that the impossible is actually possible.

SELF WORK: Brainstorm ways we can work WITH men to empower younger women.

Networking With Purpose And Passion

I must admit that because I had been so stressed out about my workshop, I skipped out on much of the conference; however, I did manage to attend an amazing networking event at the end of the two days: The Networking with Purpose and Passion event. It was held in the large ballroom, which had about 15 tables of about 10-15 people. I sat next to an African-American woman who was running a non-profit that brought inner city youth to Tokyo. She and I shared a love of guzzling water. During the session, we would take turns and sneak off to go get water for each other.

We began by talking about our dreams, what we wanted to do, any obstacles in our way, and then we got advice from others who were sat at our same table. The questions ranged from: what should I see in Tokyo, to where should I go shark diving, to how can I get more funding for my non-profit? My dream was to monetize my Happiness Workshop speaking. What was amazing was not just how everyone listened intently, but how everyone gave thoughtful advice, and not only advice, but people began connecting people WITH those they knew in the same field/industry. For example, two women offered to put me in touch WITH women they knew who were already happiness coaches and doing quite well for themselves. I offered to connect two other women with a former boss of mine who worked at the anti-trafficking non-profit where I interned many summers ago during grad school.

But the most amazing thing was yet to come: we all had to choose someone at the table to basically summarize what we did, learned, and share anything else. At most tables, the mic kept being passed around, because nobody wanted to get up in front of the 200 odd people and speak. I decided that I would, thinking it would be great practice for me, as I always did when faced with this kind of speaking opportunity. So I did. I got up and said something along the lines of this:

"I am so fortunate that I happened to sit at this table. We went around the table and had someone who was interested in shark diving get advice from someone who had done it in Fiji, someone who was interested in working for a non-profit, was given a contact by me since I used to work for a non-profit here, I mean, I didn't feel like I was sitting at a conference doing a networking session, I felt like I was having dinner with a group of girlfriends because not only did we give each other thoughtful advice, but we took it to the next level and also offered to connect each other WITH relevant people we knew. Very cool." And just like that, we had created our very own girl squad, topped WITH purpose and passion.

After the session was over, people were eagerly exchanging business cards, and I was thinking to myself: what an incredibly powerful and meaningful exercise. My thoughts were interrupted when several women came up to me and commented on what I said and how they wanted to connect with me because of what I had said. I was astounded. I mean, I didn't really think about what I was going to say, and just kind of blurted something out, but somehow that something was of value to other women there. I have never had that experience before. Then it dawned on me that women's conferences are different in that way. Women connect WITH each other on a very different level, despite the long-held notion that women compete with each other and push each other down.

But more importantly, I thought to myself: every speaking opportunity whether informal or formal is an opportunity to connect with people and change their lives.

As if the conference experience with all of these awesome and amazing women couldn't get any better, at the farewell lunch I had the opportunity to chat with the CEO Kristin (who hails from Norway) about the situation of women in Korea and how we need to empower the next generation of female leaders in Korea. After the lunch, I spoke with Dominique (who was then in charge of Speaker Relations at WIN). She had asked me how my workshop went.

"I heard that it went really well…" Dominique said with a big grin on her face.

"Well, I'm not sure what people thought (I was going to continue and put myself down by saying how few people showed up, but I stopped myself), but we all had fun!"

"You know, you should think about taking a holiday…" she continued. *Where is she going with this? I mean, why would I need to take a holiday?*

"You know, the global conference in Rome is 10 times larger than this one…You seem like someone who likes to have fun and be crazy…the Rome conference will be a lot crazier and more fun than the one here…"

I think she sensed my disappointment in how many people showed up to my workshop.

"Oh?! Yes, I like to have fun and I am definitely crazy!" I just had to make sure that she was inviting me as a speaker and not as a participant. "So, what do you think my chances of getting accepted as a speaker are if I apply?"

"Oh, pshhh…you? No problem at all."

And just like that, by being a role model for younger Asian women and perhaps women of all ages/races, I was not only invited to WIN's Global Conference in Rome, but I also learned the importance of networking WITH people.

Check out Jazmine (the woman standing to my right)'s video testimonial:

SELF WORK:
Figure out a way you can reach out to help/inspire younger women around you.

Doodles/Takeaways/Reflection Points

BEING WITH YOUR EMOTIONS

CHAPTER 13

LOVE (FALLING IN LOVE WITH YOURSELF/SOMEONE)

"Love is transparent in color, because you cannot see it but you can feel it."
~Former Japanese Middle School Student of mine

Falling In Love With Yourself

Do you love yourself?

Take some time to think about that question. Don't answer right away. Let it percolate in your mind, then your heart, and finally your body.

You can't really fall in love WITH someone else until you truly love yourself, and fall head over heels WITH yourself. Something that I learned in my 30s was to accept myself as I am: sometimes I will leave the house with toilet paper pieces still stuck on my face, I don't like brushing my hair so my hair will sometimes be in a mess, I don't like organizing so sometimes my desk is also a mess (at work and at home).

In my 20s, I used to beat myself up over these insignificant flaws. Then I would get upset when I wouldn't do anything to change. I was essentially burning the candle at both ends. When I started teaching at Yonsei, I realized that my students just loved me for who I was. The crazy, unorganized, un-brushed, toilet paper faced ME. I would hear them talk about their own flaws, and it would make me cringe. I knew it was my place to correct their grammar as they spoke about them, but was it my place to also help them fall in love WITH themselves?

Then I began telling them the story of how when I first started teaching at Yonsei I thought I had to look a certain way, dress a certain way, and act a certain way as a "professor" should. I was so stressed out trying to fit into this stereotype I had created myself in my own mind that I was not focusing on the two things that really mattered: my teaching and my students. After the first month, I started dressing my own way, teaching my own way, and not worrying about fitting in. That was when I realized my students were a lot more engaged, because I was a lot less stressed. I FORGAVE myself.

Start A Relationship With Yourself

If Chapter 3 didn't drill it into your head enough, then here is a reminder. Everything starts WITH you. If you have a strong relationship WITH yourself, your relationship WITH others will be that much stronger. We're not just talking dating relationships, but work relationships, family relationships, and any other kind of relationship you can imagine.

Don't wait to go to that travel destination. Go WITH yourself. Don't wait to go see cherry blossoms, go WITH yourself. Don't wait to try that new restaurant, go WITH yourself.

Watch your inner voice as well. That inner voice that is negative, or doubtful. Make sure that you build a relationship WITH that inner voice too. Take that inner voice out to dinner and show that inner voice a good time. Sometimes we are so focused on building relationships WITH others that we neglect the one that matters the most—the relationship WITH ourselves.

Don't Buy Into The Valentine's Day Hype!

Something I have always appreciated about my parents is that Valentine's Day was always a day to celebrate LOVE, not being in a dating relationship. My parents would send me packages filled with chocolates and other Valentine's Day goodies, my sister would send me a cheesy Valentine's Day card. Behind the roses and chocolates, Valentine's Day is about LOVE. You can celebrate this day of LOVE WITH anyone you really just LOVE being WITH. It could be a co-worker, it could be a friend, it could be someone in your family, it could be just YOU; it doesn't have to be spent feeling bad that you are single.

I know this chapter may seem like it is about mainstream LOVE (i.e. heterosexual love), but I want to make it clear that by including this chapter in my book, I also endorse that a heterosexual relationship is by no means the end all be all to happiness. Furthermore, I want to make sure you understand the amount of work I did to date WITH myself, get to know myself, build a foundation for other relationships, and I am still doing even now. It is HAAAAAAAAAAAAAAAAAAAAAARD, but worthwhile.

What I Learned Dating With Edgar About Love

Edgar literally sees LOVE in the form of hearts everywhere: in leaves, in clouds, on walls, in almost the impossibly hard to see or find. He will find that heart and point it out. Something I learned and totally appreciated early on dating WITH Edgar is that yes, love is everywhere, and yes, he totally loved me, but there was more to this love thing than I ever thought possible. He taught me to love myself first.

How? You might wonder. Well, it was in all of my insecurities: when I would flop over on the bed because I couldn't fit into a tight dress, or when I would find a pimple. He would gently hug me, and tell me that I was beautiful on the inside and out. He could tell me until he was blue in the face, but one day, I finally realized a few months into dating him that I had to put myself first regardless of what he thought about me.

So I share this, our love story, WITH a caveat: this story is about a girl who meets a boy. She falls in love WITH him, he reminds her to fall in love WITH herself, and together they work on being better versions of themselves WITH each other and WITHin themselves.

Finding Love (ie. Dating)

I am a hopeless romantic.

Everything I learned about dating from a younger age came from movies. I always thought it would be simple: girl meets boy, boy and girl fall in love, girl and boy get married, and live happily ever after. Then I realized there was a whole lot of stuff that needed to happen in between the falling in love part and the getting married part. Not to mention the fact that it's not just about heterosexual love—there's a ton of other types of love out there. Oh, and happily ever after is a work-in-progress.

I see LOVE as a WITH concept if it is done in a healthy way. I often hear my students lament about how they don't have a girlfriend or boyfriend, how it is difficult to meet other students, or how their relationships don't work out and they are single again. When you try to date someone who doesn't want to be WITH you, or doesn't feel the same way you do, it can be very frustrating, because you are trying to date/love AT someone.

Looking back at my 20s and early 30s, I will admit I did a lot of AT dating and attempted quite unsuccessfully to fall in love AT guys rather than WITH them. Definitely one of the more WITH conversations you need to have is about SEX. If you are ready, make sure that you have a conversation to set the expectations, make sure you aren't being pressured, make sure it is special, meaningful, and that you know full well what kinds of contraception to use to prevent pregnancy and STDs/HIV/AIDS. Thus, you will have sex WITH your significant other.

Ok, but before you get swept away with all of these romantic notions, you have to remember that falling completely and utterly in love WITH yourself first is the foundation on which to build every single other relationship in your life.

Are You Still A V*?

This is the question my mom asked me right around the time I wasn't a V anymore. I was fortunate to have had an older sister in my life who guided me around the French kisses, different bases, STDs, and other things you would rather *not* discuss with your parents. It was doubly awesome because she was and still is in the public health field too. I remember at boarding school, telling her about my first boyfriend, and how I wished he wasn't such a slobbery French kisser. She and her best friend (who was eavesdropping on the conversation) were laughing—in a supportive, older sister kind of way. Later, that same best friend would grill Edgar at one of the bars he worked at on MIT campus, making sure he was dating WITH me for the right reasons.

I lost my V fairly "late" in the game compared to most people. I was pretty prudish in boarding school. I mean, some male friends and I would hold hands around campus, but it didn't mean we were dating; our relationship was still purely platonic—super confusing I know. Once, my high school boyfriend P and I were caught making out in the classrooms underneath the chapel, and he was just giving me a massage, and I just had my top off. My bra was still on, as were my pants. I am not sure to what extent P was clothed. Another time, a male friend and I were at our grad night party, and I literally slept on top of him, both of us fully clothed, nothing happened. I am not sure if it was because boarding school was like a fish bowl and everyone was in everyone's business (including teachers) or if it was the stress from the amount of work we had to do, but I did not feel ready to lose my V, so I didn't.

* My mom would use the word V in place of Virgin. Don't ask me why. Asian moms, I tell you.

In college, I tried to date as well, but was quite focused on my schoolwork and doing well in my internships. Don't get me wrong, freshman year, my friends and I made a few (maybe too many) trips to Tijuana (which we nicknamed TJ) in Mexico, because we could legally drink there, but overall, there weren't many guys to date. Then I met P2 (Yes, his name also began with a P). He went to San Diego State, the cooler party school. UCSD at the time was a dry campus, meaning we were not allowed to have alcohol legally on campus. He drove a really cool red mustang, old school with a stick shift that he had tuned up himself and saved up to buy on his own. He was so cool, but he wasn't dickhead cool, he was nice cool and treated me as such.

We had been dating for several months and had come close to doing the deed, but I was never really ready. I wanted our first time to be special. It was my senior year spring, Memorial Day† weekend. We used his Sheraton points to book a hotel room nearby. I don't really remember the details, except he had brought tiny bottles of alcohol (the kind you get on the airplane) to calm his own nerves. He wanted me to have the best experience possible. I do remember afterwards, after I didn't have an orgasm and he did, exclaiming, "I didn't bleed!" And that was how I lost my V.

Although I didn't have an orgasm then, I would later have many WITH P2 and I was just grateful that on that fateful night, we had sex WITH each other.

Ex-Men

When Edgar and I first started dating, he couldn't believe that I was actually still friends WITH some of the guys I had dated. I mean to me, you spend so much time and energy developing the relationship, not to mention the level of intimacy is unparalleled, you might as well, right?

Someone once told me, "It's not about the relationship itself, it's about how it ends."

If we look at our past relationships and we are able to learn WITH our significant other, not just about ourselves, but what we are looking for in a significant other, then we can take that into the next relationship and not make the same mistakes.

---

† Memorial Day is observed on the last Monday in May to honor those who died while serving in the armed forces.

What I have learned ~~from~~ WITH guys I have dated (one date to a few months of dating):

Greek Guy: He literally almost threw his back out working for a start-up. We need to have more balance in our lives than that. Physical and mental health should be a priority.

Apply Guy: He worked on his family's apple orchard in Washington. Being a farmer can be quite rewarding work; don't need to be an office worker.

FBI Guy: Six packs aren't everything; just because you are physically strong, doesn't mean you are mentally strong too. I learned how to use a real gun! It was super heavy.

Frugal Guy: Don't be too cheap; value what is important in life. It is not about the price, but about life.

Entrepreneur Guy: Failure is not an option; diverse people lead to diverse thinking. Start your own thing now.

Lawyer Guy: Money can only get you so far; there is a level of stress that comes with that kind of money/lifestyle; his Porsche couldn't fit into a back alley; he probably didn't really even have time to enjoy it!

Spiritual Guy: Breathe. Everything happens for a reason. Look inward not outward. Seek balance within yourself. The world is beautiful and so are you. Be kind to yourself.

Friend's Co-Worker Guy: Everything in life is fleeting and temporary. He said this to me as he pointed out the sunset on his rooftop.

SELF WORK:
What have you learned from people you have dated WITH? If you haven't dated yet, what have you learned from other relationships WITH people in your life?

Setting The Ground Work (By Yourself, For Yourself + With Yourself)

I was an angsty 20 something, wanting to date, feeling ready to date. During my 20s, I heard all kinds of advice from people around me: Some good, some of it terrible, and some of it just plain awful. Before you even consider attempting to date (so you don't end up like I did when I was in my late 20s/early 30s), here is how to set the groundwork and make sure your dating relationships progress from AT → WITH:

STEP 1: TABLE FOR 1, PLEASE?!

Be happy WITH yourself. It may sound like an oversimplification, but it cannot be overlooked. If you are not happy WITH yourself when you are alone, someone else will not make you happier (for more on this see part below on YOU (DON'T) COMPLETE ME!). So this means be happy going out WITH yourself, eating WITH yourself, taking yourself out to the movies, and so on. You get the picture.

STEP 2: DESPERATE IS NOT A GOOD LOOK

Believe you me, being desperate will only get you so far. I have had my fair share of relationships where I really, really, really, did I say really (?) wanted to just be in a relationship and so you can imagine how my neediness made the guys actually run in the other direction. Think about it this way: the more you squeeze tightly on to someone, the more they will try and wriggle and writhe to get away from you.

STEP 3: DO COMPROMISE BUT DON'T COMPROMISE YOURSELF

Some of my guy friends from boarding school, at our 10-year reunion confessed to joining a yoga class in order to…wait for it…meet more women. It is laughable, because it is at least healthy if you don't end up meeting anyone, but try not to go to extremes to meet someone to date. Rather, think about the things you love doing: maybe you love hiking? Why not start a Facebook group for hikers and meet a fellow hiker?

You (Don't) Complete Me!

All of my notions of love and sex were created through movie watching. I always imagined from a young age that I would be rescued by some handsome prince on a white horse. Then as a teenager, beginning to (kind of) understand notions around sex, first in my human development course at boarding school as a sophomore, then in movies, I thought sex was something that would last 5 minutes (!). Later in my 20s, I would watch romantic comedies and follow the series *Sex & The City*‡ religiously for a slightly more realistic (still dramatized) view of relationships, dating, sex, and love.

I have always been and continue to be a hopeless romantic though. I always imagined that there would be that one person who would sweep me off my feet—and if he so happened to be a prince, that would be fine too. After watching *Jerry Maguire,* a movie that came out in 1996 (when I began my college years), I idealized Tom Cruise's character Jerry Maguire. In order to woo Renee Zellwegger's character Dorothy (a single mother), he says, "You complete me." It seemed full of romanticism, I remember crying when he delivered this line, people all across the world swooned, I am sure. However, my therapist at Harvard said this about his line, "That line is so dangerous. You should never be completed by a guy or anyone for that matter. You should complete yourself first."

Looks Are Only Skin Deep

Those of you who have seen any of the *50 Shades of Grey* movies (or read the books), may also be familiar with the critics who say if the character of Mr. Grey was a fat slob who had no money, no woman would want to touch him let alone allow him to do all kinds of kinky stuff to them in some sequestered room in his house. Our world is indeed a superficial one. Just a quick look at any magazines, commercials, models, we can easily see what kinds of people we value as "beautiful." However, your world, the world

---

‡ An American TV series that follows the dating lives of 4 American women.

that you create WITH your future partner doesn't have to be that way. Don't just judge people by what they have or what they look like. Those things will fade. It is how they treat you that should concern you the most.

You Ain't Nothing But A Gold Digger

To quote a famous line from Kanye West's song *Gold digger*, trust me, you don't want to concern yourself with how much someone has, but rather, what they value. Recently a student of mine lamented at how her ex-boyfriend had made her feel bad, because her family didn't have enough money as his. After congratulating her on the breakup, (*Imagine if they had actually gotten married?! What a disaster!*) I told her about how Edgar never judges me on how I spend my money. In fact he encourages me to spend my money on pampering myself. So rather than worrying about how much money your future partner has or may have, worry that your values align. My mom always told me, "A rich man can become poor, but a poor man, can also become rich."

Learning How To Date With: Or How I Met My Husband

It is cliché, but LOVE happens when you least expect it to and/or you're over it. It is safe to say, I spent the majority of my 20s and the early part of my 30s dating AT people. Something happened when I turned 34 though. The summer of 2012, I tried dating AT someone who was a friend, and it totally backfired. After that, I told myself: *No more.* I was done. A few weeks later, that's when I met Edgar.

"Hey, would you like a gin and tonic?" he asked innocently as he was holding not one, but three between his two hands. He went on to explain that he had originally bought the drinks for his friend who was at her bachelorette party, but upon trying to find her to bestow the drinks upon her and her friends, he had found that they had left preemptively because she had apparently already had one too many gin and tonics prior to his arrival.

It was my first time back in Boston in over 5 years. The non-profit I had worked at before, had left me with wounds so deep, it had taken 5 years to heal--finally. That summer of 2012, I had decided to stop by Boston on my way to Wisconsin. A co-worker/friend of mine from Yonsei,

L was getting married to her Korean man, so me and two other co-workers/friends decided to share a hotel room. Before heading east, I had just about had it with dating. The last straw was yet another smart, driven, yet had no time for me kind of guy. I was officially over guys.

"Remember the guy I was with for 7 years? Well, he got some girl he barely knew pregnant, and now he is going to marry her just because he feels bad, not necessarily because he loves her." My friend Jamie was not in the best of moods that night. Since we hadn't seen each other in so long, after our dinner in the North End§ with another mutual friend, I decided that we should shake things up a bit and go dancing. I wanted to return to my "old 'hood" of Cambridge. My girlfriends and I used to frequent a place called The Middlesex Lounge. It was low key, you could move your seats around, it was a great place to start the night off, so that is where we headed. The line was out the door, so Jamie suggested The Phoenix Landing in Central Square**. I had never been, but was excited to see the line was less long.

After getting in and settling down, we perused the men who were there. We sat on a couch--it was the perfect perching ground to peruse and not be seen—and we chatted, checked out guys, talked strategy, and chatted more. Once the music started and people started dancing, Jamie decided she was going to talk to one of the two Black guys in the bar. I wished her luck and told her to make smart choices, and of course, be safe. Little did I know what fate awaited me that night.

"Well, it's ok if you don't want the drinks. I guess I'll drink them." With that he decided to knock the first drink back. I looked at him. He seemed nice, fairly innocuous, and very attentive; he had that dark handsome stranger look about him. I found myself surprisingly open to talking to him. Just two short years ago, I only dated a certain type of guy. It wasn't until I came to Korea, and went out with one of my co-workers one night, that everything changed for me. Here is that story:

(May 2011)

Remember the Guy in the Corner

"Before we go, I want to dance with that guy!" D exclaimed.

I looked over at the other side of the

---

§ The North End is the "Little Italy" of Boston.

** Central Square is MIT's answer to Harvard Square.

dance floor to find not a hunk of a man, but a rather portly, shy-looking Korean guy with a wave that covered the upper part of his forehead almost to make up for the shaved back side of his head. He was standing in front of the AC-wise choice-considering the small bar/dance floor that we had happened upon randomly and happened to play awesome 70s/80s music (YMCA, U Can't Touch This, Dancing Queen to name a few) had barely any ventilation other than that one AC.

Sensing my disapproval she said, "Hey, never discount those guys in the corner. You know, I was always told that I was the prettiest girl in high school, but no one asked me to prom 'coz they were too intimidated! So it wasn't until this shy, nerdy guy asked me that I had a prom date-finally."

I couldn't imagine her not being asked to prom. At 5'7, she was a blond bombshell. Originally from Nova Scotia, Canada, one of three from her high school to actually leave her tiny insular town of Mabou, she definitely attracted an enormous amount of attention here in this tiny 80s music haven and in the outside world as well.

After telling her how much attention she was attracting, she merely shrugged and humbly said, "It's only because I am a novelty. I'm a foreigner. That's all. If they thought you were a foreigner, you'd get the same amount of attention."

She had been through a lot this past year: her husband and her were in the middle of a not-so-amicable divorce, he was trying to get half of her pension, one of her best friends had recently died, and even more recently her entire handbag had gotten stolen. This left her carrying around one of those Velcro wallets that were all the rage in the 80s.

Yet she remained stubbornly optimistic.

She put her drink down and marched purposefully towards him. He was as bewildered as the other males who had been following her every move in the bar. It was this sense of courage, this sense of I-don't-give-a-crap-about-what-others-think-yet-I-will-treat-others-with-respect confidence that I admired.

Then there was the funny dance guy who knew how to bust a move to MC Hammer's "U Can't Touch This!" It was these very moves that made D and I laugh out loud as well as the English words he so valiantly strung together, as if he were piecing a puzzle together, except the pieces somehow didn't quite fit: "I'm hot! I need shower! He said as he flapped his shirt up and down in a vain attempt to get some air up there. He would do this several times throughout the night.

I told him to take it off to which D suggested, "Why don't YOU take it off for him?!" I shied away like a timid middle school student who had been asked to partner with a cute boy for a math assignment. Where had my confidence gone? Why was I so embarrassed? Certainly I wanted to see his abs more than anyone there, yet I still couldn't muster the courage to lift his shirt up.

Then a woman approached us. "Hey, I'm KC. You guys have a lot of energy!" she said as she checked D out. Later on the dance floor, "You know, she's a lesbian right?" D winked at me. I admired her ability to be nice to everyone and have a good time with everyone whilst not giving them the cold shoulder. And by everyone I mean both the men and women who were interested in her.

Towards the end of the night, her number 1 fan was an ajoshi who only spoke in Korean, was my height, wore a baseball cap, and a fanny pack. He followed her around like a puppy, whispering sweet nothings in her ear in Korean. "What is he saying to you?!" I asked annoyed for her. "I have no idea," she shrugged without a care in the world and a big grin on her face. It's as if she had seen it all, been through so much and didn't sweat the small stuff or small guys for that matter anymore.

"I go now. I don't want. Errr...I call," he said as he held on to my hand that I had offered to say "it was nice to have met you." I thought it couldn't hurt to give funny dance guy my number, because he probably wouldn't call anyway, and even if he did, we wouldn't really be able to communicate with each other. And he seemed pretty sweet and innocuous. When D and I went to the bathroom, he thought we were leaving and like a loyal puppy, followed us to the bathroom telling me five times repeatedly after I had assured him that we were NOT leaving,

"I waiting you, always." I nodded politely and went into the bathroom.

What a sweet way to end a fun and spontaneous night; and a reminder to never overlook those guys in the corner, because at the very least, they could buy you a shot of tequila. Thanks D.

Back at the Phoenix Landing, the guy with the gin and tonics turned out to be a guy named Edgar. Edgar had told me that he was getting his Ph.D. in Bioengineering, he had sailed before, he was from Southern California, he had gone to UC Davis for undergrad where he was the graduation speaker, he had overcome seemingly insurmountable obstacles, and a whole lot more in between, but the conversation came to a screeching halt when he told me he had not one, but *two sewing machines* at home.

"Wait a second! Why do you have two sewing machines? Wait, are they Singer? My *Popo* used to sew my clothes by hand when I was growing up." He had noticed all of these details about my outfit as well. I was wearing a grey and black striped tank dress that I had gotten used at Buffalo Exchange in Berkeley. I was wearing yellow sandals with a slight heel and silver jewelry. He had noticed how well I had paired all of my jewelry. In my head I began thinking: *Wait a second, he has two sewing machines at home, he is paying attention to all of my jewelry…*

"Are you gay?!"

"Haha…funny you should mention that… my grandmother always asks me the same question because I have not given her any grandkids yet. I keep telling her that I am getting a Ph.D. at MIT." After which he sighed shaking his head. He was easy to talk WITH, not threatening nor intimidating, given his incredible academic achievements, he laughed ~~at~~ with himself, and was if anything extremely humble. I liked him, *but I would still make him work for it*, I thought.

"Would you like to take a taxi back to your hotel?" he asked sweetly worrying about my shoes. I actually wanted to walk. I love summer nights. I wanted to walk by the Charles River, so that's what we did. We walked hand in hand talking, laughing, joking. He took me through MIT and showed me a dormitory where he had previously lived and filled the night air with chatter and some kisses here and there.

"OMG! Look out!" I had been relaying the story of how I had met Edgar to my friend Katherine in Pittsburgh (my second stop on my east coast tour before going on to Wisconsin) where she had just begun her own Ph.D. program. She had come to pick me up from the airport, and almost rear-ended the car in front of us.

"I think he is great, but one of my main concerns is that he is a bit younger, and so our careers are not really at the same level." I confided in Katherine, something I had wanted to verbalize, outside of my head. "Well, does he have potential?" And it was the question that changed everything for me, because without a doubt, he did. I decided on a whim that I wanted to see him again, I wanted to invite him to be my plus one to L's wedding, so I sent him a text message asking him to come. Prior to that I quickly sent a Kakaotalk message to L asking her if it would be alright if I did end up bringing a plus one. She said it was fine and just wanted to know whether he wanted a beef/fish/vegetarian meal.

I had taken a run, and as usual, was running late. I had ended up by a park a little bit above the city. I wasn't worried about how I looked, nor the fact that I hadn't really showered, but what I would say to him. I mean, it was technically our first date, and here he was meeting me in Milwaukee of all places. Our first brunch date was perfect. We sat on a rooftop, soaking in the Wisconsin sun, chatting easily, as if we had been dating forever. Things were easy WITH Edgar. Silences were comfortable. After brunch, we sat on a patch of lawn by the hotel I was staying with my co-workers. We lay there joking about how we were the only two non-white people in the entire city, how we looked like we were running away from home, and at the laughability of the whole situation: I mean, we had just met the weekend prior, and here he was in Milwaukee. There we both were.

"I do NOT feel good…" D was throwing up in the bushes outside the church where L had just gotten married. The night before at the rehearsal dinner, D had drunk too much and literally woke up on my other co-worker's doggy bed on the floor (!). It was comical, but now, not so, because D was clearly hurting and we all still had a whole wedding reception/dancing to get to. Edgar (who had been bartending at the two bars at MIT) was no stranger to helping people with their hangovers. He quickly asked if it was ok if he ran to get her some ginger ale. I looked bewildered because he had been so thoughtful so quickly, and was running in the direction of a convenience store before I could even utter the words, "yes." D was clearly taken by how awesome Edgar was, as was I.

The following day, at L's parents' house in the suburbs, we all sat sprawled out in the back yard. L's sister was there with her three children. Two of the older girls were running around trying to hit Edgar with some small rectangular-shaped bean bags meant for playing bean bag toss. He was great with children, he was his usual innocuous self, giggling, playful, sweet. My mind wandered to an image of the two of us having children together one day, and then it was abruptly stopped by the reality of the situation: I live in Korea and he lives in Boston.

The following three years were spent doing long-distance: Skype and Kakaotalk became our best friends. I spent my vacation days in Cambridge while Edgar finished up his Ph.D. It was definitely challenging at times, but I would have to say Edgar made it work. He was always there, patiently, whether I had hit my head accidentally, or I was crying because I missed him, he was always there with a kind text or loving words.

HOW YOU KNOW YOU'RE DATING WITH SOMEONE:

- The person listens WITH you
- He/she is always there for you no matter what is going on
- The person never makes excuses to see you or spend time WITH you
- This person is extremely attentive to you and your needs
- There is no pressure to have sex or do other physical stuff
- This person is in it for the long haul

- He/she celebrates all of your quirks and idiosyncrasies
- He/she loves spending time WITH you but also WITH your friends/family
- This person appreciates who you are on the inside (not just the outside)
- He/she supports your career/dreams/goals and will be there for you when you achieve them and when you don't

When Did You Know?

I get this question from students a lot: "When did you know that he was the one?" You know, having dated guys who didn't really want to commit to me, I had a phobia that Edgar would leave. I always thought he would want to break up with me after a fight, after a particularly hard challenge, after something that was just too much. But he never did.

I think that there are pivotal moments in every relationship when you do know.

The Laundry Incident

Doing laundry in Cambridge in the winter was never my favorite thing. Since Edgar's apartment did not come with its own laundry machine, even though it was very spacious, we had to walk a block and a half to a Laundromat. Edgar would put all of our clothes in a cart and wheel it over ice, snow, slush and whatever else came between the laundromat and us. There was one particular time I put a $5 bill into the change machine and nothing came out. I was FURIOUS. Edgar calmly told me that it was not a big deal and that he would go to the 7-11 and get a roll of quarters for me instead. I threw a tantrum about losing my money, I mean, it wasn't about the $5, but it was about not getting any quarters in return. What I learned that day about Edgar and the way he sees money is that we really shouldn't sweat the small stuff in life. What was important and remains important to Edgar is that no matter how much money we have in life, money can come and money can go. We shouldn't cling on to money. It will not buy us our happiness.

The Lunch Incidences

We were in Virginia visiting my sister and brother-in-law at my brother-in-law's parents' house. My sister was pregnant at the time with my niece and putting away the leftovers of our Chinese takeout lunch. While my brother-in-law and I were enjoying our lunch and just sitting and chatting, my sister was in the kitchen clearing things away. Edgar went and helped her. He took the time to not just help her, but ask her *how* she wanted things put away, and more importantly, *how* Diane (my brother-in-law's mom) would want things put away. After another lunch outside at a Thai restaurant, my sister was craving something sweet. Edgar wasted no time, took to his phone to look up dessert places, and asked her, "Would you like cookies? Ice-cream? Cake?"

The Planned Parenthood Incident

We were out and about in Cambridge coming back from our favorite smoothie place in Central Square when Edgar was stopped by someone asking for money for Planned Parenthood. I continued walking, as I usually have no patience for these types of solicitations, but I turned back to see Edgar patiently explaining to the young representative that he already donated $5 a month to Planned Parenthood. I thought to myself: *Wow, this is how he treats complete strangers? But this is also the kind of cause he is putting what little money he had as a grad student behind? What a saint!*

The 7-11 Incident

"Hi honey, I may have to let you go." This was Edgar-speak for I have to hang up the phone for whatever reason. This particular time, he was buying something at 7-11 while chatting with me on the phone (I was in Korea and he was in Cambridge at the time) when he spotted what looked like a woman who had been abused pushing a shopping cart with her child in it. "I am going to go talk to her to see if I can help her." He ended up giving her the last $50 he had in his wallet, and calling a local domestic violence shelter, after talking to her and finding out that his hunch had indeed been correct.

So you can see, from each incident, it is not how he treated me, (because at that point in our relationship, I kind of already knew that he treated me really well and that he was really attentive to me and my needs), but rather how he treated other people around me: from complete strangers to people in need to my own friends and family. My good friend Izzy once told me that the person you end up WITH, your life partner, should be the person you respect most in this world. I never really thought I would ever be able to meet someone I respect *that* much until I met Edgar. We have been WITH each other ever since.

~~The~~ My Proposal

It was a balmy June night in Newport, Rhode Island. I had convinced Edgar to stay at a B&B, since he had never done so before. We had found this quaint B&B online. The floors creaked when we walked upstairs to our room, you could walk through the kitchen in the morning to smell the delicious aroma of a home-cooked breakfast, and there was a lovely koi pond just outside where we could munch on our home-cooked breakfast. We took some selfies in the room, in front of the ROMANCE sign in the living room downstairs and headed out to our farm-to-table dinner.

"Let's go watch the sunset!" Edgar suggested upon devouring our chocolate chip cookies. *Perfect. This is going to be easier than I thought.*

We walked to the beach, found a bench to watch the sunset holding hands, no one was around. It was the perfect place to propose, but then:

"Ahhh…I have to go pee!" I exclaimed annoyingly, knowing I might be foiling my own plans. "Yeah, me too, actually." Edgar chimed in.

After walking almost two blocks, stopping in at stores along the way to check if there were any bathrooms to relieve ourselves, we finally happened upon a bar. Without even listening to Edgar's hesitation to go in, I walked straight in, asked if we could use the bathroom, and finally felt relief. Even though it was not the bench we had previously found, we happened upon a small pier that led out to a small gazebo, which was crowded with people. We walked out, not wanting to miss the sunset, but there were too many people, so we decided upon a small humble ledge made of rock, where we sat and watched the sunset instead.

"I have a present for you…" Edgar's birthday was coming up in July, but the "present" if you will, was not intended for his birthday, it was actually for a different purpose. A month prior, I had been taken with the notion that I wanted to propose. I hated the idea that women (in heterosexual relationships) had to wait for men to decide or even worse hint at it and get into fights about it. Growing up watching movies, yes, I was taken by the fantastic proposals, and yes, it was really romantical when men got down on one knee to propose, but hold on, we are living in the 21st century, right? Women have had the right to vote for decades now, so shouldn't we also have the right to propose? So I marched out and bought a USB stick from the Yonsei bookstore with a Swarovski crystal pattern on top. I thought it was perfect because it came in a ring-like box. I also thought it would be a nice touch to download all of our photos on to this USB stick so Edgar could have them. Moreover, I thought it would be a practical gesture, because he was collecting a ton of data while getting his Ph.D. at MIT. He could use it to store all of his data.

I was beginning to really empathize WITH those men who were super nervous before they had to propose. My heart started palpitating, my palms were sweaty, the sun was setting, I knew it was now or never. My plan was to read the proposal I had written on my notepad in my iPhone, but tears started streaming down my face. Edgar was bewildered. I found out much later that he thought I had taken him there to break up with him (!). What an awkward car-ride back to Boston that would have been, we later joked.

"Here honey, can you read this?" I passed him my iphone so he could read the proposal I had written for him. It was the longest one minute of my life. He looked at me, almost in disbelief, and then said, "Yes, I would love to be your husband." After all the tears, we took more selfies, and then decided to go to an arcade to play skee ball. What better way to celebrate?

Thank you Edgar for teaching me how to date, love WITH another human. I love you.

Here are some pictures from that fateful night:

Me + Edgar | Newport Beach, Rhode Island | June 2014

Ok, but hold it right there. Cue that screeching pause music you often hear in the movies! We will not be ending this chapter just yet…

Love All Of Yourself WITH Yourself

Ok, back to YOU and falling in love WITH yourself. I had never masturbated until after I had sex for the first time. I kind of regret it. I think there is some sort of weird stigma when women talk about it or do it at all. I don't know why. So the last thing I want to say in this chapter is explore ALL of yourself WITH yourself. Men: we all know you do it too (!). Figure out the things that feel good, don't feel good, get to know the nooks and crannies of your body, such that when you have to gently guide/coach your new dating partner, it will be easier for both of you. You will be able to tell this person what works and doesn't work for you. Plus, during those dry spells of singledom, you will know how to please yourself!

And of course, enjoy pleasing yourself WITH yourself!

SELF WORK:
Ok, put this book down, and LOVE all of yourself WITH yourself, whether that is masturbating, exploring yourself sexually, or massaging parts of your body. Just physically love yourself! Write some notes of how you felt afterwards. Enjoy being truly WITH yourself!

Doodles/Takeaways/Reflection Points

TRAVELING WITH A CULTURE/COUNTRY

CHAPTER 14

TRAVEL DIARY (TRAVELING WITH YOURSELF/DESTINATION COUNTRY)

"Traveling is when true living happens WITH you if you do it right." ~me

I feel the need to justify this chapter. Perhaps it is because the relationship between traveling and WITH vs AT is not that clear, or the fact that my editor didn't understand why I had included this chapter in my book, so allow me to explain. Traveling is a luxury, and I can't even begin to describe all of the benefits. What I want to express here is that I think so many people travel without really traveling. That is to say, they travel AT cultures/people/food rather than WITH. An example of this is group bus tours, where people are dropped off at one location, they take that one selfie, upload it to Facebook, and move on to the next place. There is nothing wrong with this type of traveling, but what have you truly learned about the amazing new country you're in? What about its people? Culture? And most importantly yourself?

Something magical happens when you travel. Time stops. All your senses are heightened, because every single landscape is breathtaking, every single bite of food is mouth-watering, every single step begins an adventure, and you just never know where you will end up and what you will end up doing. You don't have to go far, you don't even have to leave your own country, but exploring new destinations pushes you to be someone you didn't think you were capable of being. It takes dating WITH yourself to new heights: you can't just run back home and hide, you have to face yourself WITH yourself in completely new environs.

The countries I chose to represent here—Rwanda, Cambodia, and Finland—I believe are not typical destinations for travelers. In each country though, I tried my best to travel WITH myself, but also WITH each country's people, culture, food, and so much more. Thereby completely pushing myself outside of my comfort zone. I dare you to do the same WITH yourself.

Oh and don't forget to journal this journey. One day, when you are 108, and you are sharing your experiences WITH your grandchildren about that time you had a Turkish bath in Turkey or that time you took a spontaneous train trip to the coast, you may just want to show them your writing, or share a story that will change their lives in ways you can never know. You may want to start journaling your very own WITH legacy.

Let's begin WITH Rwanda. Here are some excerpts from my diary which I wrote in Rwanda whilst there:

(February 2012)

RWANDA

In a land far, far away from South Korea, not only in terms of geography, but also culture, food, customs, and the list continues, my sister works in a village called Rwinkwavu. It lies in the eastern province a few hours drive from the capital city Kigali. To give you an idea of its size: there is only one restaurant called Coco Park, which doubles as a salon, a shop, and anything else you perhaps desire. She is working on her PhD. on community health and works concurrently for Partners in Health (PIH), an NGO.

DAY 1

"Do you have any brothers or sisters?" It was the most common question I had been asked whilst traveling through parts of the Middle East and parts of Africa, because it would often extend the typical small talk conversation by at least an additional five to ten minutes given large families were quite common out here.

"I am an only child. It is only me," J responded. J was a teacher my sister's co-worker had connected me with. There goes a road block for my small talk plan. I could feel my brain scrambling for another topic. After all, we had only just begun our 45-minute walk to the local elementary school.

"Do you know the war of 1994?" He was referring to the genocide.

"Yes, yes I do." I was worried where he was going with this question.

"Well, my parents were killed in that war and my brothers and sisters. So I am alone."

It was the first time I was able to put a human value and face on the genocide. Last year when I came to visit my sister, I took a taxi to the Genocide Museum outside of Kigali. I remember being so traumatized by the images and everything else I read and saw about not only Rwanda's genocide, but also other genocides around the world, that I actually walked all the way back to the town center in flip-flops. I later found out from my sister that it was a 3-mile/almost 5km walk. I mean, it's not every day in my world that you meet someone who has lost an entire family to genocide. What scared me even more was my sister had told me on one of our long car rides driving in Rwanda that people have been saying that if Paul Kagame, the current president does not get re-elected for another term, then genocide may occur again. To me, that was as incomprehensible as the images I saw at the genocide museum.

"What is genocide?" This question came up in my World Issues class at Yonsei. It made me sad to even have to define it for my students. It was almost as if any kind of definition would not do any kind of justice to all of the mothers, fathers, daughters, sons, and babies killed because of their race, religion, or some other ridiculous superficial quality.

Then I thought, genocide is the most extreme form of AT behavior against any group of people who have had to suffer from this cruel discrimination.

After the almost 45-minute walk, I was eager to see what the village elementary school looked like. I felt like a super star walking into the school, because several of the younger students were waving, racing out of their classroom, and yelling to get my attention. The muzungu ("foreigner" in Kinyarwanda) had arrived. I was told that I was to go check out a library that was built by a guy named Myles who had his frat brothers donate books. I wasn't expecting much, but was pleasantly surprised to see an array of books that were neatly placed in sections by level. There were even four packs of brand-new Crayola crayons. Ooooh I love crayons!

After the students took turns reading a book about birds and measurements, John told us to stop reading. I wasn't sure if I should at that point start teaching or what I should do, so I naturally started to teach. We played a color game, a number game, and I was just so lost for what to do with them, because I hadn't worked with kids in such a long time, I found myself stalling. The students were 6th graders and had a level of understanding similar to my 6th graders I had taught in Japan. They seemed bright-eyed and motivated, contrary to what I was expecting. Up until that point, my only interaction with Rwandan children was being pointed at, intermingled with "Good morning" and "How are you?" So you can imagine my surprise when we played the games and the students were actually able to point out colors and numbers in English.

2 hours of teaching and a 45-minute walk in the sun later, I was not only mentally exhausted, but physically exhausted. During the walk back, J drilled me on marriage culture in "my country." I was hoping he wasn't going where I thought he was going with the topic. Unfortunately he was: "So, would you marry a Black man?" That was a loaded question. I couldn't really tell him honestly that I wasn't attracted to Black men, because that would be a tad offensive, so I lied and said, "Why not? Love is love." Did that make me racist?

I later found out that he was indeed interested in dating me.

DAY 2

Today's volunteer assignment: distribute Toms' shoes to some kids in the village. It seemed like an easy enough task. I was secretly hoping that we wouldn't have to walk there, but then again, was I being too bourgeois actually hoping that I would get afforded a luxury only afforded to upper class Rwandans? My sense of guilt was replaced with relief when I saw the pick-up truck we were to take to the school, especially since we were literally mobbed by students hugging us and surrounding us once we got out of the trucks. It was the closest I have been to feeling like a movie star.

"I don't like how she gets so bossy," Jackie was referring to Hope's bossy tone with the students to get them to line up in proper lines. Jackie and Hope both worked for PIH. "She is being that muzungu in a developing country," she continued. I looked over at Hope seeing her efforts not being realized and went over to draw a line in the dirt. The students soon scuttled behind it. I wondered if any of our efforts really mattered. The students looked temporarily thrilled, akin to the first few moments you unwrap a gift only to find out later that you don't actually like it or want it. That second part was hitting the students slowly but surely as the shoes didn't seem to fit them and they wanted to return them.

"Can we have them sit down, Vincent?" I asked looking anxiously at the tiny elementary students who were getting antsy waiting for the shoes we were running out of. He was in charge of operations and Connor, another PIH staff member was working to train him. "They can stand," he commented not even really thinking about what he just said. I didn't want to overstep any boundaries. I mean, who was I to make any kind of demand? It was bothering me though. The teachers weren't really helping to keep the students in line, Hope was motioning with her hands and barking orders in English that they didn't understand, and the kids (whom I didn't blame at all) just wanted their free shoes. It was a bit of a mess. Later on Hope asked Vincent if they could sit down and he finally relented.

Finally, I thought.

So, this is when you wonder: what difference are we making if any? Are these kids really going to wear their new Toms' shoes? On the way to the school, Connor said that because the kids walk around bare-footed so frequently, their feet were often wider, which proved to be difficult when trying to find shoes for them. I looked around at the tiny feet covered in the ubiquitous red dirt that was now a part of my clothing too and noticed that most of the students were wearing plastic open-toed shoes of neon colored variety. Was squeezing into tight or loose Toms shoes better than going bare foot? Toms made sure that every pair they sold in the developed world, a pair would be given for free to those in the developing world. How noble, but was it actually practical, realistic? I am still left wondering. The people here are very relaxed. People will wait at the cashier for you and not even yell at you or give you a dirty look if you are delayed in finding your wallet or pulling out money. It seems as if everything runs in slow motion. During a golden monkey trekking expedition in the northern part of Rwanda, I was speaking with our guide, Paul. He asked where I was from and I told him that I was teaching in South Korea and how it couldn't be more different. He asked how different and I went on to explain the slowness. I didn't want it to seem as if I was one of those negative muzungu who complain about everything under the sun, because it is NOT like their home country. I went on to say that it made me feel relaxed, unhurried, and it was a welcome respite from Seoul. He laughed and agreed.

I returned to Seoul, turned on my lights with the touch of a switch. I had a hot shower, running water, a multitude of restaurants to eat at, public transportation to hop on and off of. I was suddenly grateful for all of it and never took any of it for granted after my trip to Rwanda.

Thank you, Miu for sharing your Rwanda WITH me.

My conclusion: Everyone should go to a country in Africa in his/her lifetime. It is a truly eye-opening and humbling experience. And if you can, rather than superficially touring a country from the confines of an air-conditioned tour bus, actually get out there and mingle WITH the locals. It may just change your perspective on life.

At a school in Rwanda about to hand out Toms' shoes | Rwanda | February 2012

School children waiting eagerly for their new shoes | Rwanda | February 2012

A closer look at the shoes | Rwanda | February 2012

A truck carrying boxes of shoes in the background and students waiting around in the foreground | Rwanda | February 2012

(February 2016)

CAMBODIA (2/17–2/24/16)

"You know we drivers don't really make enough," the taxi driver lamented.

"Oh really? What kinds of professions make enough here?" I asked wanting to know more. I always found taxi drivers to be a terrific source of local information.

"People in IT, good with computers, business..."

"Oh I see."

"Yeah, for me, I make $180/month and one room to rent here in Phnom Penh is $150/month. One meal is about $3 so it is hard for me to support my family. My wife works in the rural area and she makes $120/month as a teacher. You know only 35% of the population here lives in Phnom Penh. The rest go back to the countryside because they cannot afford to live here."

I was trying to wrap my head around all of these numbers. I was still in that excitement phase of having just landed in a new country. Looking out at the streets, from what little I could see through the haze and darkness, I could already understand what my driver was talking about. The stark contrast between the haves and have-nots was already apparent. Most people were driving motorcycles with not just one person, sometimes an entire family on board, often without even helmets. Then there were the tuk tuk drivers (I later found out that foreigners were the only ones who actually used tuk tuks at about $2-5 a ride). Finally, those that really had that much more, drove SUVs.

Here is a selfie video of me on a tuk tuk. My driver Vincent (who is featured) was totally loyal. He waited for me throughout my stay in Phnom Penh, and picked me up on time whenever I needed him to:

In Korea, there is more of a middle class. The contrast between the haves and have-nots was not as stark, even though it is perhaps headed that way. I began to wonder: perhaps all developing countries look like this, no matter where in the world they are located. Shrouded in haze, trash here and there, a huge gap between the rich and poor, motorcycles, incomplete construction, mosquitoes everywhere. It kind of felt like Ecuador, Tanzania, Thailand, and other developing countries I had been to before. Perhaps I had been spoiled living in countries that had significantly developed economies. I read somewhere once (in grad school I think) that half of the world's population lives on less than a dollar a day. I believe it.

"I struggle with trying to wrap my head around the reality of the situation here and what I am preaching in my workshop. I mean, how can I really help the masses out on the streets just from my workshop?" I confided in Edgar during one of our conversations and later MK too. But then I thought back to Originals, Adam Grant's latest book on how people challenge the status quo and are actually extremely successful at it going on to change the world.

Grant brings up the story of a woman named Medina in the CIA who wanted to create an online system to share information. She found the archaic way of sharing information offline to be exceedingly slow and inefficient. She received a lot of backlash from her colleagues saying that because the information they were sharing was so sensitive, they had to share it offline. Fast forward, this same woman had moved up the ranks and become more senior. Two colleagues approach her about her previous idea to get information online and she was then able to convince those in power to create this online system. What was the difference between when she first brought it up to when she brought it up again the second time? She had more status within the organization, so people were more likely to listen to her. Grant argues, "Once Medina had accumulated enough wins, she started speaking up again-and this time, people were ready to listen."[1] He is basically saying that without power, you cannot create change, so you have to first work hard within an establishment or organization in order to then create change later. It is also important to note that Medina (the woman he talks about) is Puerto Rican and a woman. Thus, she had the double whammy of being a woman and a minority in a Caucasian male dominated industry.

Edgar voiced similar sentiments during our conversation and told me that when he went away to college in northern California, he felt bad leaving behind his family, friends, his community back in southern California. He wanted to help them, give back to them, and be the first in his family to attain a college degree. His mentor at the time, now an 85-year-old Irish grandpa of a man, said this to him, " If you cannot help yourself, you cannot help anybody." He was right. You have to help yourself first. I liken it to drowning. If you are drowning, and you want to try to save other people around you, you will all drown together, right? So I soothed my bourgeois guilt conscious by telling myself that I would be able to create change later. MK further noted, " Well, it is a good thing that you are thinking about all of this stuff, right? It will help inform your writing for your book. It is good to think of these things now, so later you can do something about it." It made sense.

I decided to spend some of my free time outside of my workshop to check out some organizations that were actually helping people change and better their lives for some inspiration.

I happened upon one in Phnom Penh, and two in Siem Reap. Since I have always been interested in the plight of women, I decided to check out Daughters of Cambodia in Phnom Penh, and Blossom Café and Vimean Beauty Salon in Siem Reap.

Daughters of Cambodia began as a non-profit helping survivors of human trafficking. Several years ago, they decided to open a store that sells goods made by these women and a café where the women worked. The result: a two-storey building with a café on top and a store on the bottom. I brought my conference buddy Kirk (an American guy who is a professor in Japan), and the two of us very much enjoyed being a part of something that would help these women. Kirk picked out necklaces for his wife and daughter, and I bought lots of omiyage ("souvenirs" in Japanese) presents for friends/students.

In Siem Reap, I went to the Blossom Café, which doubles as a training center for women. The cakes and cupcakes were absolutely divine, and the café itself acts as a wonderful reprieve on a hot humid afternoon. The women who work there are extremely *professional and kind. I enjoyed a banana cupcake with an iced chai latte my first visit, and then a caramel cupcake and an iced milk tea my second visit. Finally, I decided to get my hair cut and straight permed in Siem Reap and happened upon this beauty salon that also trains women. So I went and got my hair done. I was the only patron at the time, but I found all of the women to be very well trained. I had a lovely experience. They were even willing to go back to my hotel room with me to finish off the hot ironing when the power went out. Fortunately, it came back on within a few minutes, so we didn't have to resort to that.*

Here is a selfie video shot at the Blossom Café:

All in all, it was wonderful to see the change that people are truly creating in different ways. Perhaps I was not so far away from hatching a plan to help people lift themselves out of desperate situations. My workshops and my classrooms always prescribe action over passiveness, happiness over

complacency, helping others to help yourself, giving back to move forward, and social entrepreneurship. Perhaps I was more on my way than I thought?

Having conversations WITH local people from the taxi driver to the tuk tuk driver, to the empowered women was deeply inspiring.

(April 2016)

Finland (4/14-4/22/16)

"I am so incredibly grateful that all of you took time out of your busy schedules to come to this Global Leadership dinner that Ilkka put together. I thought: How could I possibly show my gratitude to all of you? So I decided to write cards to you, inspired by Ilkka's students who did something similar in their Happy Laurea* videos," I said nervously handing out my hand drawn and handwritten cards.

I looked out at the 20 or so people whom Ilkka had handpicked to come meet me in person, support me, share

---

* Laurea University of Applied Sciences in Finland (where Ilkka was a Digital Business lecturer at the time) is the place where I gave The Happiness Workshop to his students.

ideas WITH me, and of course eat WITH me. It had begun as it always did with Ilkka and me: on a weekly Skype call. We would talk about our week, discuss ways in which we could collaborate, and hash out our crazy ideas WITH each other. The Skype calls began at a lull in my career: during the winter of 2016, as with most winters, I was in a fog of depression and a blanket of self-doubt in deep hibernation. I wanted to move forward with my ideas of public speaking, get the happiness workshop more out there, start getting paid to speak, and so much more, but I was incapacitated by my fear of failure. Ilkka and I began our Skype calls just to hash out ideas, but then most of our ideas became realized. We became each other's support, mentor, collaborator, and then I thought, Hey why not go to Finland again, meet Ilkka's students in person, and see what other craziness we could get up to? Ilkka was beyond himself when I finally decided to tell him.

Monday, April 18th 2016

We decided to keep my visit a secret so we could surprise his students. He was teaching a Digital Business course during the spring, and his students had interacted with my students respectively in the form of selfie videos. My students had come up with the idea for me to bring Korean snacks and real letters over as a gift, and in return, Ilkka's Finnish students would send me back with the Finnish equivalent. Ilkka and I could barely contain our excitement, nervousness, and anticipation. Ilkka came up with the idea for me to pretend I was on a Skype call with them, when really I was in the next room "hiding" out with his team-teacher Anna. I walked in to Pharrell's Happy song, a song I liked to begin my Happiness Workshops with, and everybody was clapping! It was the closest I have ever been to feeling like a celeb-with the exception of that time I walked into a village full of children in Rwanda; in fact, I felt like I was walking in to the Ellen Degeneres Show (!)-one of my favorite shows.

The day went by in a blur. Here is the link to the edited version on YouTube that was created by Ilkka's students:

I was nervous as all hell, because I didn't realize that Ilkka was going to broadcast it live, but he gave me the best advice, which I often overlook: "Hey, just be yourself." So good.

Tuesday, April 19th, 2016

We returned to the place where one of Ilkka's fantastic students Melissa had created a response video after watching my TED talk. Ilkka had the idea to create a third video in the trilogy: 1) My TED Talk; 2) Melissa's video in response; 3) Collaborative WITH vs AT video. We began at a beautiful café that overlooked a lake, over salmon soup, we talked about what we would do, our ideas, and how they thought the week went. It was awesome to have that one-on-one time WITH two of his students. Melissa had brought Ile, another one of Ilkka's outstanding students, who helped out as our cameraman.

Melissa directed like a pro, coaching me on what to say, where to move, how to act, and interviewed me on the origins of WITH vs AT. Honestly, beyond the chilly weather conditions, it was one of the more challenging things I have had to do, because it had been a while since I had actually thought about my TED talk. I really dug deep about what it all even means. I am forever grateful to Ilkka, Melissa, and Ile for truly believing in my WITH vs AT idea, but also for pushing me both physically and mentally. I never imagined in my wildest dreams that I would be acting in this kind of video production in a forest in Finland. You can check out the video here:

Wednesday, April 20th, 2016

I must admit, I was a bit mentally and physically exhausted than I was on Monday. I was however, looking forward to watching the HAPPY LAUREA videos the groups put together. As always, when I assign this task, I am never sure how the videos will turn out, whether the students will actually do them, and the list of uncertainties continue to run through my mind. While I was filling out paperwork in Ilkka's office, one of the groups who was working on their HAPPY LAUREA video, actually came in and gave us both roses. It was so awesome. Ilkka mentioned that those students don't usually try that hard in class, so it made me smile even more.

The atmosphere in the auditorium had changed over night. Students were calmer, happier, they wanted to be there, it was such a change from Monday morning's class when students seemed really uneasy, tired, didn't want to be there. The student groups presented their HAPPY LAUREA videos one by one, and touched our hearts the more we saw. Ilkka and Anna were so touched that they were moved to tears in the back of the lecture hall. I was of course too.

Thursday, April 21st, 2016

The afternoon got off to a great start. I took myself out to the Helsinki Day Spa where I had a massage. My masseuse was an Indian man from Goa. He told me this hilarious story of how his son (he is married to a Finnish woman) went and told his teachers at school that his father spanked him, so my masseuse had to go down to the police station twice. My masseuse had to explain that in his culture, spanking lightly was a way to not only punish, but show affection. He said he never did it again after getting called to the police station (!). But all jokes aside, it really shows how seriously Finland takes child abuse.

Ilkka invited us (another Polish professor named Jacek and I) to his apartment; we got to meet his three-year old daughter Hilma and his wife Anna. I was amazed at how minimalist the apartment was and how uncluttered it was given they had a 3 year-old child. Apparently, Finnish babies are put outside (even in the winters!) to nap, because parents believe that the fresh air is healthier for their babies. They just wrap them up in a ton of blankets.

So, back to The Global Leadership Dinner that began as an idea on Skype, as with all things that Ilkka and I try to create, then became a Facebook event, and it was finally time for the actual dinner. Walking in to the private room at Blue Peter and meeting all of the guests was like walking into a house party. No one felt like a stranger, everyone felt like someone I knew, because everyone knew Ilkka. I had this crazy idea to have everybody draw what comes to mind when they think of a GLOBAL LEADER and then redefine what it means to be a GLOBAL LEADER in a selfie video. I was hesitant thinking that no one would want to do it, but everyone was extremely enthusiastic. Of course they would be, they are Ilkka's friends!

I naturally gravitated towards the women at the dinner. Camilla: she wrote a book in 6 months in which she also did all of the illustrations herself, created an Emotion Tracker app, and a company by the same name. You can check out her website here:

Riika: she is a corporate trainer. In her own words, she says, "I help people find their dream jobs." Very cool. Aida: originally from Sarajevo, Aida survived the war and is one of the warmest/kindest people I met that night. I unabashedly whispered to Riika and Aida: "I know this might sound *crazy, but if I lived in Finland, I feel like we would be besties."*

Anna (Ilkka's team teacher) and me | Finland | April 2016

Camilla's husband Pekka, me, Ilkka and Camilla | Finland | April 2016

Riikka and me | Finland | April 2016

Friday, April 22nd, 2016

Things I learned about myself while in Finland:

1. *Wow! When you put yourself out there, the sky really is the limit.*

2. *Perhaps there is more to WITH vs AT than I could have ever imagined, and thanks to positive people like Ilkka and his students/friends, I am now sure of this and myself more than before.*

3. *Everyone should be in the minority in their lifetime, because it is when you are in this state, true self-exploration, growth, depth happens.*

4. *Even though I didn't really know Ilkka that well before going to Finland, I can now call him a brother. He is*

truly a good person (and doesn't want anything in return), willing to help others, promote others, provide me WITH a platform (the dinner) in which to launch me and my work.

5. I am worth it! Sometimes you need a little push from those around you to remind you of that!

6. Perhaps there is a link between Bullying and AT.

7. I can be thought of as a future book writer (one of Ilkka's friends at the dinner asked if I have written a book-as if it were a very natural thing to have under my belt).

8. The Happiness Workshop can have profound effects on people (ie. Ilkka and Anna cried, the students pushed themselves beyond what they knew was actually possible). When I asked if I could include her blog link (which has since expired) in this book on Facebook Messenger, this was her response:

"Sounds great!!! I wish you all the luck and patience WITH your writing! I'm sure it'll turn out to be a great success and inspiration! Kyla, if only you knew how much you have given me *in the form of inspiration and belief that I will always find the truth when I'm open and willing to listen to my heart!!"*

9. *I still LOVE traveling (<3). I want to travel more, more, more.*
10. *Finnish food is so fresh and delicious. Yes, I could eat salmon 3 meals a day, everyday. I love me some Omega 3s.*

Oh, and here is the best advice Ilkka gave me the day before my Happiness Workshop when I was super nervous, when I told him my mom may have early onset dementia, and at every other super critical moment in my life:

Doodles/Takeaways/Reflection Points

AFTERWORD

At a café in *Gwanghwamun* after a lovely Thai dinner, there we were again, 8 years later: Jae-kyung, Ji Hye, and me. I had sent them a Kakaotalk message super spontaneously and asked if they could join me for dinner and an interview. We had been meeting once every few months prior to that to update each other on our lives, talk about life, and they were always ever so supportive of my latest crazy ventures, and I of theirs. As always, our laughter filled the café and overflowed with positive energy. It came to me that I wasn't really sure how to end this book, maybe I didn't want it to end, but that what I did know was that it began WITH them and how appropriate to end WITH them.

What has always struck me and impressed me about both of them is that they are extremely open-minded: Ji Hye was in her late 20s, she decided to quit her job last year as a clinical research associate and focus on studying German everyday intensively so that she can eventually be a "digital nomad" in her words and live and work in Germany. Jae-kyung, who just celebrated her 60th birthday last year, spent her summer vacations traveling to learn about new cultures and spent her winter vacations upgrading her skills or learning new ones (sewing, painting, art therapy to name a few). She recently revealed to us that night that she had founded her very own choir and they would be performing this Saturday evening—WHAT?! Of course, Ji Hye and I were overjoyed at the prospect of seeing our friend Jae-kyung sing for the first time and we were excited we could support her by attending.

> Kyla: Why do you think you are both so open?
>
> Ji Hye: (pointing to Jae-kyung) It's because of her! I never expected students at FLI would be her age, I assumed that they would all be in their 20s like I was at the time. But getting to know Jae-kyung who was always eager to learn something new like English, I thought was really inspiring. She changed my view on learning—it's never too late to learn something. I thought to myself that older people can be self-motivated and that they have no *grenze* ("barrier" in German).
>
> Jae-kyung: I also was used to working WITH younger people. I worked with a lot of younger people when I was teaching English at middle school. So it wasn't a big deal for me. When my second son was in 5th grade, I went back

into teaching English in middle school and I would tutor socioeconomically disadvantaged students for free.

Kyla: What?! That is so amazing. How did you find those students to tutor?

Jae-kyung: Well, I could just sense that they either didn't have a father or didn't have a mother at home.

Ji Hye: What? How?

Jae-kyung: I would look at their clothes. If their uniforms were super clean, but then they lacked confidence or looked super shy, I just knew intuitively they didn't have a father at home. If their uniforms were dirty, then they didn't have a mother at home. I would then ask their homeroom teacher, and I was always right. You know they are like little puppies in a big rainstorm—downtrodden. Yeah, some of those students are now in their 20s and they will call me and help me too! (She was beaming from ear to ear!) I am very good at first impressions.

Ji Hye: Wait, what was your first impression of me?

Jae-kyung: That you had a good mom and dad.

Ji Hye: Phew!

Kyla: What about me?!

Jae-kyung: You too. I could tell you had a very supportive childhood and you were really loved.

Kyla: Yes, that is totally true! Wow! Ok, what advice would you give our readers?

Jae-kyung: Break the *GRENZE!* Everyone has his/her own barriers WITHin which they have created themselves. But if you can really break free from your own barriers, you can live a really fantastic life. One of my former students, she always wanted to live in the U.S. for 6 months, so she did! Then she wanted to live in Jeju Island, so she is living there now and posting all kinds of beautiful photos on Facebook. She told me recently that the next time I go to Jeju, she would pick me up from the airport!

Ji Hye: I would tell a younger version of myself to talk more WITH my family. After my mom got cancer, and then survived cancer, I changed. I started saying "I love you" more to my mom, my dad, and even my brother.

Jae-kyung: I envy your mom!!

Ji Hye: It is still difficult at times. I try a little each week, and I try to remember to do it. Sometimes it is challenging to do it WITH my brother, but I still try. I wish I had done it sooner.

Kyla: But the important thing is that you are doing it now.

Ji Hye: Right. That's why I have always really liked Min Ju's (my husband's) family. They will often have spontaneous family meetings with wine and cheese, talk about life, and just be WITH each other. I realized after spending time WITH them, that I wanted to have that kind of family too with Min Ju.

(Ji Hye and Min Ju had just started dating when the three of us met at FLI in 2010. They stayed together over the years, and recently their parents met each other for the first time. A meeting called *Sanggyun rye* in Korean. Ji Hye had said the meeting went really well and she wasn't super nervous about it. They recently got married in September 2018! Edgar, Jae-kyung and I got to attend the wedding together.)

Kyla and Jae-kyung: How cool!

Jae-kyung: My advice would be to read more books. Real books like literature, humanities, and philosophy.

Ji Hye: Like our book club!!

Kyla: Great advice! Thank you. So I can hear readers and imagine them asking, "*How* do we overcome our own *grenze*?

Ji Hye: Start with small things. I hug my mom once a week.

Jae-kyung: Not every morning?! (Jokingly) One thing I learned is you can count down from 5,4,3,2,1, and then start! Also, say your intentions out loud in front of a mirror.

Kyla: Wow, that's a great strategy. How do you think our friendship has changed you? And over the years?

Jae-kyung: We could all be friends naturally, thanks to Kyla.

Ji Hye: Your smile!

Kyla: Awww…thanks!

Jae-kyung: Remember that time we went to that *mandu* ("dumpling" in Korean) restaurant? And you told us about Edgar for the first time? I still remember what you were wearing, your earrings. That was the first time I felt like we were all really friends because you were sharing WITH us something so deeply personal. And then we went to that temple nearby…

Ji Hye: Your laugh (looking at both me and Jae-kyung) always helps to break the ice!! I actually never felt bad about the fact that I couldn't communicate that well in English or that you would judge me. Sometimes I worry about that when I hangout with other people, but not you two.

Jae-kyung: Me too!

Kyla: Me three!

Jae-kyung: I was actually really impressed that you had gone to do volunteer work in Uganda…

Ji Hye: Oh, thank you. You remember that?!

Jae-kyung: Actually, talking with you both now, I realize that I am enough! I mean, even if I die tomorrow, I am enough.

(I was brought back to our conversation about legacy and funerals back at FLI.)

Kyla: That is so interesting you bring that up, because I often have that conversation WITH my students about living each day as if it is your last. What would you do differently if you knew this was your last presentation? Your last conversation WITH a friend? Your parents? Would you still live your life for someone else rather than yourself?

Ji Hye: I think about that with my parents. (Ji Hye began to cry.)

Jae-kyung: I think about that with my husband and my sons. (Jae-kyung began to cry too.) Sometimes when I am angry or upset I think about saying angry things, but then when I think about my words as being my last words to them I rephrase what I want to say in a kinder manner. It's like that TED Talk by that conductor[1]. He talks about meeting an Auschwitz survivor who was upset with her brother when they were children. Her last words to him were scolding words because he had forgotten his shoes. Now she says, "I will never say anything that couldn't stand as the last thing I ever say."

Kyla: Oh my gosh! I had that exact quote on my cupboard when I was living at Yonsei and teaching at FLI! Whoa…Thank you so much for coming here. I really appreciate your friendship and how you are both pioneers of your own generations. I hope the readers get inspired by your openness, your ability to overcome your own *grenze*, and create change WITH yourselves and WITH others around you. You are both true inspirations, really. I love how our friendship transcends age, *grenze*, and everything else.

I love you both, Jae-kyung and Ji Hye.

Then and now:

Me, Jae-kyung, and Ji Hye at FLI, Seoul, South Korea | 2010

Ji Hye, me, and Jae-kyung | At a café in Gwanghwamun | 2017

Jae-kyung, Ji Hye, and me | On our very first trip together in Namhae, South Korea | February 2018

GRATITUDE (OR ACKNOWLEDGMENTS)

The idea of writing a book is like running a marathon. Good on the outset, but once you start actually doing it, halfway, you're like: *Ummm…what was I thinking?!* Having written one now, I totally get why Murakami Haruki likens book writing to running marathons: it is all mind over matter.

Having said all of that, this book would not have been possible if it had not been for several amazing people in my life.

Everyone who had a starring role in this book: Thank you, thank you, thank you. You made this book shine!

My family (mom, dad, Miu, Bobo, LG, and Edgar): Thank you for your unconditional love and support, as well as being WITH me every step of the way.

My GIRL SQUADS around the globe: you know who you are. Thank you for never judging me, but believing in me so deeply. And being there through the good, the bad, and the ugly WITH me. Ling Cult: Thank you for 20+ years of support, drag downs, and friendship. Songdo Sistahs: Thank you for immediately accepting me into one of the most inspiring sisterhoods I have been a part of. WINners: Thank you for changing my life, and being an incredible global network to be reckoned WITH. Harvard + UCSD Ladies: Thank you for never settling on love, life, career and so much more, and inspiring me to do the same.

My editor Luke and translator Youngmi: if it weren't for your technical support, I would not have been able to pull this off. But beyond your technical support, it was your unwavering belief in me and WITH vs AT that really made this book come to life.

Bo: The Graphic Designer who said we could! Thank you for your talent, creativity, and vision.

My students: thank you for inspiring this book, pushing me and encouraging me to finish it and teaching, learning and growing WITH me. I am forever grateful.

My family spirit guides: *Popo*, Grandma Kay, Grandpa Mike. I will always love you and you will always be WITH me in my heart.

Ilkka: I'm not sure how my life would have turned out if I hadn't met you, or if you hadn't introduced me to the most amazing + inspiring network of people in Finland—your network. But I know that my world and my life have become that much more positive and awesome since we started collaborating. Thank you for everything.

My Coach friends: Thank you for doing the work on yourself WITH yourself and inspiring me to do the same. Dom (PHD): Thank you for EMPIRING me and being WITH me at mile 25.

Maxine: My life coach extraordinaire! Thank you for pushing this project forward and reminding me of the fierce woman I am.

Szilvia: My Frisky Friend/Spiritual Coach! You have been an incredible gift from this universe. Thank you for believing in me and this journey since the very first time we met in Bali. I love you!

MK: You supported this book from beginning to end. Every time I doubted this book, or myself you were there WITH an encouraging word, text, hug. Thank you for believing in this project so deeply and profoundly. Looking forward to being 90 WITH you!

Edgar: The human I respect the most in this world, my best friend, the love of my life, my partner-in-crime, my biggest support system, my rock, the most positive person on this planet. I yobb you. High 4!

Finally, anyone and everyone who has touched my life and therefore this book, WITH a conversation here, a comment of support there, a Facebook post, a text message, an email, a phone call-- I will never forget how much you have given me and helped me grow WITH you.

ABOUT THE AUTHOR

KYLA MITSUNAGA is a Global Happiness Coach/Women's Empowerment Coach/Speaker/Award-Winning Professor/Founder of The Happiness Workshop. She realized her true calling and passion when she won her first teaching award at Harvard. She went on to teach at Yonsei University in Seoul for several years creating unique and innovative content for classes such as Career Development, Global Issues, Cross-Cultural Communication. She even created a course on Happiness for Freshman and won multiple teaching awards. In 2012, she was invited to be a TED@Seoul speaker; she recently trademarked her TED Talk title WITH vs AT. She has delivered innovative and dynamic corporate workshops as well as practiced one-on-one coaching all over the globe.

When not speaking or workshopping globally, you can find Kyla swimming, baking (without processed sugar), writing, finding the best eats in Korea, and mulling over women's rights.

Kyla has traveled to 46 countries and called 5 countries "home."

You can communicate WITH her here: www.kylamitsunaga.com

Author's Note

[1] Mathews, Jay. *Work Hard. Be Nice: How Two Inspired Teachers Created the Most Promising Schools in America.* Algonquin Books of Chapel Hill, 2009.

[2] Sandel, Michael J. *Justice: What's the Right Thing to Do?* Langara College, 2016.

[3] The Conan O'Brien Show: http://teamcoco.com/

Chapter 1

[1] Alter, Adam L. *Drunk Tank Pink: and Other Unexpected Forces That Shape How We Think, Feel, and Behave.* Penguin Books, 2013.

Chapter 1.5

[1] Watson, Leon. "Humans Have Shorter Attention Span than Goldfish, Thanks to Smartphones." *The Telegraph*, Telegraph Media Group, 12 Mar. 2016, www.telegraph.co.uk/science/2016/03/12/humans-have-shorter-attention-span-than-goldfish-thanks-to-smart/.

[2] "Learning Pyramid." *The Peak Performance Center*, http://www.thepeakperformancecenter.com/educational-learning/learning/principles-of-learning/learning-pyramid/.

[3] "How I Built This with Guy Raz." *NPR*, NPR, http://www.npr.org/podcasts/510313/how-i-built-this.

[4] Gebbia, Joe. "How Airbnb Designs for Trust." *TED: Ideas Worth Spreading*, http://www.ted.com/talks/joe_gebbia_how_airbnb_designs_for_trust.

[5] M., Jan. "Why Dutch Children Are the Happiest Children in the World." *Netherlands Tourism*, 26 Feb. 2015, http://www.netherlands-tourism.com/why-dutch-children-are-the-happiest-children-in-the-world/.

Chapter 2

[1] Tatlow, Didi Kirsten. "Q. And A.: Shawna Yang Ryan on the 1947 Incident That Shaped Taiwan's Identity." *The New York Times*, The New York Times, 22 Jan. 2016,

http://www.nytimes.com/2016/01/23/world/asia/taiwan-shawna-yang-ryan-green-island.html.

[2] Cooper, Robert K. *Get Out of Your Own Way: the Keys to Surpassing Everyone's Expectations.* Crown Publishers, 2006.

[3] Cooper, Robert K. *The Other 90%: How to Unlock Your Vast Untapped Potential for Leadership and Life.* Crown, 2003.

[4] Johnson, Whitney. "What First Class Travel Says About Gender Inequality." *Time*, Time, 26 May 2016, http://time.com/4329919/flying-gender-inequality/.

[5] Edwards, Samantha. "New Study Says Hiking Makes You Happier." *Cottage Life*, 12 June 2017, http://cottagelife.com/news/new-study-says-hiking-makes-you-happier.

Chapter 3

[1] Ryan, Tim. *A Mindful Nation: How a Simple Practice Can Help Us Reduce Stress, Improve Performance, and Recapture the American Spirit.* Hay House, 2013.

[2] Kim, Larry. "Multitasking Is Killing Your Brain." *The Huffington Post*, TheHuffingtonPost.com, 7 Dec. 2017, http://www.huffingtonpost.com/larry-kim/multitasking-is-killing-your_b_9821244.html.

[3] "Dan Millman Presents The Peaceful Warrior's Way." *The Peaceful Warrior's Way*, http://www.peacefulwarrior.com/.

Chapter 4

[1] Waldinger, Robert. "What Makes a Good Life? Lessons from the Longest Study on Happiness." *TED: Ideas Worth Spreading*, 23 Dec. 2015, www.ted.com/talks/robert_waldinger_what_makes_a_good_life_lessons_from_the_longest_study_on_happiness?

[2] Grant, Adam M. *Give and Take: a Revolutionary Approach to Success.* Phoenix/ Orion Books, 2014.

[3] . "Monday Convocation | Kyla Mitsunaga '96." *Cate School*, 10 Feb. 2017, http://www.cate.org/2017/01/monday-night-convocation-kyla-mitsunaga-96/.

[4] "Health Status - Suicide Rates - OECD Data." *TheOECD*, https://data.oecd.org/healthstat/suicide-rates.htm.

[5] Walters, Natalie. "Brothers Who Cofounded a $100 Million Company Say This Question Their Mom Asked Every Night at Dinner Is What Inspired Their Business." *Business Insider*, Business Insider, 17 Dec. 2015, http://www.businessinsider.com/life-is-good-founders-say-this-question-inspired-their-business-2015-12.

Chapter 5

[1] That "it" is job hopping. A new study networking site LinkedIn found that young people really do change jobs a lot more than their parents did. "The New Normal: 4 Job Changes by the Time You're 32." *CNNMoney*, Cable News Network, https://money.cnn.com/2016/04/12/news/economy/millennials-change-jobs-frequently/.

[2] "Youth Unemployment Rate in Korea Reaches Highest in 15 Years." *The Korea Herald*, 26 July 2015, http://www.koreaherald.com/view.php?ud=20150726000328.

[3] Markowitz, Eric. "Entrepreneur of the Year: Aaron Levie, CEO of Box." *Inc.com*, Inc., 26 Nov. 2013, http://www.inc.com/magazine/201312/eric-markowitz/aaron-levie-entrepreneur-of-the-year.html.

Chapter 7

[1] Spiegel, Alix. "She Offered the Robber A Glass of Wine, And that Flipped the Script." *NPR*, NPR, 15 July 2016, http://www.npr.org/sections/health-shots/2016/07/15/485843453/npr.org/485900076.

[2] "The Aarhus Model: How Denmark Prevents Jihad Fighters." *The Borgen Project*, 21 June 2017, http://borgenproject.org/aarhus-model-denmark-prevents-jihad-fighters/.

Chapter 8

[1] "In a Final Videotaped Message, a Sad Reflection of the Sexist Stories We so Often See on Screen." *The Washington Post*, WP Company, 25 May 2014, http://www.washingtonpost.com/lifestyle/style/in-a-final-videotaped-message-a-sad-reflection-of-the-sexist-stories-we-so-often-see-on-screen/2014/05/25/dec7e7ea-e40d-11e3-afc6-a1dd9407abcf_story.html?utm_term=.ba9a418ff90b.

[2] Plait, Phil. "#NotAllMen: How Not to Derail Discussions of Women's Issues." *Slate Magazine*, Slate, 27 May 2014, http://www.slate.com/blogs/bad_astronomy/2014/05/27/not_all_men_how_discussing_women_s_issues_gets_derailed.html.

[3] Piff, Paul. "Does Money Make You Mean?" *TED: Ideas Worth Spreading*, 20 Dec. 2013, http://www.ted.com/talks/paul_piff_does_money_make_you_mean?language=en.

[4] "Violence against Women." *World Health Organization*, World Health Organization, http://www.who.int/mediacentre/factsheets/fs239/en/.

Chapter 9

[1] Ramirez, Elaine. "The 'Escort Bars' That Uber Execs Reportedly Visited Are A Regular Affair In South Korea." *Forbes*, Forbes Magazine, 28 Mar. 2017, http://www.forbes.com/sites/elaineramirez/2017/03/27/the-escort-bars-that-uber-execs-reportedly-visited-are-a-regular-affair-in-south-korea/ - 5e56c5512f17.

[2] Lockwood, Amy. "Selling Condoms in the Congo." *TED: Ideas Worth Spreading*, 15 July 2011, http://www.ted.com/talks/amy_lockwood_selling_condoms_in_the_congo.

[3] Herald. "Gay Rights Groups Call for LGBT-Inclusive Education at School." *The Korea Herald*, 8 Feb. 2017, http://www.koreaherald.com/view.php?ud=20170208000720.

Chapter 10

[1] "The Bechdel Test for Women in Movies." *Feminist Frequency*, 9 Aug. 2016, http://feministfrequency.com/video/the-bechdel-test-for-women-in-movies/.

[2] Torres, Nicole. "It's Better to Avoid a Toxic Employee than Hire a Superstar." *Harvard Business Review*, 9 Dec. 2015, http://hbr.org/2015/12/its-better-to-avoid-a-toxic-employee-than-hire-a-superstar.

[3] Spiegel, Alix. "She Offered The Robber A Glass Of Wine, And That Flipped The Script." *NPR*, NPR, 15 July 2016, http://www.npr.org/sections/health-shots/2016/07/15/485843453/it-was-a-mellow-summer-dinner-party-then-the-gunman-appeared.

[4] Cuddy, Amy. "Your Body Language May Shape Who You Are." *TED: Ideas Worth Spreading*, http://www.ted.com/talks/amy_cuddy_your_body_language_shapes_who_you_are.

[5] Cuddy, Amy Joy Casselberry. *Presence: Bringing Your Boldest Self to Your Biggest Challenges.* Back Bay Books, 2018.

Chapter 11

[1] Holodny, Elena. "South Koreans Could Be 'Extinct' by 2750." *Business Insider*, Business Insider, 19 June 2015, http://www.businessinsider.com/south-koreans-could-be-extinct-by-2750-2015-6.

[2] "The Best-and Worst-Places to Be a Working Woman." *The Economist*, The Economist Newspaper, 3 Mar. 2016, http://www.economist.com/blogs/graphicdetail/2016/03/daily-chart-0.

[3] "The Glass-Ceiling Index." *The Economist*, The Economist Newspaper, 5 Mar. 2015, http://www.economist.com/blogs/graphicdetail/2015/03/daily-chart-1.

[4] "The Glass-Ceiling Index." *The Economist*, The Economist Newspaper, 7 Mar. 2014, http://www.economist.com/news/business/21598669-bestand-worstplaces-be-working-woman-glass-ceiling-index.

[5] Matsui, Kathy, et al. *Womenomics 4.0: Time to Walk the Talk*. 2014, *Womenomics 4.0: Time to Walk the Talk*, http://www.goldmansachs.com/our-thinking/pages/macroeconomic-insights-folder/womenomics4-folder/womenomics4-time-to-walk-the-talk.pdf.

[6] Grant, David RockHeidi. "Why Diverse Teams Are Smarter." *Harvard Business Review*, 4 Nov. 2016, http://hbr.org/2016/11/why-diverse-teams-are-smarter.

Chapter 12

[1] "Key Characteristics of Parental Leave Systems." *OECD Family Database*, 26 Oct. 2017, http://www.oecd.org/els/soc/PF2_1_Parental_leave_systems.pdf.

[2] *KELA Benefit in Euros 2018. KELA Benefit in Euros 2018*, http://www.kela.fi/documents/12099/6889543/Kela_benefits_in_euros_2018.pdf/23cc6882-1755-442c-bf5e-5f4595d64fbc.

[3] Slaughter, Anne-Marie. "Why Women Still Can't Have It All." *The Atlantic*, Atlantic Media Company, 20 June 2018, http://www.theatlantic.com/magazine/archive/2012/07/why-women-still-cant-have-it-all/309020/.

[4] "Orchestrating Impartiality: The Impact of 'Blind' Auditions on Female Musicians." *Gender Action Portal*, 1 Jan. 1970, http://gap.hks.harvard.edu/orchestrating-impartiality-impact-"blind"-auditions-female-musicians.

[5] Matsui, Kathy, et al. *Womenomics: Japan's Hidden Asset*. 2005, *Womenomics: Japan's Hidden Asset*, http://www.goldmansachs.com/insights/investing-in-women/bios-pdfs/womenomics-pdf.pdf.

[6] *KELA Benefit in Euros 2018. KELA Benefit in Euros 2018*, http://www.kela.fi/documents/12099/6889543/Kela_benefits_in_euros_2018.pdf/23cc6882-1755-442c-bf5e-5f4595d64fbc.

[7] Cohen, Rhaina. "Who Took Care of Rosie the Riveter's Kids?" *The Atlantic*, Atlantic Media Company, 18 Nov. 2015, http://www.theatlantic.com/business/archive/2015/11/daycare-world-war-rosie-riveter/415650/.

[8] Korean Daily News, News Report, Posted: Mar 15, 2016. "Spirits' Homecoming, Movie About Comfort Women, Is a Miraculous Success."

New America Media, http://newamericamedia.org/2016/03/spirits-homecoming-movie-about-comfort-women-is-a-miraculous-success.php.

Chapter 14

[1] Grant, Adam, and Sheryl Sandberg. *Originals: How Non-Conformists Move the World.* Penguin Publishing Group, 2017.

Afterword

[1] Zander, Benjamin. "The Transformative Power of Classical Music." *TED: Ideas Worth Spreading,* 24 June 2008, http://www.ted.com/talks/benjamin_zander_on_music_and_passion.

Made in the USA
San Bernardino, CA
24 July 2019